HAWKER'S SECRET
COLD WAR AIRFIELD

HAWKER'S SECRET

COLD WAR AIRFIELD

DUNSFOLD: HOME OF THE HUNTER AND HARRIER

CHRISTOPHER BUDGEN

AIR WORLD

AIR WORLD

HAWKER'S SECRET COLD WAR AIRFIELD
Dunsfold: Home of the Hunter and Harrier

First published in Great Britain in 2020 by
Air World
An imprint of
Pen & Sword Books Ltd
Yorkshire – Philadelphia

Copyright © Christopher Budgen, 2020

ISBN 978 1 52677 175 9

The right of Christopher Budgen to be identified as Author of this work has been
asserted by him in accordance with the Copyright, Designs and Patents Act 1988.

A CIP catalogue record for this book is available from the British Library.

Typeset by SJmagic DESIGN SERVICES, India.

Printed and bound in the UK by TJ International Ltd.

Pen & Sword Books Limited incorporates the imprints of Atlas, Archaeology,
Aviation, Discovery, Family History, Fiction, History, Maritime, Military, Military
Classics, Politics, Select, Transport, True Crime, Air World, Frontline Publishing, Leo
Cooper, Remember When, Seaforth Publishing, The Praetorian Press, Wharncliffe
Local History, Wharncliffe Transport, Wharncliffe True Crime and White Owl.

For a complete list of Pen & Sword titles please contact

PEN & SWORD BOOKS LIMITED
47 Church Street, Barnsley, South Yorkshire, S70 2AS, England
E-mail: enquiries@pen-and-sword.co.uk
Website: www.pen-and-sword.co.uk

Or
PEN AND SWORD BOOKS
1950 Lawrence Rd, Havertown, PA 19083, USA
E-mail: Uspen-and-sword@casematepublishers.com
Website: www.penandswordbooks.com

MIX
Paper from
responsible sources
FSC® C013056

Contents

Foreword

Once you have been part of Dunsfold it will always be part of you. Experiencing the unique culture, enjoying so much exciting success whilst being at the core of British aviation history was fulfilling and rewarding.

I clearly remember the first time I saw Dunsfold; it was in June 1971. I had just parked my Red Arrows Gnat on the west end ORP from where there was a panoramic view of the aerodrome. We were using Dunsfold for our displays at the Biggin Hill Air Show. A mixture of wartime Nissen huts and old buildings, but dominated by the large hangars that towered over the industrial site on the north side, Dunsfold made an immediate and big impression on me as I looked around. This was somewhere that I would like to be part of.

Not having been fully aware of what went on at Dunsfold, I had no real knowledge of what it represented as one of Britain's foremost flight test centres. Having landed in a Gnat I did at least know that it was from there that they had been delivered to the RAF; the original Folland Gnat trainer production aircraft were all Dunsfold-built. I did know something about the great Hawker aircraft company at Kingston, having flown the Hunter on 20 Squadron and at RAF Valley as a flying instructor but, at only 26-years-old, the full history of Dunsfold and Hawkers had largely escaped me. I was still in the little bubble that surrounded my early career as an RAF pilot but in my defence it is fair to point out that Dunsfold had much more to its history than most people are aware.

Our host was Duncan Simpson, the newly-appointed Chief Test Pilot, and during the next few days I found him sufficiently personable to feel comfortable with asking him what the prospects were for future employment. The answer was simple and tactful; a test pilot qualification was a pre-requisite. This only served to enhance a long-held desire for exactly that, and that conversation was part of the impetus that put me onto the right route through the Empire Test Pilots' School and Boscombe Down.

Finally, it was John Farley who offered me a job there, and over the subsequent forty years we became very close friends.

My experience is typical of how Dunsfold immediately got under your skin. The atmosphere at this quiet countryside location in Surrey, surrounded by trees and with an olde-worlde appearance, belied what was an efficient and highly productive manufacturing and assembly plant. Add the smell of aviation fuel and you have Heaven on Earth for pilots, engineers and enthusiasts. All of the miscellaneous trades and the support staff who made essential and important contributions are included in the collective term 'enthusiasts' – because that is what they were. The local population, however, had a love/hate relationship with Dunsfold being a noise nuisance but also providing a good source of local employment.

It took me eight years before I set foot on the site as an employee and it proved to be everything that it promised to be. Shortly before I started work there it had become part of British Aerospace, but to us it was still 'Hawkers'. During those eight years I had reason to visit Dunsfold a number of times associated with Harrier and Hawk programmes; every visit only served to make the appeal grow stronger. The more I got to know company people in the various roles at Dunsfold the more I came to appreciate that everyone pulled in the same direction, everyone loved and respected the products and everyone would go the extra mile to keep the aircraft rolling off the production line.

Everyone was interested in the aircraft that they were part of and, as we developed them out of the Experimental Hangar, there was always excitement around the site about progress and new activities. The Hunter, Harrier and Hawk were aircraft that nobody ever got tired of watching, except perhaps some of the neighbours who constantly complained about the noise; they somehow missed the point about the 'sound of freedom'. Such was the disadvantage of operating out of the 'gin and Jaguar' belt in Surrey.

One could easily believe that foreign forces were the biggest obstacle to the success of Britain's aircraft industry. However, it has been a peculiar characteristic of British governments and bureaucrats that obstacles, project cancellations and company amalgamations handicapped our aviation potential. Whilst this has forced some excellent compromises and products, it has not been foreign action that has sometimes limited British aviation: it has been the peculiar national characteristic to knock what is ours and give succour to what is foreign. Meanwhile, all too often we shared our expertise and gave away leads.

FOREWORD

Yet when the chips were down it was our own industry that gave us the means to protect ourselves. Hawkers played a big part in that but did not always have the fullest and deserved recognition. The origin of Hawkers was in the Sopwith Aircraft Company, producer of 16,000 aircraft for the First World War. Yet the company was driven into liquidation after the war due to a misconceived purge on profit making. Like the Phoenix, Hawkers rose from ashes to fly again, later making a decision unique in aviation history. With another war looming in 1936, the production of 1,000 Hurricanes was set up without a government contract. Thus the United Kingdom had the product ready when it needed it for action. The media continues to push the Spitfire as the icon of the Battle of Britain, but the Hurricane played the bigger part.

That was not the only time that Hawker products were at the forefront of action when needed. If it was not for the Sea Harrier one wonders what would have happened to the Falklands. Air superiority was essential there, but it was only the combination of the small carrier and STOVL that was practicable in the awful sea states that prevailed. The Sea Harrier was developed at Dunsfold and for the UK it would have been worth it all for that alone.

After the Second World War, Hawkers moved to jet engines and all-metal airframes. From Dunsfold came the 'Big Three' – the Hunter, Harrier and Hawk – that have collectively sold in bigger numbers than such a combination of aircraft from any other British manufacturer during a similar period. And with a score of thirty-three, they have sold to more countries. The United States, with all its might in aviation, has been a customer for both the Harrier and the Hawk, whilst India has been for all three. India, a very exacting customer, also had the Sea Hawk, so they have operated all the Hawker jet fighters.

Of course, the birthplace of the 'Big Three' was the factory on Richmond Road in Kingston-upon-Thames, but the flight test centre at Dunsfold was where they came alive. In Kingston aircraft production at various sites went on for nearly a century and the RAF has always had Kingston aircraft in service. Longevity in service has reached legendary numbers. Presently the Hunter is approaching seventy years and is on course to become the world's longest-serving post-war jet fighter. The Harrier, discarded unwisely by the UK for dubious reasons not fully supported by an adequate defence review, is on course to serve the United States until an equal seventy years has passed. The Hawk, still in production after forty-five years, is expected to be in service until 2050. That being the case, it will top the Hunter and Harrier by another five years, and would ultimately be a British record.

I flew these three types of aircraft for almost thirty years, all initially whilst I was in the RAF, so I feel that I have Hawker products in my blood. I had the very great privilege to routinely fly all three types in the course of a week's work at Dunsfold. The role of an industry test pilot was not all test flying; indeed the larger part was various support tasks including marketing, customer training and deliveries. At Kingston, Hawkers had a unique approach to product sales – they funded company demonstrators. These aircraft gave the workforce an added feeling of being part of the whole process from design and development, through sales to production and deliveries. Production aircraft came, in pieces, and went, but company-owned demonstrators become part of the workforce. They even seemed to develop personalities of their own.

Over the years we saw a lot of activity as prospective customers 'tried out' the product. Dunsfold was good at having the aeroplanes ready and serviceable at the right time but it was quite a game flying with visitors of unknown quality. Often we needed to temper an ego and in some cases they were hell-bent on showing off. Sometimes our competitors had passed on bad information about our products and they were trying to find problems that did not exist. For me the occasional narrow squeak with a customer pilot was far riskier than any of the test flying I was involved in, perhaps more so when we were away from Dunsfold in foreign places. Demonstration flying was far harder than test flying and, in this context, it also includes classic low-level aerobatic displays, an area of aviation that I had always been involved in, but never really enjoyed, having known too many good pilots who came to an untimely end.

For many the iconic photographs of Bill Bedford spinning the two-seat Hunter demonstrator in Switzerland as part of the sales campaign is a classic. The movie is even more impressive! Eventually, in 1967 that Hunter T.66, G-APUX, was refurbished and sold to Chile, so we have no knowledge of whether it still exists. Later at Dunsfold we had the two-seat Harrier Mk 52 demonstrator G-VTOL, and used it internationally on development and marketing exercises. It is now at Brooklands in the museum with the Hawk Mk 50 demonstrator G-HAWK standing alongside. This Hawk operated for many years from our site and around the world before leaving with the rest of the Hawk programme, by which time we had developed and tested seventeen versions of Hawk. Demonstration tours were a normal part of the workforce's activities and their culture and hard work produced many outstanding results that became sales.

FOREWORD

I have so many fond memories of Dunsfold. I hope that I enjoyed my fifteen years there as much as, looking back, I realise that I should have. My first impressions of the site were well proven to be right: it was a unique place and the achievements of those who worked there made a big contribution to the UK, both in financial terms and to the defence of the realm. I am proud to have been involved albeit playing a small part and for a relatively short period, perhaps only about a third of the time Hawkers and British Aerospace operated from there.

But those fifteen years are a big part of me.

Enjoy the book!

Chris Roberts
Dunsfold Chief Test Pilot 1990-1994

Acknowledgements

As with any work of this scope, the number of people and organisations kind enough to assist with my research has been many and varied and inevitably there will be those whose names have slipped through the net.

In particular, I would like to extend my grateful thanks to Peter Amos whose knowledge of aviation is truly encyclopaedic. Similarly, Chris Farara, at Brooklands Museum, has been most helpful in answering my numerous queries by drawing on his many years at Hawker Siddeley and British Aerospace. Chris Roberts, Heinz Frick and John Farley, all test pilots with a wealth of knowledge of both Dunsfold and its products, have been invaluable in their guidance.

I would also like to extend my thanks to the following for sharing with me their stories and memories of the years at Dunsfold: Bill Anderson, Colin Balchin, Keith Bollands, Mick Cooper, Stewart Courtnell, Malcolm Francis, Mark Gerrard, Norman Hayler, Terry Hill, Rod Hunt, Allen Jennings, Stan Lawson, Dick Longhurst, Malcolm Mills, Pat Moran, John Parrott, Dick Poole, Mike Robins, Peter Rolfe, Mick Simmonds, Roy Upjohn, Danny White and Dick Wise.

Thanks are also due to Andrew Lewis, Trevor Clarke, David Potter, Barry Guess, Kieron Kirk, David Griffin, Darren Pitcher and Andy Lawson for their assistance.

Finally, my thanks to BAE Systems, The National Archives, Brooklands Museum and Tangmere Military Aviation Museum, and to the small team of proofers – Sue, Elaine, Allison and Bob – who have waded through the text seeking out my errors.

Glossary

A.C.	Alternating current
A&AEE	Aeroplane and Armament Experimental Establishment, later Aircraft & Armament Evaluation Establishment.
AAA	Anti-Aircraft Artillery
AAIB	Air Accident Investigation Board
AAM	Air-to-Air missile
AFB	Air Force Base
AHU	Aircraft Holding/Handling Unit
AM	Air Ministry
AMRAAM	Advanced Medium Range Air-to-Air Missile
AN/ALE	Threat Countermeasures System
APU	Auxiliary Power Unit
ARBS	Angle Rate Bombing System
ASI	Air Speed Indicator
ASR	Air Staff Requirement
AST	Air Staff Target
ATC	Air Traffic Control
AWA	Armstrong Whitworth Aircraft
BAC	British Aircraft Corporation
BAe	British Aerospace
BEA	British European Airways
BEAC	British European Airways Corporation (formal title for BEA)
BOAC	British Overseas Airways Corporation
BSEL	Bristol Siddeley Engines Ltd
BVR	Beyond Visual Range
CA	Controller Aircraft

CAP	Combat Air Patrol
CAS	Close Air Support
CASOM	Conventionally Armed Stand Off Missile
CCTV	Closed Circuit Television
CEPE	Central Experimental and Proving Establishment
CG	Centre of Gravity
CIA	Central Intelligence Agency (USA)
CO	Commanding Officer
CofA	Certificate of Airworthiness
CSEU	Confederation of Shipbuilding and Engineering Unions
CTP	Chief Test Pilot
DASG	Development Aircraft Support Group
DB	Development Batch
D.C.	Direct Current
DECS	Digital Engine Control System
DH	de Havilland
DME	Distance Measuring Equipment
EFA	European Fighter Aircraft
ETPS	Empire Test Pilots' School
FAA	Fleet Air Arm
FAMA	*Flota Aérea Mercante Argentina* – Argentine Merchant Airline (Argentina's first national airline)
FGA	Fighter, Ground Attack
FLIR	Forward Looking Infra-Red
FOD	Foreign Object Debris/Damage
FR	Flight Refuelling
FTE	Flight Test Engineer
FTO	Flight Test Operations
FTS	Flight Test Schedule
GTS	Gas Turbine Starter
HAS	Hardened Aircraft Shelter
HM	Her/His Majesty
HOTAS	Hand On Throttle And Stick
HP	High Pressure
HRDC	Hambledon Rural District Council
IAC	Intercontinental Armament Corporation

GLOSSARY

IAS	Indicated Air Speed
IFF	Identification Friend or Foe
IMN	Indicated Mach Number
IN/GPS	Inertial Navigation/Global Positioning System
INS	Inertial Navigation System
JPT	Jet Pipe Temperature
JTIDS	Joint Tactical Information Distribution System
LERX	Leading-Edge Root Extension
LGB	Laser-Guided Bomb
LIDS	Lift Improvement Devices
LP	Low Pressure
LRMTS	Laser-Ranging and Marked Target System
LRU	Line Replaceable Unit
MA&A	Military Aircraft and Aerostructures
MAD	Military Aircraft Division
MADGE	Microwave Aircraft Digital Guidance Equipment
MAWS	Missile Approach Warning System
MBB	Messerschmitt-Bölkow-Blohm
MCAS	[US] Marine Corps Air Station
MDAP	Mutual Defense Assistance Program
MDC	McDonnell Douglas Corporation
mdc	Miniature Detonating Cord
MEXE	Military Engineering Experimental Establishment
MFCS	Manual Fuel Control System
MFD	Multi-Function Display
MIRLS	Miniature Infra-Red Line Scan
ML	ML Aviation, named for Eric Mobbs and Marcel Lobelle
MLU	Mid-Life Update
MoA	Ministry of Aviation
MoD	Ministry of Defence
MoS	Ministry of Supply
MoU	Memorandum of Understanding
MRU	Medical Rehabilitation Unit
MTCP	Ministry of Town and Country Planning
MU	Maintenance Unit

MWDA	Mutual Weapons Development Agency
MWDP	Mutual Weapons Development Pact
NACA	National Advisory Committee for Aeronautics
NARDA	Supplier of measuring equipment in the EMF Safety, RF Test & Measurement and EMC sectors
NASA	National Aeronautics and Space Administration
NATO	North Atlantic Treaty Organisation
NBMR	NATO Basic Military Requirement
NGTE	National Gas Turbine Establishment
OAT	Outside Air Temperature
OCU	Operational Conversion Unit
OR	Operational Requirement
ORP	Operational Readiness Platform
PCB	Printed Circuit Board
PFTS	Production Flight Test Schedule
PoW	Prisoner of War
PSP	Pierced Steel Planking
PTFE	Polytetrafluoroethylene – a plastic cable insulation
QFI	Qualified Flying Instructor
QWI	Qualified Weapons Instructor
R&D	Research and Development
RAE	Royal Aircraft/Aerospace Establishment
RAF	Royal Air Force
RAFVR	RAF Volunteer Reserve
RATOG	Rocket Assisted Take Off Gear
RCAF	Royal Canadian Air Force
REG	Radio Frequency Environment Generator
RF	Radio Frequency
RFC	Royal Flying Corps
RFD	Reginald Foster Dagnall, company founder
RFP	Request for Prices
RNAS	Royal Naval Air Station
RNEC	Royal Naval Engineering College
RNVR	Royal Naval Volunteer Reserve
ROC	Royal Observer Corps
RPM	Revolutions Per Minute

GLOSSARY

RTW	Return to Work
RWR	Radar Warning Receiver
SAM	Surface-to-Air Missile
SBAC	Society of British Aircraft Constructors/Aerospace Companies
SCC	Surrey County Council
SEPECAT	The Société Européenne de Production de l'avion École de Combat et d'Appui Tactique
SHAPE	Supreme Headquarters, Allied Powers Europe
SI	Systeme International
STO	Short Take Off
TES	Tripartite Evaluation Squadron
TIALD	Thermal Imaging and Laser Designator
TWU	Tactical Weapons Unit
u/c	Undercarriage
UHF	Ultra-High Frequency
UN	United Nations
U/S	Unserviceable
USAF	United States Air Force
USMC	United States Marine Corps
USN	United States Navy
USSR	Union of Soviet Socialist Republics
V/STOL	Vertical/Short Take Off and Landing
VE	Victory in Europe
VHF	Very High Frequency
VTO	Vertical Take Off
VTOL	Vertical Take Off and Landing
ZEUS	Radar warning and automatic jamming system

Introduction

One day in 1895 a heavily laden cart slowly wound its way up from the depths of the Sussex Weald to its destination over the county border in Surrey. Its cargo comprised the worldly effects of Richard Budgen – my great grandfather – and his family, moving to new work on the Hall Place Estate between Dunsfold and Alfold. His home for the next forty-seven years – Hawkins Farm – sat at the top of a ridge from where the road swept down across a flat plain on its way to Horsham. His job would be the rearing of cattle for the estate on this land below the cottage until, in 1942, this part of the estate, and contiguous parcels, was requisitioned by the government for use as an aerodrome for the RAF, much to the chagrin of the landowner but … 'there's a war on you know'.

The land in question lay athwart the main A281 road between Guildford in Surrey and Horsham in Sussex. It comprised level agricultural land studded with several small farms and cottages, woodland and fields. The eastern area formed part of the Hall Place Estate under the ownership of the Rowcliffe family, the current incumbent – Hugh – being the one unlucky enough to receive the bad news of the loss of this land and also land to the north of the house for the foreseeable future.

Richard's grandson Maurice, my father, by then a plucky 14-year-old apprentice with the Guildford Gas Light and Coke Company Ltd was involved with the job of laying the 11,000-volt underground electrical cable into the west end of what would become RAF Dunsfold, the trench being dug by a group of fifty men from the Pioneer Corps of the British Army. Maurice's princely wage for a forty-seven-hour week was 15 shillings (75p).

As a large area of the estate disappeared behind barbed wire, the estate somehow continued to function as the new aerodrome took shape on the fields below the cottage. The work was carried out by men of the Canadian Army to provide an air base for the Royal Canadian Air Force which would provide an Army co-operation role for the men on the ground once they arrived on the continent. Completed as a standard three-runway layout, the work included a three-mile perimeter track and multiple hardstandings for aircraft dispersal, all in concrete. Later would be added two T2 type hangars and an array of Nissen huts to provide service, maintenance and technical facilities.

By October 1942 the aerodrome infrastructure was broadly complete and work proceeded on the domestic sites to the north of the aerodrome to billet squadron and administrative staff; the facilities would include a hospital and cinema, all connected to its own sewage treatment farm. On the 16th, the aerodrome was officially handed over to the Royal Canadian Air Force at Dunsfold and in December the first aircraft – P.51 Mustang 1s – arrived courtesy of 400 and 414 Squadrons RCAF, later joined by 430 Squadron. From here, once training was complete, armed raids over the continent would become the order of the day.

Richard Budgen, by then eighty-six-years-old, lived just long enough to see the aerodrome become operational, dying in January 1943. He left the estate as he had arrived, by horse-drawn waggon to burial in Hascombe churchyard. Another departure of the old order was Major Rowcliffe, the estate owner, who found that, not only had his estate been requisitioned but his capacious house as well! However, life must go on, so alternative accommodation was arranged for him at the Dower House at Stovolds Hill just down the road.

With the movement of the Canadian squadrons away in July 1943, on 18 August the first aircraft of the new squadrons began to arrive – North American B-25 Mitchell medium bombers of 98 and 180 Squadrons RAF, later joined by 320 Squadron of the Netherlands Naval Aviation Service, the aerodrome now becoming RAF Station Dunsfold and bombing raids on the continent soon became part of life.

The advent of D Day, the invasion of Europe under the codename OVERLORD, saw security at Dunsfold tightened rigorously and the squadrons detailed to attack troop and transport movements in the vicinity of the invasion beaches and, later, more widely in harassing attacks against the enemy transport infrastructure in support of the ground war. These included participation in Operation MARKET GARDEN, the attempt to leap-frog progress towards Germany by the capture of strategic bridges at Nijmegen, Son, Veghel, Grave and Arnhem in the Netherlands. October 1944 saw the Dunsfold squadrons preparing to leave for the continent, destination Melsbroek aerodrome in Belgium. At the beginning of 1945 Dunsfold welcomed the arrival of 83 Group Support Unit and their disparate collection of aircraft including Spitfires, Typhoons and Tempests from their main base at RAF Westhampnett in Sussex and in April, with the war on the continent coming to an end, plans were laid to use RAF Dunsfold as a PoW repatriation centre for returning servicemen. On 21 April the first of the PoW return flights landed at the aerodrome, soon followed by a constant stream of aircraft ferrying the former prisoners home. By the end of the air movement of PoWs, nearly 48,000 had passed through the Air Arrival Centre at the aerodrome on their way to freedom.

VE Day – 8 May 1945 – saw the official end of the war in Europe thanks to the remarkable efforts of the men and women of the allied services. The aerodrome would next see use as a disbandment centre where demobilising squadrons could deposit their mounts. Dunsfold thus became temporary home to a large and varied selection of aircraft types pending their onward flights to RAF maintenance units for storage or scrapping. By 1946 RAF Dunsfold was being held on a care and maintenance basis with no squadrons present, being declared inactive in August of that year. At Hall Place hopes were raised that the end of war would also see the aerodrome returned to its rightful owners, though not just yet. Surrey County Council, in attempting to confirm the longer-term plans for the aerodrome, was told that its use by the RAF would be required for the foreseeable future.

With war's end, the resumption of civil flying in the UK would be under the auspices of the Ministry of Civil Aviation. In the summer of 1946 they had sought Air Ministry approval for temporary use of RAF Dunsfold as a maintenance base by a civil air charter company called Skyways, of which, more later. Well placed to offer its services at the start of the blockade of Berlin by the USSR in June 1948, the subsequent airlift, Operation PLAINFARE, saw a massive increase in operations and staff by the company at Dunsfold. One of those newly employed was Maurice, grandson of Richard Budgen, who had recently completed his national service in India on Liberator transport aircraft. Thus well-schooled in multi-engine aircraft maintenance, Maurice began work at Dunsfold for Skyways but fell foul of the slowdown in work following the end of the Berlin Airlift and the subsequent woes of the company that saw it pass into liquidation soon after.

The Berlin Blockade by the eastern bloc saw the scales fall from the eyes of Western governments and the realisation that a new period of conflict was about to start. Dubbed the 'Cold War', it would confirm the future of Dunsfold for the next fifty years, prevent the return of the land to the original owners and provide expertise to the nation and employment for a disparate cross-section of the local population.

INTRODUCTION

By 1954 Maurice had returned yet again to Dunsfold, this time as an employee of Hawker Aircraft Ltd to work on their new jet fighter, the Hunter, and would remain for over forty years, finally leaving in 1992. So where do I – Richard's great grandson – fit into this story? In 1979 I had secured work at Dunsfold, by then with British Aerospace and remained until closure in 2000. Thus the family's close connection with the land had been retained, apart from a few years, for over a hundred years and for nearly its entire life as an operational aerodrome. Very shortly, after a long and bruising campaign, the aerodrome will disappear under a sea of housing; a sad end to a fascinating location.

Dunsfold Aerodrome

NO ENTRY TO UNAUTHORISED PERSONNEL
All visitors park in lay-by and report to Reception.
This is a Prohibited Place within the meaning of the Official Secrets Acts.
This is a CAA Licenced Aerodrome, trespass is a criminal offence.

No Photography or Video Recording

No Mobile Phones or CB Radios

No Dogs

Warning: Radar Emissions may affect wearers of pacemakers and hearing aids

Sign at the entrance to British Aerospace's facility at Dunsfold Aerodrome 2000. (Author's collection).

Chapter 1

Hawker's Search for a New Home

As the Second World War drew to a close in the summer of 1945 and demands on the production lines decreased, thoughts at Hawker Aircraft Ltd turned to the future and what peace would mean. Throughout the war, the company had been forced to operate from a disparate number of locations. It might be thought that the Hurricanes, Typhoons and Tempests with which the company had supplied the RAF had all come from the great works at Richmond Road at Ham Common, Kingston-upon-Thames – part of the National Aircraft Factory expansion of the Great War – but remarkably, throughout the 1939-45 war, this site had not been available, having been bought in 1920 by Leyland Motors (though it took until 1928 for purchase to be completed). This situation had grown out of the distaste for all things military which had pervaded the country at the end of the Great War.

The Sopwith Aviation Company, created by T.O.M. Sopwith had responded to the realisation that aircraft would play an increasingly important role in modern warfare, by producing ever increasing numbers of aircraft to fulfil government orders throughout the Great War. Eventually the works at Canbury Park Road and, latterly, Richmond Road had produced over 16,000 aircraft for the Royal Flying Corps (RFC) and Admiralty by the time of the ceasefire in November 1918. As existing and future orders for aircraft were successively reduced or cancelled outright with the advent of peace, production was vastly scaled back and staff, many women included, returned to peacetime activity. With almost no orders coming through the door, Sopwith gave up the lease on the Richmond Road factory and retrenched in the old Canbury Park Road premises. These were straitened times for Sopwith Aviation but plans to diversify were quickly brought in in an effort to keep a core of skilled employees occupied.

But then, in 1920, with world disarmament the dream of many, the company was hit with a swingeing tax bill, ostensibly for 'excess war profits'. Such was the cost of this that Sopwith and the company directors had no choice but to place the firm in liquidation and Sopwith Aviation, the company that had conceived many winning designs such as the Pup and Camel fighters, ceased to exist. Somehow, Sopwith was able not only to pay the onerous tax bill but also to clear all the creditors' bills as well. The paucity of government thinking engendered in such actions should come as no surprise, but the lack of vision that such actions represented was to be a recurring theme throughout the 1920s and well into the '30s.

Never one to be dejected at what life threw at him, in 1920 Sopwith brought together a small band of skilled workers and designers, including Harry Hawker, an Australian pilot who had been with Sopwith from the earliest days, to set up the H.G. Hawker Engineering Company. Its remit was the production of new, and modification of existing, aircraft to fulfil what small government orders filtered out of Whitehall and to produce sporting aircraft for the many who had learned to fly during the Great War. This sparse workload was bolstered to a modest degree by general engineering projects such as cars and motorcycles, that were just enough to keep a core group of committed individuals together until matters improved. Unfortunately, tragedy struck the following year when Hawker was killed practising for an aircraft race challenge. Thus were the unpromising beginnings of what would become one of the leading aircraft companies in the world.

Slowly, over the next ten years, the Hawker Engineering Company worked its way back to prominence, designing biplane fighters that filled the squadrons of the post-war RAF. There were still lean periods but the early 1930s brought better conditions with orders for Hart light bombers, Audax and Fury fighters to such an extent that the company had to subcontract work to other companies. Also at this time, the H.G. Hawker Engineering Company was subsumed into a public company – Hawker Aircraft Ltd – in May 1933 and later that year purchased Gloster Aircraft Company, one of the largest aircraft manufacturers at the time. Such was the success now of the company that something like 85 per cent of all aircraft serving with the RAF were Hawker designs.

The year 1934 was significant for Hawker Aircraft. Work began on acquiring the shares of the Armstrong-Siddeley Development Company to create a public holding company called Hawker Siddeley Aircraft Company Ltd. Thus was created a powerful aviation concern that included not only Hawker and Gloster Aircraft, but also Sir W.G. Armstrong-Whitworth Aircraft, A.V. Roe (later Avro) & Company, together with Armstrong-Siddeley Motors and Air Service Training Ltd. Under this umbrella, the Kingston-based company continued to trade as Hawker Aircraft Ltd. Also in 1934 Hawker's inspired designer, Sidney Camm, began to scheme a low-wing monoplane fighter which would revolutionise the war in the air. First flown in 1935, the Hurricane became the saviour of the UK during the forthcoming Battle of Britain, claiming the destruction of more enemy aircraft than the efforts of other fighters and anti-aircraft defences combined.

As the UK belatedly woke up to the fallacy that 'world peace' represented, and Nazi Germany's secret rearmament programme became known, the government hastily set about a major expansion of the country's armed forces. In the aviation world, expansion schemes followed hard on the heels of each other as orders were frantically placed with aviation companies for up-to-date aircraft, of which (given almost total disinterest by successive governments in the previous twenty years) few designs were to be had. The Hurricane, and later the Supermarine Spitfire however, were to form the backbone of the coming air war. It was about this time that the lack of proper factory space (Hawker was still occupying the former skating rink and factory in Canbury Park Road at Kingston) or any dedicated airfield (all Hawker aircraft were taken by road to Brooklands at Weybridge for flight testing) became a serious impediment to production. With the Ham works not available, if the Kingston team were not to contract out all their work, premises would be required to continue the high output of aircraft required by the country.

In 1936 a purchase was made of Parlaunt Park Farm at Langley on the outskirts of Slough. Here was constructed factory space, flight sheds and an airfield, eventually allowing Hawker's transport of all their aircraft to Brooklands for testing to cease. By the outbreak of war in September 1939, output of Hurricanes was well advanced at Kingston, Brooklands and Langley, as well as Gloster Aircraft, and later the Austin Motor Company and the Canadian Car and Foundry Company and by war's end, over 14,500 Hurricanes had been built. Following the Hurricane through the production shops came improved aircraft – the Typhoon and Tempest fighters in many different marks.

As the war ended in the late summer of 1945, Hawker Aircraft was busy on its latest design, the Fury for the RAF and the Sea Fury, for the Royal Navy, and already orders for aircraft production were being scaled back by a government brought to the brink of insolvency by war. In the latter stages of the conflict new aircraft powered by jet engines had emerged and initial schemes were studied at Kingston for aircraft powered by the new engines.

By 1947 Camm had produced an early exercise coded P.1040, a fairly conventional airframe with the Rolls Royce Nene centrifugal jet engine midships. During initial testing and ground runs at Langley, it soon became

Dunsfold Aerodrome under construction in 1942. Note the extensive dispersed hardstandings. (Author's collection)

apparent that flight testing needed to be moved away from the grass airfield and, following first flight at A&AEE Boscombe Down on 18 August 1947, the company leased land at RAE Farnborough by October 1948 for the construction of a hangar, at a cost of £10,157, and continued testing from there. While the P.1040 might be considered a research aircraft, it did spawn a large production contract for the Royal Navy under the project code N7/46, who named the developed version the Sea Hawk, some of which were still in service in the mid-1960s.

Hard on the heels of the P.1040, a straight-wing design with bifurcated jet exhaust, came the P.1052, with swept wings and the P.1072, with a rocket motor in the tail. Finally came the P.1081, with swept surfaces and straight-through jet exhaust. Testing of these aircraft all took place at Farnborough with the rocket motor flights based at Bitteswell, an Armstrong-Whitworth airfield in Leicestershire.

By then, these various jet aircraft designs had, between them, tested the various new design parameters that would come together to become the leading British fighter of the 1950s – the Hawker Hunter. Coded by Hawker P.1067, the design led to Air Ministry specification F3/48. As with the Hurricane fifteen years previously, it seemed that the Hunter would fill a desperately felt need just in time.

All the while that Langley had continued to turn out propeller-driven aircraft, the facilities at the Slough airfield had been perfectly adequate but, as the 1940s played out, several developments were coming together to conspire to spell an end to flying from the airfield. With the advent of the early jet designs, the requirement for aircraft facilities changed from grass flying fields to concrete paved runways – and long ones at that since initial acceleration could be sluggish. However, in the years since Langley had been constructed, the town of Slough had crept ever closer and the local authority wanted rid of the site, both to quash complaints of noise from the houses crowding its boundary and as a location into which to expand. The last nail in the coffin for Langley's flying aspirations was the continued growth of the Great West Aerodrome just to the east. This site had been chosen as the location for London's first airport, and named Heathrow. Traffic from the two almost contiguous airfields was beginning to conflict; there could only be one winner and it would not be Langley.

While Hawker, in 1945, had considered the merit of a complete move out of Kingston to a centralised grouping of facilities at Langley, it was now evident that such a move would not have been a wise one. The idea was quickly abandoned and the Kingston locations retained. In addition, in 1948, Hawker Aircraft offered the Leyland Motor Company £585,000 for

RAF Dunsfold post-war. This view gives a good indication of that which greeted Hawker Aircraft Ltd On their arrival in 1951. (Author's collection)

the Ham works, the offer being quickly accepted, allowing them to return to Richmond Road; but this left the question of where to carry out flight testing of the new jets which was now becoming an urgent problem. Accordingly, in early 1948, the company approached the Ministry of Supply in an effort to secure facilities at one of the aerodromes in the area left vacant following the end of the war. An assessment of many locations in the south revealed only two realistic options – Blackbushe in Hampshire or Dunsfold in Surrey. Blackbushe was quickly removed from the equation due to requirements by several other parties for its use and the problems associated with any expansion of the site, much of which was on common land. That left only Dunsfold, and following much correspondence and many meetings throughout 1950, the Ministry of Supply finally gained Air Ministry approval and acquiescence from the other ministries for its temporary use in February 1951.[1]

What were the problems that had resulted in the search for flight facilities taking almost three years?

The Ministry of Supply's role was overtly straightforward; in the case of the Air Ministry, it was tasked with supplying aircraft to the RAF against specifications issued to industry. However, behind the scenes, this role was complicated by secret government plans intended to disperse essential industry away from the south-east and, particularly, London. As the country's leading supplier of fighter aircraft, Hawker Aircraft Ltd were high on the list of companies whose presence in Kingston-upon-Thames, so close to the capital, caused great concern within government. There was therefore pressure applied to the ministry to force Hawker out of Kingston and to relocate to the north, to Squires Gate airfield at Blackpool.[2] Hawker steadfastly refused the offer of Squires Gate as an alternative to remaining at Kingston, rightly pointing out that such a move would result in the break-up of their design team and create competition for labour with Avro and English Electric, both active in the area. In the event, some production would move to Squires Gates but the problem would bubble away in the background for several years to come.[3]

For the Air Ministry, a move for Hawker into Dunsfold could only be bad news. Via the Ministry of Civil Aviation, their tenant Skyways Ltd was using the airfield for maintenance of its freight operation and servicing contracts for the Anglo-Iranian Oil Company and contracts for BOAC and BEA. These operations were important to the Treasury for they generated much needed dollar exports at a time when the country's coffers were dangerously low. All well and good, but the concomitant of Dunsfold as

Dunsfold Aerodrome, c.1965 showing how the northern site was developed up to 1980. (Courtesy Peter Amos)

a maintenance base was the disturbance that this caused all day and much of the night as the company's aircraft – Avro Yorks and Lancastrians – were powered up, took off and landed, and the subsequent complaints from some rather important neighbours about this, including the previous owner of the land upon which the aerodrome had been built, who was pressing for the derequisition of the airfield and return to its former owners.

Also of concern to the Air Ministry was the small issue of their own plans for Dunsfold. In the event of war, Dunsfold was to be one of the airfields in the south which would be allocated to RAF squadrons. Their ideal was therefore that there should be no lodgers at Dunsfold, which would be maintained on a care and maintenance basis until required. Eventually, as the problem of Skyways receded into the background, the company becoming insolvent in 1950 and placing its aircraft up for sale, the Ministry of Civil Aviation, Skyways' sponsor, and the Air Ministry would drop objection to Hawker's tenancy but with the rider that this would be for a temporary period and that the RAF would have priority in war.

The Ministry of Town and Country Planning (MTCP) also had a say in the matter as did Surrey County Council (SCC) and Hambledon Rural

District Council (HRDC). From the national perspective, MTCP had a duty to implement the dispersal of war industry previously alluded to, while SCC was concerned about the potential for the industrialisation of the airfield site, something to be avoided at all costs. HRDC's concerns were rather more prosaic. They were concerned that increased use of the airfield would result in an influx of people seeking work and therefore also housing, for which they were responsible. The district council was already stretched in this regard and had implemented, with SCC, a modest building programme of council housing in the villages round about. What they did not need, therefore, was a flood of new labour coming into the area and becoming a drain on their slender resources.

Eventually, in February 1951, all these concerns had been temporarily papered over and Hawker Aircraft Ltd was given the green light to move into the airfield. But what was the urgency of the situation? Hawker still had Langley and their various concerns in Kingston-upon-Thames to fall back on. The urgency arose from two government contracts that Hawker Aircraft had been awarded against a background of the realisation that the next war, against the USSR, could start at any moment and the current aircraft in the RAF's inventory were woefully unequal to the task of the defence of the country.

Accordingly, HM Government had issued two contracts to Hawker – N7/46 for a developed version of the P.1040 for the Royal Navy, to be known as Sea Hawk, and F3/48 for an interceptor based on the P.1067 for the RAF, which would become the Hunter.

Thus it was that Hawker Aircraft had found themselves, as in the Kingston/Brooklands days, in a position where they possessed no airfield of their own from which to fly these new aircraft. The acquisition of Dunsfold had arrived in the nick of time for their new jet aircraft. These jets included the P.1040 VP401, later modified to become the P.1072; the two N7/46 prototypes VP413 and VP422; and the two P.1052 prototypes VX272 and VX279, later modified to become the P.1081. With quantity production of the N7/46 Sea Hawk and, now, also for the Hunter, Hawker were once again in the position of receiving orders they could not complete successfully from Kingston alone and as yet, no airfield to fly the aircraft from.

So it was that by the start of 1951, Hawker Aircraft had approval to use RAF Dunsfold for the flight testing of the N7/46 Sea Hawk and F3/48 Hunter. But just what did this approval give them in terms of infrastructure? The grudging approval, obtained through the Ministry of Supply, was,

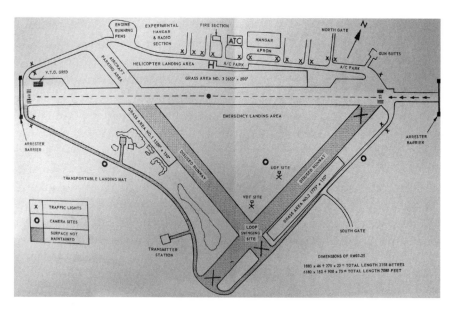

Schematic view of Dunsfold, c.1980. Not shown are the T2A and T2B hangars. (BAE Systems, courtesy of Brooklands Museum)

as far as the Air Ministry was concerned, quite restricted – use of one of the T2 hangars (the other was still tenanted by the remains of Skyways), which was in a poor state of repair; the technical site between the two hangars, which amounted to a collection of Nissen huts; use of the runways and dispersals, themselves in disrepair, and that was pretty much all. There was good reason for this, since the Air Ministry had other plans for the station – plans which did not include Hawker Aircraft Ltd.

Hawker, on the other hand, had entirely different plans in mind when they accepted Dunsfold for a temporary period and either with, or without, MoS connivance, began to prepare for an upgrade of the facilities available.

At a meeting on 22 February 1951 with the Ministry of Supply, Hawker presented their proposals for increasing their production of F3/48 Hunter aircraft, which revolved around the construction of three new B1 type hangars to form a flight test complex measuring 360 feet by 250 feet which, with offices and other accommodation, would give a total area of 105,000 square feet.[4]

On 7 May 1951 the ministry wrote to Hawker, noting that 'we are in touch with the Air Ministry on final clearances for your use of the airfield and we hope to be able to give permission for your occupation of hangar T2B'.[5] This was not sufficient to delay Hawker's plans and contractors were approached for the supply of steel to construct the three B1 type hangars, while the ministry was busy estimating the cost of this together with essential repairs to T2B hangar. On 16 May Macks Structures responded to Hawker's approaches to confirm that they were confident that they could fulfil the order from existing stocks, estimating a six to eight week lead time for materials delivery to site for the first bay, and twelve to fourteen weeks for the remainder. As ever in the commercial world, Macks were careful to advise that they had other customers keen to snap up materials and so Hawker should not delay placing their order.

By 9 July initial approval to fund the construction work via the Capital Assistance Scheme was approved for the creation of a 'new final assembly and flight test centre' at Dunsfold for an estimated cost of £200,000 to cover the new hangars and provision of main services, and a further £5,000 for the repair and installation of services of hangar T2B, this finance being subject to the company agreeing a suitable rent for the completed works. The new centre would, on Air Ministry instruction, have to be 'concentrated in an area to the west of Skyways hangar 2A'. This would not stop the Ministry later complaining that the work had blocked sight lines from the control tower.

By August Hawker had placed orders with Mack Structures for the steel and, typically, the company had exhausted their stock of second-hand hangar

Some of the many original wartime Nissen huts and blister hangars that comprised the accommodation for technical and aerodrome services during Hawker Aircraft's tenure, only replaced by modern buildings in the 1980s. This view looking north gives a good feel for the rural nature of the site and includes the main water tower sited to the north of the aerodrome within the dispersed camps, early 1960s. (BAE Systems, courtesy of Brooklands Museum)

sections and were trying to source alternative supplies.[6] Other contractors were approached for the supply of a steam-heating system for the flight sheds. This delay in obtaining suitable facilities was not playing well with Hawker Aircraft, who were keen to push on with the Hunter and Sea Hawk programmes. The Ministry of Supply in an internal memo of 12 October noted that work was being carried out at Dunsfold that did not form part of the current Capital Assistance agreement:

> There has been a great deal of misunderstanding about Dunsfold. At the moment the Air Ministry have not even agreed that Hangar no 2A can be made available for Hawkers although Hawkers are busily repairing this hangar. However we had a meeting with the company and the air ministry yesterday and I have no doubt that matters will soon sort themselves out.

As summer waned and the autumn of 1951 approached, an inspector from the Ministry of Supply visited the site to assess the progress of Messrs Ides of Kingston, the principal contractor. Although happy with progress on the repair and installation of services to T2B hangar – 90 per cent complete – the new hangars were another story; no materials had been delivered for the buildings and therefore progress was painfully slow. Excavations for the hangars were 75 per cent complete but with only thirty-one men on site, the work was proceeding slowly towards a target completion date of March 1952.

On 6 June 1951, Neville Duke – Hawker's experimental test pilot – had flown into Dunsfold from Langley airfield in Rapide G-AHGC, making it perhaps the first Hawker aircraft to visit the aerodrome and was back the following month, this time in the Whitney Straight.

At the next inspection, just before Christmas 1951, things had picked up. Hangar T2B was complete and in use. Levelling of the site for the new hangars was 90 per cent complete though casting of the concrete bases for the steel stanchions was being disrupted due to the site being waterlogged following bad weather.[7]

By January 1952 Hawker's plans had evolved further and now included a canteen and a larger paint shop, for which further funding had been agreed. Macks Structures were still chasing steel supplies and had approached the MoS for assistance in obtaining materials.

At the 5 February inspection, work had not progressed much, partially due to continued bad weather. Levelling of the hangar site was still not complete nor excavation for the stanchion bases. Macks were still claiming supply problems for their lack of progress in getting the hangar materials on site. However, there were now ninety-three men available, the floor of the first bay was complete and work had started on the second bay floor. The inspector was of the opinion that completion date, the new target being 5 July, would not be achievable till December that year.[8] On 18 March, the next site inspection revealed both progress and the continual evolution of Hawker's plans. Steelwork had arrived and work had started on erection of the first bay. The Capital Assistance Agreement value now stood at £204,000, plus another £9,000 for the canteen. Departures from the authorised work, and for which no doubt Hawker hoped to be reimbursed, included alterations and painting to hangar T2A, extra work in hangar T2B, alterations to the watch office/control tower (the addition of a third storey), the conversion of building 28 Nissen hut from a store to a crash tender and ambulance station bay and construction of a road from that building to the perimeter track.

Hawker's push to move properly into Dunsfold as soon as possible received good news on 13 April when planning approval was received from the local authority – Hambledon Rural District Council – for the 'erection, repair and flight testing of aircraft' by Hawker Aircraft Ltd. Strangely, while the permission was limited only to a 'temporary period', the various

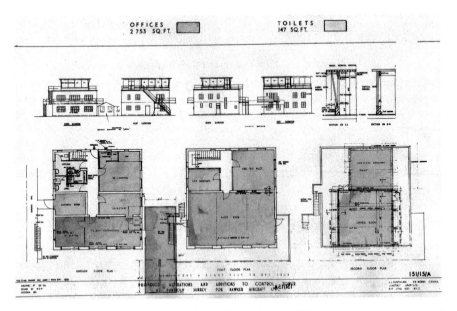

Plan showing alterations to Watch Office, c.1951. (BAE Systems, courtesy of Brooklands Museum)

ministries became convinced that this period would be one of seven years, but Hawker were not privy to this misunderstanding until 1957 when approached by HRDC asking for their future plans for the airfield since their permission was shortly to expire! However, all that was still in the future; for now, work continued, steelwork for the first bay was complete and the second bay was coming along nicely. The foundations for the boiler house and paint shop were proceeding, as was the canteen.

On 15 May 1952 the inspector's visit showed good progress, steelwork for the first two bays was complete and both had a roof.[9] The Ministry of Supply appeared to be coming around to acceptance that the additional works carried out would likely fall to them and now included the repairs to hangar T2A and the erection of security fencing, the new costs likely to be in the region of £359,050. By June, perhaps on the basis that the ministry had covered Hawker's costs for the various additional works carried out at Dunsfold, the company had approached MoS for reimbursement of costs to acquire various vehicles required for the site, together with agreement that the ministry would cover the cost of the cutting of the extensive grass areas of the airfield. Suffice to say the ministry was not amused and declined to play.

The various material shortages were continuing to cause problems into mid-summer of 1952, the requirement to rebuild substantial areas of the major towns destroyed during the war was of critical importance and affected the supply of materials for the construction work at Dunsfold. Steel for the boiler house was on site but that for the paint shop was still short, the building being partly erected. The London Brick Company in their pursuit of 100,000 bricks for the project were moved to remind Hawker that, although the works themselves benefitted from Super Priority status, the supply of bricks did not! It was left to the Ministry of Supply to progress with the Ministry of Works this thorny subject. The good news was that the hangar doors were now erected and cladding could begin.[10]

As Hawker's construction programme at Dunsfold approached completion in October 1952, the costs to the Capital Assistance Agreement operated by the Ministry of Supply were becoming clear. Costs were confirmed as: supply and erection of three B1 hangars to include boiler house, dope shop and roads – £297,330; repairs to T2B hangar – £10,800 and T2A hangar – £10,800; alterations to the control tower – £5,350; installation of security fencing – £4,000; construction of new canteen – £12,620; sundry building work – £16,150; supply of professional services – £29,000; a total of £386,050.

Meanwhile, over at the Air Ministry, concerns were growing about the whole situation. Its officers appear to have assumed that Hawker would clear a space in the corner of one of the hangars and carry out the occasional flight in furtherance of their R&D requirements for Hunter development, while at all times following any rules that the AM laid down. The reality was very different and seems to have shocked and bewildered staff at the ministry. Internal memos asserted that Hawker had 'infiltrated' the site to a far greater degree than had been anticipated and bemoaned the buildings demolished to make way for the new hangars. Hawker Aircraft was part of the national Hawker Siddeley Group, by far the largest and most powerful aircraft construction concern in the country. The company had emerged from the war with illustrious aircraft names to its credit – supplying the RAF with Hurricane, Typhoon and Tempest – while post-war it was busy supplying the Royal Navy with the superlative Sea Fury and Hawker's first production jet, the Sea Hawk. The order book was buoyant, and the coffers healthy. Now, with their second-generation F3/48 Hunter about to enter service, the company was in no mood to pussyfoot around. Facilities were urgently needed to develop the first of what would turn out to be one of their most popular aircraft and Dunsfold was central to that plan.

Having agreed with the Ministry of Supply that Hawker could use Dunsfold for Hunter work, the Air Ministry was now stuck with trying to square this with the requirement to allow the RAF to use the airfield in time of war. The Air Ministry response was to try to get Hawker out of the airfield by 1954 by offering alternative facilities but this was too little, too late – Hawker were in, new facilities were being constructed and the first aircraft would soon be arriving. In an attempt to mollify the Air Ministry, the Ministry of Supply mooted the idea of 'making a present' of the new facilities although, since they were built on AM property, it could hardly do any else.

As the work at Dunsfold progressed, another project was also maturing, one which would once again bring Hawker into conflict with the Air Ministry.

As the Second World War drew to a close in the summer of 1945 with the unconditional surrender of Germany and Japan, the Allies had, not unreasonably, expected that life could now get back to something approaching normality. As part of this expectation, hundreds of thousands of prisoners of war were being returned to their countries, and men of the three services looked forward to imminent demobilisation back to a life made safe again by the enormous cost and suffering of the second

Production hangar under construction. In the foreground is the Experimental hangar with the 'Black hangar' in the top left background. (BAE Systems courtesy of Brooklands Museum)

global conflict in twenty-five years. However, such expectations did not take account of the plans of the third ally in the triumvirate of the United Kingdom, United States of America and the Soviet Union.

Stalin was by now confident that he could retain a hold over the countries of Eastern Europe so recently under German rule that the Soviet Union had 'liberated', either through direct occupation or through malleable administrations sympathetic to the Communist/Soviet view. By this means he believed that he could obtain security for himself, his repressive regime, his country and his ideology. This control included the area of Germany which Soviet forces had been in possession of at VE day. As part of the immediate post-war plans for administration of a defeated Germany, it was agreed that the Allies would continue to hold the areas that they had liberated and Berlin itself would also be divided between the Allies. To this end, by 1946, Germany was under the control of the Soviet Union in the east and the UK and USA in the west together with France who had graciously been allowed to play a part by the Allies. Berlin was similarly split with the

Soviet Union in possession of East Berlin and the UK, the USA and France in control of West Berlin. Thus was the ground laid for the beginning of the Cold War.

Stalin had hoped that eventually the situation in Berlin, completely surrounded by Soviet held territory, would change to one where the entire city came under his control, but the Allies, awakening to Stalin's post-war expansionist plans, remained firmly in control of their area of the city. Eventually in June 1948 Stalin ordered the closure of the road and rail links that passed through Soviet East Germany to West Berlin and along which the majority of the city's requirements passed. The action set in motion a number of plans and commitments for which Stalin had not accounted. By any measure, his plans to force the Allies out of Berlin and perhaps even West Germany badly backfired.

As a massive airlift swung into action to keep West Berlin supplied with essentials through the winter and spring of 1948-49, three groups of American B-29 heavy bombers were flown across the Atlantic and based in Britain for the duration of the emergency.[11] Finally convinced of Stalin's aggressive intent, the USA came together with the countries of Western Europe to create the North Atlantic Treaty Organisation – NATO – duly inaugurated in the midst of the Berlin Crisis in April 1949.

Following the cessation of the Berlin Blockade, it had become apparent to the allies that the requirement to reinforce the defensive capability of the UK might arise again in the future and that plans should be formulated to deal with such an event. From this realisation, Operation GALLOPER was conceived.

In informal talks between the RAF and the USAF, future plans for heavy bomber deployment to Britain had first centred around requirements identified by the USAF for airfields capable of taking the B-29 Superfortress. Although bases in Norfolk had been used during the Berlin Crisis, the Americans felt that these were too close to the coast and were therefore vulnerable in wartime to attack with atomic weapons by the Soviet Union. To this end they requested that four bases in 'the Midlands' – in reality in the Cotswolds – be made available instead. Costs to bring these bases up to a suitable level for heavy bomber deployment were estimated at some £6-8 million, the majority of the cost to be borne by UK government.

Since the UK was at this time nearly bankrupt following the war, the government baulked at such a cost. Whatever finance they were to grant for such work could only come from funds already earmarked for the RAF;

there was no spare cash to be had. However, in the long term, a compromise was agreed which saw the costs of the works, reckoned at some £45 million, covered equally by the UK and USA.

If the owners of the lands requisitioned during the war had expected to have them handed back following the cessation of hostilities, they were to be disappointed. As the planning for GALLOPER matured, it became apparent that further resources would be needed to support a heavy bomber deployment, including escort and defensive fighter squadrons, and ground-based artillery. Suitable airfields for all these aircraft would need to be identified and brought up to standard, to be maintained on a care and maintenance basis in expectation of future deployments in time of war.

As early as June 1948, as the Berlin Blockade got underway, the UK and the United States held informal talks aimed at agreeing to a reciprocal arrangement whereby they could share each other's airfield facilities.[12] By April 1950 this exploration had hardened into the so-called 'Ambassadors Agreement' to allow US heavy and medium bomber forces and their escort and defence fighters to use RAF air bases in the UK. The bomber deployment was covered under the codename GALLOPER while the fighter deployments were covered under OFF-TACKLE, both operations attracting Top Secret status.[13]

So, out of Operation GALLOPER grew Plan OFF-TACKLE, covering the deployment of fighter squadrons to the UK. Eighteen airfields for these were identified in the requisite areas and allocated fighter wings were to be split between the individual airfields. It was at this point that it became clear that there were insufficient airfields available to contain the many squadrons which were required to support offensive operations from the UK. RAF Station Dunsfold, although considered redundant and now in the hands of the Air Ministry, was not going to be ploughed up anytime soon.

The southern sector of air bases for defence fighters was to comprise the airfields of Dunsfold, Tarrant Rushton and Blackbushe, which were already war reserve bases for the RAF having been allocated as early as December 1949.[14] The fighter strength was to be one group (three squadrons) with one squadron at each airfield comprising twenty-five aircraft, although by November 1951 this had increased to two squadrons (fifty aircraft) at Dunsfold. The fighters would likely be F-84E Thunderjet or F-86A Sabre aircraft with deployment to be complete by D + 30 days.[15] By the end of December 1950, the southern sector airfields had changed to Dunsfold, Lasham and Beaulieu. In September of that year the airfields had been surveyed to ascertain the runway length to ensure that a minimum of

6,000 feet was available for the defence fighter stations and if not, whether the runways could be extended, if necessary, with PSP planking.[16]

At Dunsfold, in August 1952, works were to be put in hand to improve the main runway, taxiways and hardstandings together with the addition of 'scramble aprons', operational readiness platforms.[17] The requirement of a minimum of forty-four single or twenty-two double hardstandings should not have been a problem for Dunsfold since it had been designed thus from inception; also required would be bulk fuel and technical facilities and VHF equipment. The main runway was barely long enough to accommodate the American jets and so urgent enquiries were made to begin the process of buying up land at each end of the runway to allow extension and clearance of any obstacles. Technical and domestic sites would also be required to accommodate, at Dunsfold, an initial base population of some 696 personnel. With Dunsfold's future becoming clear, the Air Ministry, in January 1951, concluded a deal with the previous owner of the majority of the site – Edward Hugh Rowcliffe – to purchase just over 276 acres for £22,175.

By May 1951 it was noted that the contract for the resurfacing of the runway and taxiways had been agreed in March, Fighter Command had carried out their accommodation survey and this was being reviewed by HQ 3rd USAF.[18] It was about this time that the American planners become aware that Hawker Aircraft Ltd was also intending to operate from Dunsfold but were assured by the Air Ministry that the US would have priority for use in time of war. On this basis they raised no objection.[19]

Thus was set in train a clash in requirements between the Air Ministry, Fighter Command and US 3rd Air Force, charged with the defence of the UK on the one hand and the Ministry of Supply and Hawker Aircraft, charged with supplying the means to equip that defence on the other.

By November 1951 the Ministry of Supply was making representations to Fighter Command on behalf of Hawker that they be allowed to continue to use Dunsfold in time of peace and would be expected to remain at Dunsfold in war and to share the airfield with USAF, a proposal to which Fighter Command was opposed. In early February 1953 a plan of a new technical site at Dunsfold was inadvertently passed to USAF by the Air Ministry which let the cat out of the bag with regard to what facilities would be available to the American forces in wartime.[20] Since moving into the airfield Hawker had taken over the technical site for their own work, a facility that USAF considered essential for their own use at each airfield. Although a new technical site was being offered, the USAF did not feel that they could wait for it to be built and, on 17 April 1953, announced that Dunsfold would no longer be suitable for their deployment and urgently requested an alternative airfield to replace Dunsfold.[21]

Ford was then offered to USAF as an alternative, and accepted, and refund of the costs of the abortive works at Dunsfold requested; Ford would be dropped from USAF plans in 1956. By this time, between 1951 and 1953, the Air Ministry had spent some £227,000 on OFF-TACKLE improvements at Dunsfold. In the event, 1953 saw the end of American interest in Dunsfold as far as the GALLOPER and OFF-TACKLE plans were concerned.[22]

Ironically, in May 1966, long after HM Government thought that the question of repayment of the cost of works at Dunsfold to USAF had gone away, the government suddenly received a request for the outstanding sum to be repaid. The unilateral action of France under de Gaulle, in withdrawing from NATO and requiring removal of foreign forces from its territory resulted in an urgent requirement to rehouse American personnel in the UK and funds to pay for the works, hence the sudden emergence of the repayment request.[23] By 1967 the outstanding sum was reckoned to be £228,000 specifically owing to the Special Construction Programme Fund, with £174,456 to be credited by the UK back to the fund and £53,438 to be credited to cover cost overruns on various USAF projects. This was finally agreed in October 1967.[24]

Chapter 2

Early Jet Experiments

Given the importance of Dunsfold to the future of Hawker Aircraft – it would after all be the sole centre for flight development of their jet fighter aircraft – it may be helpful to look at just how the company got into the jet aircraft business.

The Hawker design team had turned its mind to the use of jet-turbine engines relatively late in the war; de Havilland and Supermarine had produced jet-powered designs before Hawker while another Hawker Siddeley Group company – Gloster Aircraft – was selected by the Ministry of Aircraft Production to construct a prototype to flight test Frank Whittle's new engine design, the Power Jets W.1. This was not because the ministry felt that Hawker would not make a first-class job of the requirement but that its design team and factory floors were fully occupied with the supply of fighters for the RAF and Royal Navy and there was little spare capacity for the design of an experimental airframe not directly related to the war effort. That said, some design work had been carried out in the Hawker Project Office under Robert Lickley and a preliminary design schemed in 1941 and given the project number P.1011, consisting of two Power Jets' units installed in the P.1004 high-altitude fighter design. Nothing came of this but in 1944 a design was schemed and given the project number P.1035, broadly a Nene jet engine encased in a F2/43 Fury fuselage. Later in the year this project had been refined to include a jet engine mounted midships fed by wing-root inlets and exhausting via bifurcated outlets at the back of the wing.[1] This design – P.1040 – now had almost nothing in common with the Fury but the company decided to construct a single aircraft, later increased to three, to test the various new technologies introduced into the design. As work began on the first aircraft, with metal cutting in October 1945, the design office was already thinking about its development and produced two additional designs around the basic P.1040; the P.1052, with a swept wing and the P.1072 with an Armstrong-Siddeley Snarler rocket motor installed

P.1040 VP401 at Hawker's Langley facility carrying out engine run, June 1947. The aircraft was later taxied around on the grass prior to delivery by road to Boscombe Down for first flight. (BAE Systems, courtesy of Brooklands Museum)

in addition to the Rolls Royce Nene engine. Following on from these studies came the P.1081, which retained the swept wing of the P.1052 but deleted the bifurcated exhaust, replacing it with a straight-through jet pipe, and, finally, the P.1067 – which would become the Hawker Hunter.

The P.1040, serialled VP401, left Hawker's Canbury Park Road, Kingston, premises in early May 1947 and was delivered to Langley by road for installation of the Rolls Royce RB.41 Nene engine, a derated unit of 4,500lb static thrust. Following engine runs, in June 1947 the aircraft was taxied around the airfield minus its canopy before being broken down for transport to the Aircraft and Armament Experimental Establishment (A&AEE) at Boscombe Down. There it was re-assembled and first flown on 2 September 1947 at the hands of the company test pilot Bill Humble – Hawker Aircraft had entered the jet age.[2] Although the Air Ministry felt that the new jet did not offer sufficient advance on the Gloster Meteor to be considered worthy of an order, the Admiralty saw an opportunity to gain experience of jet aircraft and increase their striking power at sea, with aircraft based on the P.1040 flying from its carriers. Thus, in February 1946, the Admiralty had issued contract cover for the P.1040, until then a private venture project, and the second and third aircraft were constructed under the designation N7/46 to be developed as a carrier-borne jet fighter, later to be named Sea Hawk. These aircraft first flew on 3 September 1948 (VP413) and 17 October 1949 (VP422) as fully-navalised aircraft with folding wings, four-cannon armament and arrestor hook.[3] Meanwhile, VP401 was raced in the SBAC Challenge Cup at Elmdon on 1 August 1949, reaching a speed of 510mph; one run was clocked at 562mph. During subsequent testing, an indicated Mach number (IMN) of 0.845 was achieved.

The P.1052 was proposed as a basic N7/46 but with a 35-degree swept wing and straight tail surfaces and powered by a Rolls Royce Nene RN.2. A research specification issued to Hawker under E38/46 for the aircraft was received on 16 January 1947, and contract cover confirmed in May for two airframes to be serialled VX272 and VX279. By early 1948 Hawker had re-acquired the Richmond Road, Kingston, premises, making VX272 the first jet aircraft manufactured there. This was transported to Boscombe Down and first flight completed in the hands of Hawker test pilot Squadron Leader T.S. 'Wimpy' Wade on 19 November 1948 with VX279 following

P.1040 VP401 at A&AEE Boscombe Down just prior to first flight, 2 September 1947 by Bill Humble. (BAE Systems, courtesy of Brooklands Museum)

on 12 April 1949, from Farnborough.[4] These aircraft remained with Farnborough and its outstations for a variety of flight test trials, undergoing a number of trial installations and suffering several minor accidents, such as wrinkled wing and fuselage skins following a 10g manoeuvre, by Neville Duke on 9 September 1949 during a demonstration at that year's SBAC display. Eventually, in April 1950, VX279 was returned to Kingston for modification work to allow a straight-through tail exhaust and swept tail surfaces to project code P.1081.

Hawker's temporary sojourn at Farnborough with the new jets proved useful for the RAE since it allowed their pilots and scientists access to a swept-wing design to further the country's understanding of the potentialities and pitfalls of high-speed flight. P.1052 VX272 bore the brunt of these flights, VX279 having been withdrawn for modification, and consequently suffered more than its share of accidents, including three engine failures in the space of a year. These included (all from Farnborough):

29 September 1949: engine failure, forced landing in a farmyard at Cove.

17 April 1950: engine failure due to fuel pump failure. Wheels-up landing.

17 July 1950: engine failure; aircraft crashed onto Farnborough cycle sheds killing a painter.

31 August 1953: hydraulic failure. Into Odiham and landed on nose and starboard main undercarriage. Flown back to Dunsfold for repair 3/9/53.

25 September 1953: engine failure while fitted with variable incidence tailplane.

The sole P.1040, VP401 having completed its research programme, had been returned to works for modification in September 1949. Under project code P.1072, the aircraft was equipped with an Armstrong Siddeley Snarler rocket motor in the extreme tail, providing 2,000lb additional thrust, the Nene engine being retained in the centre fuselage. Fuel was to be a water/methanol and liquid oxygen mixture, giving 2.75 minutes thrust duration. In September 1950 the aircraft, complete with rocket motor, was transported to Bitteswell from where the limited test flying was performed. Although the results were promising, the airframe design's limiting Mach number and lack of pressurised cockpit limited testing, as did the early design of the motor. Following an explosion in the rocket motor while being flown by Duke on 19 May 1951,

'Wimpy' Wade aloft in P.1052 VX279, 1949. (BAE Systems, courtesy of Brooklands Museum)

the trials were terminated and no further work carried out by Hawker, the installation being considered rather a high risk to the pilot.

The P.1081 – the modified P.1052 VX279 – was ready for its first flight by early June 1950. The aircraft had been schemed to take the Rolls Royce Tay engine with reheat but, due to delayed development, VX279 flew with a Nene instead. The aircraft took to the air under 'Wimpy' Wade on 19 June 1950 at Farnborough. This aircraft, too, had its share of problems, making a forced landing at RAF Odiham with hydraulic and undercarriage problems and was flown back to Farnborough for repair but, by February 1951, Duke had pushed the speed up to a Mach number of 0.94.[5] However, two months later, this aircraft crashed, resulting in the death of Wade.

The two N7/46 aircraft continued to develop the specification for what would become the Sea Hawk, being used for all manner of trials, both with Hawker and with the Admiralty including deck-landing trials aboard HMS *Illustrious* and on 22 November 1949 the company was awarded a contract for the supply of 151 examples of a developed version of the P.1040 to the Royal Navy under the name Sea Hawk F. Mk 1. The first production

Sea Hawk, WF143, would make its first flight on 14 November 1951 from Dunsfold powered by a Rolls Royce Nene 4 engine of 5,000lb thrust.

Thus, over a number of what were essentially research airframes Sidney Camm and the Hawker design team had demonstrated successfully the various elements that would come together to become one of the greatest aircraft of the age – the P.1067 Hunter.

While the Power Jets and early Rolls Royce engines had proved the concept of jet turbine propulsion, they had all utilised a centrifugal compressor whereby the compression of the incoming air was achieved by centrifugal force, the air being pushed to the periphery of the compressor and then into the combustion area. While this design was relatively straightforward, it did impose a penalty in terms of airframe design, since the compressor wheel – to obtain sufficient efficiency – resulted in an engine with a significant diameter, in turn resulting in airframes that were quite tubby and therefore limited in terms of aerodynamic efficiency. RAE Farnborough, in the person of Dr A.A. Griffith, had been working towards a design for another

P.1072 VP401, reconfigured from P.1040 with Armstrong Siddeley Snarler rocket motor in the tail in addition to the Nene engine, 1950. (BAE Systems, courtesy of Brooklands Museum)

P.1081 VX279 reconfigured from P.1052 at Farnborough. Note straight-through jet pipe, swept wing and tail surfaces, 1950. (BAE Systems, courtesy of Brooklands Museum)

type of engine altogether, with an axial-flow compressor. In this design multiple compression stages progressively compressed the airflow prior to its entry into the combustion area. The advantages of such a design were two-fold. Firstly, the number of compressors could be increased, allowing for greater power and, secondly, because the compressor was a multi-stage unit, the overall diameter could be kept to a much slimmer profile. The disadvantage was that stresses in the axial-type engine were far higher and therefore material strength, design tolerances and lubrication requirements all conspired to delay the arrival of a reliable engine.

Work on what would become the Hunter originated in the Kingston Design Office with initial responses to Air Staff specification F43/46 of 1946 for a single-seat day fighter to replace the Gloster Meteor. While this specification did not produce much in the way of realistic proposals, it did lead to a refined specification F3/48 which Hawker felt was a more realistic attempt to draft a new fighter. The early responses to this, given the project code P.1067, resulted in an airframe rather larger than the P.1040 and featuring swept wings, high fin-mounted swept tail and nose air intake. As the design matured, the tailplane was brought down to sit at approximately one third the height of the fin and wing-root intakes replaced the nose intake. Most importantly of all, Hawker had been briefed on a new engine being planned by Rolls Royce – the AJ.65 – an axial-flow design which promised far greater power, once developed, than the centrifugal-flow designs. This engine became the Rolls Royce Avon, one of the most successful designs of the time. However, Griffith, the former axial-compressor guru at RAE but now head of design at Rolls Royce, in failing to appreciate the need to closely follow the design rules to be applied to compressors originating from the fertile mind of Alun Howell at the National Gas Turbine Establishment (NGTE) Pyestock, had produced an engine which in its early years possessed several detrimental attributes that required much further development work to bring the Avon to its later superlative peak. These faults would do much to delay the entry into service of the Hunter in later years. Harry Pearson at Rolls Royce had perhaps the last word on the early Griffith Avon: 'Yes, he designed it. I just had to make the bloody thing work!'[6]

The proposed aircraft would carry the unprecedented armament of four 30mm Aden cannon in a detachable nose-pack, allowing rearming in a matter of minutes. With detail design work underway by May 1948, a contract was raised for three prototypes on 25 June 1948, two to be powered by the Avon and the third by the Armstrong Siddeley Sapphire engine as an insurance should the Avon fail to deliver on its early promise. Work on the first aircraft began in December 1949 at Kingston and was complete by July 1951. At this point, the aircraft was transported to Boscombe Down for its initial flights. The aircraft, WB188, made its first flight on 20 July 1951 at the hands of Squadron Leader Neville Duke powered by an Avon RA.7 of 7,500lb thrust – uprated from RA.3. After several flights, the aircraft was transferred to RAE Farnborough to continue its development and was flown into Dunsfold for the first time on 7 September 1951 for a demonstration the following day to a delegation from the USAF before returning to Farnborough ready for the SBAC display the following week where, under Duke's inspired piloting, it would be the star of the show. In May 1952 representatives from the USAF returned to England and travelled to Dunsfold with at least one F-86 Sabre in order to carry out comparison flying between their aircraft and the Hunter, using either WB188 or WB195. The party consisted of Colonel Fred Ascani, Major General Albert Boyd and Lieutenant Colonel Richard Johnson, all highly-qualified test pilots. Unfortunately, their assessment report has not come to light.

Even before the first prototype had flown, on 14 March 1951 an order was received for the manufacture of 113 Avon-powered F. Mk 1 Hunters

P.1081 VX279 up from Farnborough, fitted with wing fences, 1951. This aircraft would crash months later, killing its pilot. (BAE Systems, courtesy of Brooklands Museum)

(later increased to 139 aircraft) and then later a further order for forty-five Sapphire-powered F. Mk 2 aircraft which would be built by Armstrong Whitworth Aircraft at Coventry.

Such then were the aircraft that Hawker was intent on producing in quantity for Britain's armed forces. But before they could be allocated to squadron use, a long and involved period of testing would be required to take the raw machine to the standard required by the Air Ministry and Ministry of Supply. The men who carried out this process were a disparate group of people, mostly ex-RAF or FAA and at the peak of their abilities. Indeed, they would need to be since the company and its new aircraft were entering a world where very few had gone before. The, for the most part, swept-wing transonic aircraft that they would be testing were completely different in aerodynamic terms from what had been available during the war. Spin recovery, for example, was a completely unknown quantity in these new jets and yet the test pilots would have to investigate this and a host of other new situations to ensure that the correct recovery procedures could be identified and passed on to the end user. Yet for all the care taken by these men, far too many would lose their lives or be seriously injured in testing the limits of what the aircraft could do. Before we return to Dunsfold, a look at the pilots who would be testing the aircraft in the fifties might prove instructive.

Bill Humble was born in 1911. He had joined the Royal Air Force Volunteer Reserve (RAFVR) pre-war and on outbreak of war was posted to 11 Flying Training School (FTS) but, due to an apprenticeship in mining engineering, was seconded back into the coalmining industry. Having eventually extricated himself from this situation, Humble was posted to Hawker's airfield at Langley in 1943 as production test pilot on Hurricanes and Typhoons and, later, Tempests and Furies. In 1945 he became Chief Test Pilot on the retirement of Philip Lucas. His career had a fitting finale when he became the first man to fly a Hawker jet – the first flight of the P.1040 VP401 at Boscombe Down on 18 August 1947 – retiring the following year to be succeeded by Wade.

Trevor 'Wimpy' Wade was born in 1920. Like Humble he had joined the RAFVR in 1938. On the outbreak of war, Wade was posted to a Spitfire squadron, remaining on this aircraft for the next two years. In 1943 he found himself posted to Wittering to take charge of the Air Fighting Development Unit, testing captured German aircraft. Following on from this work, in 1945 he was part of a team sent to the USA to assess captured Japanese aircraft. Wade left RAF service in 1946 to work for an aviation magazine but joined Hawker Aircraft at Langley in 1947 at the invitation of Bill Humble. Humble retired in 1948 and Wade took over as Chief Test Pilot. He had started his test piloting career with Hawker on production Sea Furies but, on Humble's retirement, took over the work on Hawker's first jets and Sea Hawk prototypes. However, on a flight in the P.1081 VX279 out of Farnborough on 3 April 1951, the aircraft failed to pull out of a dive and, although apparently initiating a late ejection, Wade died in the subsequent crash.

Born in 1917, Frank (Francis) 'Spud' Murphy had joined the Royal New Zealand Air Force in 1941 before travelling to England and flying Hurricanes and Typhoons with the RAF. Seconded to Hawker at Langley on test pilot duties, he found himself flying Hurricanes, Typhoons and Tempests. On leaving the RAF as a squadron leader, Murphy joined Hawker in July 1945, remaining at Langley on test pilot duties, taking the position of Chief Production Test Pilot in 1948.

Neville Frederick Duke was born in 1922. A well-known and respected wartime squadron leader, who ended his operational tours as the top scoring pilot in the Mediterranean theatre with twenty-seven victories, Duke had joined the RAF in 1940, mainly flying Spitfires before a posting to North

Africa and Italy where his mounts were various marks of Tomahawk and Kittyhawk. By January 1945, at the end of his third tour, he had been seconded to Langley as a production test pilot for a year. The first of Hawker's test pilots to pass through the Empire Test Pilots' School, he graduated from course No. 4 in 1946. Following this period, he was posted to the High-Speed Flight at Tangmere in June 1946 before moving to A&AEE Boscombe Down. Duke left the RAF in June 1948, managing to get a flight in the P.1040 just prior to doing so, and, at Bill Humble's invitation, to work for Hawker back at Langley as a production test pilot in August on Tempest and Sea Fury as well as sharing the test flying on early Sea Hawk trials.[7] Following his earlier work with the High-Speed Flight, Duke was involved in display flying of the N7/46 Sea Hawk prototype at the SBAC shows at Farnborough in 1949 and 1950 and the P.1052 aircraft VX272 at the 1951 show. The 1949 show had been Duke's debut as a display pilot at Farnborough and the event had nearly ended in disaster. Flying the first N7/46 prototype VP413 on 9 September, his characteristic entry run at high speed, low level – and inverted – was a sensation for all the wrong reasons. Seeking to roll the aircraft upright at the end of the run down the display line, he let the nose drop, very close to the ground and in a desperate attempt to right the aircraft and climb away, suffered a high-speed stall and pulled 10g before successfully completing the display. On landing, the airframe was found to have wrinkled skins on the wings and fuselage which laid up the aircraft for repairs. After the display, in Duke's words, 'On landing, I walked to the pilots' tent. I found it hushed – and the bar open, early.'[8] Duke and Wade had known each other since their early days in the RAF at Biggin Hill and so were able to form a close partnership with Wade as chief and Duke as his number two. With Wade's death in April 1951, Duke became Chief Test Pilot.

Frank Bullen, born 1921, had joined the RAF, mainly flying Spitfires and Mustangs. On leaving the service in 1946 he had moved to Blackburn & General Aircraft at Brough in Yorkshire as a production test pilot before joining Hawker in July 1949, based at Langley.

Bill Bedford was born in 1920. Following wartime service with the RAF on Hurricanes, P.47 Thunderbolts and P.51 Mustangs, he became a qualified flying instructor (QFI) at Upavon until 1949 when he attended the ETPS, graduating from course No. 8 and completing periods as instructor with the school and also with RAE Aero Flight and NGTE. While at Farnborough, he met Duke and was recruited to the team at Hawker Aircraft in 1951 as an Experimental Test Pilot.[9]

Thomas 'Don' Lucey was born in 1922. After wartime service in the RNVR, Lucey took a degree in Mechanical Sciences before joining Hawker Aircraft as a production test pilot in 1953.

Lest the impression be gained from the above that Dunsfold was to be a centre for the latest and most advanced aircraft of the time, there was another flight of aircraft regularly seen at the aerodrome that had their origins in another world entirely. This was Hawker's fleet of heritage aircraft, put to use on a variety of purposes including chase aircraft and communications or 'hack' aircraft. These were a very necessary part of Hawker's operation since, although the pilots' office had migrated to Dunsfold under Duke in early 1952, there was still a heavy commitment at Langley, and later at Squires Gate, Blackpool, for the production testing of Sea Furies for the RN and Furies for export customers to be covered by pilots from Dunsfold.

Arguably the most famous of these aircraft was the last Hurricane of some 14,000 ever built – a Mk IIc version constructed at Langley in July 1944 and named 'The Last of the Many'. Registered initially as PZ865, it was used at Langley for communications work and, at the end of 1945, was purchased by the company for private use. Eventually going into storage, it was later converted to civil use in May 1950 and placed on the civil register as G-AMAU. With the cannon armament removed and a Rolls Royce Merlin 24 engine fitted, later replaced by a Merlin 500, it was used by Hawker as a chase and observation aircraft during flight testing of other types. The aircraft was much in demand at various displays, service and industry garden parties, participating also in a variety of air races, a popular feature of life after the war, and had a starring role in the 1950 film *Angels One Five*. The aircraft was retained at Langley while Dunsfold was developed but was a regular visitor to the aerodrome from October 1951, Dunsfold soon becoming its new home.

Another well-known and rare aircraft was the Hawker Hart registered G-ABMR, powered by a Rolls Royce Kestrel 16 Special. Built by Hawker in 1930, it was the thirteenth of its type off the production line and was retained by the company for demonstration purposes. This aircraft was again a great favourite at garden parties and service demonstrations and paid its way as an occasional aerial photographic platform for company use. Both this and the Hurricane were for a time painted in the Hawker company 'racing' colours of dark blue with gold cheat lines but later reverted to more representative colour schemes.

Two further Hawker aircraft graced Dunsfold in the 1950s, the first of which had been Sidney Camm's first 'clean-sheet' design for Hawker.

The Hawker Cygnet, registered G-EBMB, was one of two, designed to a requirement for a light sporting aircraft to compete in the 1924 Light Aeroplane Competition at Lympne. Powered by an ABC Scorpion but later fitted with a 34hp Bristol Cherub III, as Camm's first solo design, at a mere 442lb, it was considered highly successful and had a place close to his heart. As the oldest and most fragile of the company airframes, the Cygnet led a relaxed life, being used primarily for demonstrations at company events and garden parties.

The final Hawker airframe was the Tomtit, registered G-AFTA and powered by a 130hp Armstrong Siddeley Mongoose IIIc, built in 1928 as Hawker's submission to an Air Ministry specification for a light trainer aircraft. Some 100 aircraft were produced for the RAF but with the rapid advances in aircraft design during the 1930s, the aircraft were withdrawn and offered for sale on the civil market in 1935. The aircraft was refurbished in 1939, given its civil registration and passed through a series of owners before purchase by Neville Duke as a private runabout in 1948. When Duke moved to Hawker, naturally the aircraft came with him and eventually joined the fleet as an occasional air taxi.

As well as these Hawker machines, others were on the books. A Miles Whitney Straight had been acquired by the company in March 1941. Serialled G-AEUJ, and powered by a Gipsy Major engine, the aircraft was used as a two-seat communications aircraft, often making the journey from Dunsfold to Langley to ferry a pilot for testing duties at the Slough site.

Also used, as the principal means of commuting between sites were two DH Rapide biplane passenger aircraft, sometimes described by its RAF name of Dominie. These aircraft, G-AHGC, acquired in March 1946, and G-ACPP were busy machines. With its enclosed cabin, G-AHGC proved to be the transport of choice when senior management were required to commute to Blackpool in connection with the setting up of a further Hunter production facility at Squires Gate, piloted by Duke or Murphy. The aircraft was also in demand when pilots' presence was required at the RN bases at Anthorn and Renfrew in Scotland. In September 1952, following an air test by J.F. Robertson, G-AHGC appears to have been replaced for a while by G-AHPP on the Dunsfold–Langley runs, not appearing again until mid-December. Thereafter, both machines were retained for communications duties.

The last of the civil fleet at this time was Avro C.19 Anson, G-AHXK, acquired prior to 1952. This proved useful for airborne wireless and navigation aid checks but also found work as a longer distance transport when a Rapide was not available.

Meanwhile, back at Dunsfold, with the T2B hangar ready for occupancy, no time had been lost in closing down Hawker's flight test facilities at Farnborough. While the arrangement at RAE had been to the benefit of the establishment's scientific community, it had proved irksome for the company test pilots who were still based at Langley, since each test flight at Farnborough necessitated a flight to and from RAE in one of the company hacks. Accordingly, on 19 September 1951, Duke flew the N7/46 prototype VP413 from Farnborough to its new home at Dunsfold, where it remained. This was followed by the other N7/46, VP422 on 17 October. The first P.1052 VX272, having been laid up following a crash landing earlier in the year, had suffered the embarrassment of a further forced landing on its first flight after repair and put down at Langley on 4 September 1951, losing a wheel in the process. However, it was quickly repaired at the airfield in time for the SBAC display at Farnborough on the 11th and was also flown into Dunsfold on 19 September, making one other flight before being laid up until March 1952 for various works, including the addition of a bullet fairing at the fin/tailplane intersection in preparation for high-speed flight trials. On 21 September P.1067 WB188 flew in to its new home and, in January 1952, the Test Pilot office relocated to Dunsfold's tower. The irksome commutes from Langley could at last be forgotten.

An interesting diversion from the efforts at Dunsfold to prepare the airfield occurred in the summer of 1951. As part of the research work being undertaken by Avro at Woodford in preparation for the Avro 698 Vulcan bomber, several scale aircraft were constructed to air test the radical delta wing planform prior to its utilisation on the full-sized aircraft. The first of these test aircraft – the Avro 707 – flew in September 1949 but crashed soon afterwards near Blackbushe on a flight out of Farnborough. The second airframe – the Avro 707B – first flew in September 1950 in the hands of Roly Falk. This version was used to collect data on the delta wing at low airspeeds and had its public debut at the SBAC Show that year. The following year, on 31 July 1951, the 707B, serialled VX790, was brought over to Dunsfold from Boscombe Down and shown to the press both on the ground and in the air. It is a little hard to understand the reason for this since the aircraft would be available for all to see at the Farnborough Show the following week. On 5 June 1952 Avro 707B VX790 was again brought over to Dunsfold from Boscombe Down and some test flights made the next day, together with a display for selected guests before return to Boscombe Down. Perhaps as a quid pro quo for this facility, Duke was able to get a flight in the Avro 707A at Woodford on 23 October.

SEA HAWK F. MK. 1
NENE 4
NOV 1951

N7/46 Sea Hawk WF143, the first production example at Dunsfold. Note absence of tail bullet fairing, November 1951. (BAE Systems, courtesy of Brooklands Museum)

By October 1951 the cracks papered over at the beginning of the year were already showing through. The Air Ministry, already jittery regarding the efforts to host Hawker at Dunsfold as well as future squadrons of USAF fighters, complained to the Ministry of Supply on 25 October that 'we are disturbed to find now at this stage that Hawkers have already gone far beyond the agreement … by removing the experimental section of their company from Farnborough to Dunsfold'.[10] In an effort to influence a situation that was fast spinning out of their control, the Air Ministry felt forced to restate the conditions under which the Ministry of Supply had been permitted to approve Hawker's move into the airfield: that occupation be limited to five years and that, as soon as conditions permit, Hawker to vacate the airfield and move elsewhere; additional hangar space not to exceed 90,000 square feet; persons employed not to exceed 300, of whom not more than 140 to be recruited from local labour resources; Ministry of Civil Aviation to approve ATC facilities at Dunsfold. In a further effort to shorten or stop altogether Hawker's moves to bed in at Dunsfold, the Air Ministry, in the person of Air Marshal Sharp had approached Hawker's management with an offer of alternative airfields – at Finmere, Oakley, Grove and Ramsbury – to the fury of the Ministry of Supply and Hawker.[11] In an extraordinary blast to Robbins at the Ministry on 7 January 1952, John Lidbury, Hawker's company secretary stated that:

In short, we are being asked to scrap the Dunsfold project and start again … . We must put on record the following points:

1) Dunsfold was allocated to the company in February 1951 after a most exhaustive survey of available aerodromes in the south.
2) The allocation was agreed, after full discussion at many meetings, by all interested departments of HM Government.
3) Dunsfold is the only suitable aerodrome, by reason of its proximity to Kingston and the travelling facilities available, to which our existing skilled production and experimental erection and flight labour can be transferred.
4) As will be seen from the file, the negotiations for a suitable aerodrome were so protracted that by the time the allocation was made, it left this company with a race against time to prepare for Sea Hawk production flying.
5) Since February last, a great deal of work has gone into making this aerodrome ready and extraordinary measures have had to be taken to this end. Labour has successfully been transferred; the experimental flight section has been installed; our experimental facilities at Langley and Farnborough have been given up, and all our experimental flying and our first production Sea Hawk flying is now being completely and successfully carried out from Dunsfold.

We therefore submit … we are entitled to look to the Ministry of Supply to support us to the full in our occupation of Dunsfold, and therefore, we do not propose to contemplate an alternative location unless we are directly instructed by the Ministry of Supply to cease our occupation of Dunsfold.[12]

This appeared to settle the matter for a while and allowed Hawker to get on with their job – to manufacture and deliver to Britain's armed forces the equipment required to defend the country – there was much to do and little time to do it.

By the summer of 1952 things were settling down. The T2B hangar, henceforth known as 'Experimental' was complete and in full use. Closely surrounded by security fencing, entry was through a guard-controlled gate. The three-bay Production Hangar was coming into use with bays 1 and 2

Sea Hawk F.1s in Production hangar at Dunsfold. Tail bullet fairing now fitted, probably 1953. (BAE Systems, courtesy of Brooklands Museum)

broadly complete. With Skyways eventual vacation of hangar T2A, Hawker were busy refurbishing this for their own use, again to the chagrin of the Air Ministry who had not given permission. The runway and taxiways had been resurfaced and operational readiness platforms completed at each end of the runway. Hawker's research and experimental aircraft were safely ensconced and the first production Sea Hawks were being completed, the first production Sea Hawk Mk 1 aircraft, WF143, having made its maiden flight on 14 November 1951 in the hands of Duke, the second aircraft WF144 not flying until 21 February 1952 and the third, WF145, on 23 March, all from Dunsfold. Joining the first P.1067 was the second prototype WB195 which flew for the first time on 5 May 1952 and the first Armstrong-Siddeley Sapphire-powered Hunter, WB202, effectively the prototype for the F.2 Hunter which would fly on 30 November that year, both from Dunsfold.

With Sea Hawk production underway, airframes were available to join the trials work being undertaken by the development N7/46 aircraft. Trials work was split between the first eight airframes thus:

WF143 first production Sea Hawk: general development work both at Dunsfold and at Farnborough and Boscombe Down, including RATOG and fuel-systems trials.

WF144, under CS(A) control remained at Dunsfold on general development duties.

WF145 was retained by RAE Farnborough for radio trials including IFF Mk 10 and Green Salad.

WF146 allocated to Boscombe Down for flight trials to clear the aircraft for drop-tank carriage and generator-cooling trials.

WF147 effectively became the prototype F.2 Sea Hawk, retained at Dunsfold under Hawker Aircraft testing the installation of powered ailerons, first flown 20 November 1952.

WF148 was allocated to winterisation trials at the Winter Experimental Establishment (CEPE) at Namao near Edmonton in Canada. Due to a disappointing 'season' following unserviceability, it was retained into 1953.

WF149 allocated to Boscombe Down for gun-firing trials. It crashed there due to faulty wire-locking.

WF150 allocated to Rolls Royce for engine trials.

Additionally, WF157 became the prototype F.3 with pressurised cabin. This was allocated to Boscombe Down for bombing trials.

WF161 also moved to Boscombe Down for refrigeration trials.

Finally, WM901, part of the last Kingston-built batch, was used by Boscombe Down for gun-heating trials.

Because of the necessity of clearing the aircraft through its many upgrades and development trials, by 1 July 1952, only two aircraft had reached CS(A), while eight more were at Dunsfold for final assembly and testing and none had been delivered to the Admiralty. By March 1953 the situation had improved slightly with five aircraft in the hands of the first Sea Hawk operational unit – 806 Naval Air Squadron – at Brawdy.

Matters were not helped by the congestion at Kingston caused by the large orders arriving for Hunters. In the event, all thirty-five Sea Hawks, in three batches, would be completed in the Experimental Department before being roaded to Dunsfold. By the end of 1952 some eighteen aircraft had been flown. By the end of the following year, the entire batch of thirty-five aircraft that Kingston would build were broadly complete and had been delivered to service or government facilities.

Not all flight testing went smoothly. On 5 January 1953, WF154, under test by Bedford, had suffered an engine failure at 10,000 feet after inverted flight to check oil pressure behaviour. Electing to make a forced landing on runway 07, and with dubious undercarriage and flap performance, Bedford saw the runway pass by before getting the aircraft down on the grass, ploughing on across the airfield and two ditches, crossing the A281 road and coming to rest in the field beyond, minus his main undercarriage. Murphy also had an interesting few minutes in WF159 on 19 December 1952. Having taken off from Dunsfold on a production test flight, the engine caught fire forcing him into an emergency landing at RNAS Ford. With his engine producing a 15-foot flame from the rear and failing hydraulics, the entire length of the wet runway was required to bring the aircraft safely to a halt during his wheels-up landing. It would be the first of too many forced landings that the company pilots would undertake at Ford.

Of the many former employees interviewed for this book, none recalls production Sea Hawks in the hangars after 1953, although some test airframes were in evidence for the next couple of years. In all, some 435 Sea Hawks of various marks were delivered to the Admiralty and were well liked, the aircraft seeing action during the Suez campaign in the fighter-bomber and fighter-ground-attack configurations. The aircraft was also successfully exported for use by the Royal Netherlands Navy, by the German Marineflieger and by the Indian Navy, being used in the Indo-Pakistan Wars of 1965 and 1971. While the Sea Hawk started to leave the RN inventory around 1960, they were employed by specialist units such as the Fleet Requirement Unit (FRU) into the mid-1960s. The Indian versions did not leave service until replaced by the Sea Harrier from 1983.

Because of the initial delays in getting the flying characteristics right on the early aircraft, and the requirement to re-equip the RAF with the Hunter becoming paramount, only thirty-five aircraft were completed by Kingston and Dunsfold. All remaining production and design authority was handed off to Sir W.G. Armstrong Whitworth Aircraft Ltd, another company within the Hawker Siddeley Group, to allow Kingston, Langley and Dunsfold to concentrate on the Hunter. In total over 539 Sea Hawks of all marks, plus a number of refurbishments, were manufactured, mostly at Armstrong Whitworth's facilities at Coventry and Bitteswell.

With regard to Hunter progress, there were still no production aircraft available to assist with the flight development work being undertaken by the three prototype airframes. Some early progress had been made, however. Duke had quickly identified two major problems with the aircraft: a severe 'buzz' emanating from the rear at fairly high speeds and the reluctance of the aircraft to slow down when required. Although this may sound like a desirable asset in fast jet aircraft, the lack of ability to decelerate quickly, either in combat or for landing etc., was a severe disadvantage and not one that the services would accept. Therefore, plans were swiftly put in hand to find the best location for the mounting of an airbrake. The high speed 'buzz' was cured by the fitting of a streamlined conical fairing at the fin/tailplane interface, similar to the cure for the vibration problems with the Sea Hawk but at the back of the fin rather than the front. Notwithstanding the problems being experienced, which were common on new designs, Duke was able to take Hunter WB188 through the 'sound barrier' on 24 June 1952 for the first time.[13] In fact, this may not have been his first venture into the realms of Mach 1 flight. In his autobiography *Test Pilot*, Duke describes a conversation with a bemused Frank Bullen in the flight office one morning. Bullen had been driving down to his home the previous day at Northchapel and had been approached by some villagers who enquired of him whether there had been a crash at the aerodrome that might account for 'queer bangs' heard about the locality. Duke had been up in the Hunter at the time and Bullen and Duke quickly realised that what the locals were describing must have been sonic booms created by Duke's flight.[14]

With no production Hunters in the offing at Dunsfold, production testing of Sea Hawks continued under Murphy while work on development flying of the Hunter and N7/46 prototypes continued under Chief Test Pilot Neville Duke.

Meanwhile events on the other side of the world were about to intrude on the British Government and the country's aircraft industry, not necessarily to Hawker's disadvantage. The Korean War, triggered by the invasion of Communist forces across the UN mandated border into South Korea, had pitched US and Commonwealth forces into a shooting war on the other side of the globe. The appearance of Russian-built MiG-15 jet aircraft in the conflict had quickly brought about the realisation that, after five years of Government parsimony in respect of aircraft research and development funds, Britain was ill-equipped to fight an aerial war, relying as it did on obsolescent Gloster Meteors and DH Vampires for its offensive fighter cover. The absence of a transonic aircraft, which the Hunter represented, with which to combat the MiG was felt keenly in the corridors of Whitehall, and unusual steps were taken to remedy the situation. With the defeat of the Labour administration under Attlee and the return of Churchill in October 1951, a scheme was enacted which gave certain aircraft projects 'Super-Priority' status within the industry and ministries involved. Two of the aircraft thus benefitting were the Hunter and Sea Hawk. Yet it would be another eighteen months-plus before the first production Hunter would be ready to fly from Dunsfold. In an effort to speed up production, Hawker had been persuaded to take a lease on facilities at Squires Gate in Blackpool and effectively set up a shadow factory for Hunter production. Thus, beginning in May 1951, Duke and fellow pilots were involved in flying various of the Hawker Aircraft directors and senior managers to and from Blackpool as the production operation in the north got under way.[15]

Chapter 3

Hunter into Production

On 19 May 1953 HRH Prince Philip visited Hawker Aircraft at Kingston-upon-Thames and, in the afternoon, drove down to Dunsfold for a tour of the premises. As the husband of the new Queen, Philip was a consort in search of a purpose and gaining an insight into British aircraft manufacturing with a view to promoting the country's abilities abroad seemed one way of achieving this.[1]

Describing the occasion, *The Aeroplane* magazine's reporter noted that:

> Few companies in this country would be able to provide as representative a collection of their designs as was lined up for the Duke to inspect at Dunsfold. Starting with the delightful little Cygnet biplane (G-EBMB) of 30 years ago, the party inspected, in turn, the Tom Tit (G-AFTA), the Hart (G-ABMR), the last Hurricane (G-AMAU), a Tempest TT.5 target tug, a Sea Fury FB.11 for the R.C.N, the navalized P.1052 swept-wing prototype, a Sea Hawk F.Mk 1, the second prototype Avon-Hunter (WB195), the Sapphire-engined Hunter F. Mk 2 (WB202) and in pride of place at the end of the line, the first production Hunter F. Mk 1 (WT555), which had flown for the first time four days previously.[2]

Accompanied by Hawker Directors Sir Frank Spriggs, Neville Spriggs and Chief Designer Sydney Camm, a tour of the production hangars revealed the last of the Sea Hawks and some of the first production Hunters undergoing finals preparatory to flight. WB188, the first P.1067, was not available for viewing, having been transported back to Kingston on 3 December 1952 to transform it into the first, and only, Mk 3 Hunter.[3] Following a display of flying by the company test pilots in various of the older aircraft, Neville Duke took Hunter WB195 up to altitude and dived on the airfield to produce a satisfying sonic boom for the assembled worthies. Later in the afternoon,

P.1067 mock-up at Richmond Road Kingston Experimental Department 1949. By this time the nose intake had been deleted but the T-tail remained. (BAE Systems, courtesy of Brooklands Museum)

the Duke unveiled his crest painted on the nose of the first production Hunter before this and the two prototype Hunters were taken up and flown in formation – the first time that more than one Hunter had been seen in the air at one time. Altogether a successful day for Hawker management and a fitting 'official' opening of the Dunsfold production facilities.

The first production Hunter, of 113 in the first Kingston batch, WT555, had in fact first flown on 16 May in the hands of Duke.[4] Thereafter, one Hunter per month was rolled out of the Production hangar for its first flight. By September the company was managing two aircraft per month and by December of that year six aircraft passed out of the hangar. This unpromising start was soon overtaken by better rates. January 1954 saw ten aircraft take to the air for the first time and by September the factory was managing to push twenty-three aircraft through the door. By the end of the year the first batch of Mk 1 aircraft was complete. With a further twenty-six aircraft built in the new Hawker factory at Squires Gate Blackpool, Hunter Mk 1 production was terminated. Henceforth subsequent marks of aircraft would fill the production lines. It must be said that, due to the urgency of bringing the Hunter into service, aircraft in this first batch were of varying modification states, the earliest not having the 'flying-tail' or a definitive air brake solution, these concerns being addressed as and when testing was complete and final modification drawings were available.

While work progressed on the F.1, at Coventry and Bitteswell a further production line was getting into gear to produce the Sapphire-engined version of the Hunter, the F.2, the prototype for which – WB202 – had been flown at Dunsfold on 30 November 1952. It was joined in December 1953 by WN888, the first production F.2 built at Coventry and retained at Dunsfold for various trials to clear the aircraft for CA release.

As the early Mk 1 aircraft came off test at Dunsfold they were quickly called upon to plug the shortfall in development flying that the initial order of only three prototype aircraft had made inevitable. The two most urgent concerns with regard to preparing the Hunter for operational use were the buffet at the rear of the aircraft at high speed and insufficient air braking capability.

While the buffet was cleared fairly quickly with the addition of a conical fairing aft of the fin/tailplane joint, the airbrake problem was not so easily solved. Camm's original design had indeed understood the requirement for air braking and had incorporated this in the split flap arrangement on the rear

P.1067 WB188, Hunter prototype at Boscombe Down prior to first flight on 20 July 1951. (BAE Systems, courtesy of Brooklands Museum)

of the wing. However, the extension of flap at speed and low level resulted in an invigorating response. 'When the selection was made, the nose of the Hunter went hard down, while the pilot headed for the canopy. The trim was such that it was totally operationally unacceptable.' So said Air Vice Marshal Bird-Wilson, at the time Wing Commander and Officer Commanding the Air Fighting Development Squadron at the Central Fighter Establishment at West Raynham, who had been ordered to Dunsfold to fly the first production Hunter WT555.[5] By all accounts Camm was not amused to be told his design was no good and that he would have to revise it. The problem with the airbrake was not news to Hawker, who had fitted side airbrakes to the rear fuselage of WB188 for the speed record attempts in the summer of 1953. However, these were found to be unacceptable for service aircraft.

Having toyed with slotted flaps and flaps mounted above the wings, an installation was mounted under the tail with a single brake installed. Various extension angles were flown on the prototypes in February 1954 before the fix was applied to production aircraft WT556, Frank Murphy taking it up to Mach 1.05 and 610 knots IAS with acceptable

Erection of Hunter F.1 at Dunsfold, middle bay of the Production Hangar, 1953. WT575 in the foreground first flown in January 1954 by Duke. (BAE Systems, courtesy of Brooklands Museum)

trim change and buffet levels. Eventually a 67-degree extension angle was incorporated and Bird-Wilson declared the airbrake operationally acceptable. Notwithstanding service acceptance, Hawker continued to experiment with airbrake location, even moving the Vernier rail assembly upon which the test airbrake was mounted to a position under the cockpit but with no improvement. The rear position was the one that went into production.

As noted above, WB188 had been withdrawn from flying for modifications to be made to the airframe to incorporate a reheated Avon engine as part of the trials to produce a developed Hunter under project code P.1083, which would feature a 50-degree swept wing and an Avon RA14R engine rated at 9,600lb thrust with reheat engaged. P.1083 would give the RAF a truly supersonic fighter with which to arm the service and keep its abilities in the forefront for years to come. But, as work continued on the prototype at Kingston, the end of the Korean conflict brought sudden cancellation and the chance of Britain having a supersonic fighter in the early 1950s was lost. Instead it was left to English Electric's Lightning to fulfil the requirement ten years later. Rather than a reheated Avon, work would now progress on development of a 'dry' engine of higher performance, this work in its turn leading to the Hunter F.6 with an engine rated at 10,000lb thrust.

With the cancellation of P.1083 the work being undertaken to flight test the reheated Avon had little purpose but it was decided that the opportunity existed to make some progress with reheated engine technology and, at the same time, make an attempt on the world absolute air speed record. Accordingly, the engine was installed in WB188 together with the afterburning tailpipe, ventral NACA intake for cooling the aft fuselage and clam-shell airbrakes. A sharply pointed nose was fitted and a raked fairing for the windscreen installed, the work being carried out at Kingston. Finally, a gloss red paint scheme was applied and flight testing commenced. Prior to the work up on the south coast, Duke took the aircraft up from Dunsfold for tests of the reheat system for the first time on 7 July 1953, the installation being largely trouble free.[6]

Practice flights along the course, off the coast at Littlehampton, were made in August and, when all was ready, the aircraft was based at Tangmere, just minutes from the course and from where the attempts would be flown. As noted earlier, Duke had been involved in the High-Speed Flight of the RAF when a Meteor was used, also out of Tangmere, for an earlier series of attempts on the record in 1946. He was thus well versed in the procedures for the attempt and on 7 September returned an average speed round the low-level course of 727.63mph or Mach 0.92. On the 19th Duke flew the 100-kilometre course at an average of 709.2mph, a new world record.

P.1067 Sapphire-engined prototype for Hunter F.2 at Dunsfold. Note in the background Sea Fury VX283 and Sea Hawk in front of the Experimental Hangar. (BAE Systems, courtesy Brooklands Museum)

Hunter F.3 WB188 being prepared for its record attempt at Dunsfold prior to despatch to Tangmere. Note the modified sharp nose profile, August 1953. (BAE Systems, courtesy of Brooklands Museum)

Although Duke had achieved an unofficial run of 741.76mph on 30 August, representing Mach 0.94, both this and the official speed record pointed up the limiting effect of the aircraft's swept wing and the short-sightedness of the cancellation of the P.1083 with its 50-degree sweep.

As the successful launch of Hunter production got underway at Dunsfold it became apparent fairly quickly that the early Avon engines were noisy items of equipment. At the time there were no engine detuners available on the airfield to mute the various ground engine runs that were required to clear the aircraft for flight. With upwards of twenty aircraft per month rolling out the door ready for engine runs, thanks to seven-day-per-week two-shift working, together with the various air tests required, Dunsfold became a very noisy place in which to live and work. Pretty soon, complaints were reaching the Air Ministry and local authority about the situation, but there was little that could be done. The Hunter was desperately needed by the armed forces and nothing short of a nuclear blast was going to change that.

The blast in question would come soon enough. A landowner on the south side of the airfield, one Colonel Thomas Houssemayne du Boulay, had tired of writing letters of complaint to the authorities and Hawker and had turned to the more effective remedy of legal action. On 1 March 1954 a writ was issued against Hawker Aircraft alleging nuisance and the seeking of an interim injunction to ban all engine running threatened. The concern at the ministry was that an action to seek an injunction might well succeed in temporarily achieving its aim of bringing silence to Dunsfold and, in so doing, threaten the supply of aircraft to the services.[7]

A move to grant immunity to Hawker's activity at Dunsfold was felt to be fully justified. The action was believed to be necessary to cover a serious gap in legislation by which an individual could interrupt a major part of the defence programme and that, while full consideration should be given to private interest, it was unreasonable that the state should be exposed to such a risk.

Within days the Ministry of Supply was examining various courses of action with which to fight this threat by bringing the activity at the aerodrome under government control. Various proposals were mooted by the Under-Secretary Air including:

1) The Ministry of Transport and Civil Aviation to license Dunsfold so that it notionally came under their control.
2) Make an Order in Council under the Civil Aviation Act to give the aerodrome immunity under the Act such as already enjoyed by government sites.

3) The Ministry of Supply to appoint a Controller for Dunsfold so that Hawker would notionally be under government control.
4) 'Inducing the MP for the division in which Dunsfold lies to appeal to the better nature and sweet reason of the man who is causing the trouble.'

Such was the concern raised by this question that within a matter of hours, orders had been given to prepare paperwork etc. for each of the above contingencies. Part of this concern resulted from the realisation that the situation at Dunsfold, and the threatened action to prevent testing of aircraft, could equally be applied to other airfields, thus reducing the country's aircraft production programme to tatters. It was estimated that a further forty-six airfields fell into this category. As the various alternative remedies were further considered, it was quickly decided that the making of an Order in Council under the Civil Aviation Act would provide the best answer and steps were taken to prepare for this eventuality. Behind the scenes other remedies were being sought, including some means of noise attenuation.

On the basis that it appeared that the complainant was seeking genuine remediation of the noise problem rather than financial damages, it was decided early in April that a two-pronged approach be taken. Firstly, that Colonel du Boulay would be assured that everything possible was being done to reduce the noise nuisance and that might include an agreed undertaking between Hawker and du Boulay. Secondly, once such agreement was in place, the government would proceed with its order in council to achieve immunity for airfields including Dunsfold in the future. This plan was soon scuppered when it became clear that the complainant was indeed seeking financial damages, both to recover his own costs and cover claimed physical damage to his property but also on the basis of a back-dated payment for each month of disturbance suffered, his solicitors suggesting payment of some £3,587 as recompense, later reduced to £1,200.

By the end of the month, the various ministerial departments, in an uncharacteristic burst of speed, had affidavits ready for ministers to sign should this be necessary to support Hawker in court. In parallel, government solicitors had prepared a draft for an Order in Council to apply Section 40 of the Civil Aviation Act 1949 to Crown aircraft, which would include those being produced by Hawker Aircraft Ltd.

In the event, on 1 June 1954, du Boulay settled for £750 together with an undertaking from Hawker that they would do everything possible to minimise future disturbance from aircraft noise and, directly the settlement was confirmed by all parties, an Order in Council was presented on the evening of the 3rd and issued under the Air Navigation Order (seventh amendment) 1954, to give future immunity from legal action to airfields including those occupied by government contractors.

When the news of this order was announced in the press on the 4th, an outraged du Boulay lost no time in slating the authorities. The *Daily Mail*, under the headline 'Jet noise pact wiped out', claimed that his agreement with the company was just twelve hours old when it was invalidated by the new legislation. Du Boulay complained: 'This Order in Council makes sheer nonsense of the agreement that Hawkers signed. It makes it impossible for me to take any further legal action against them.' That was not strictly true; he could still hold Hawker to account if they went back on their undertaking, although no-one was in any hurry to tell him so, but du Boulay could no longer successfully threaten the cessation of aircraft testing in law.[8]

The work to mitigate noise propagation from aircraft engines included the use of portable screens around the intakes of the aircraft and at the rear. Hawker had approached the National Physical Laboratory along these lines and was planning to acquire some 'baffles' so that they could experiment. One has to have some sympathy for Colonel du Boulay; the ministry noted that, on an average day in January and February 1954, some nine engine runs had been carried out. The author clearly remembers as a child the constant background roar of jet engines from the aerodrome in Cranleigh, some four miles distant, even in the later 1950s. Although du Boulay continued to seek support for his complaints in the press and in parliament for some months, the noise concern was finally addressed with the construction of three engine-running pens on the north side of the airfield and the installation of 'mufflers' from Detuners Ltd, into which the aircraft exhaust was channelled, effectively reducing the noise by an order of magnitude. That work was complete by the end of 1954.[9]

In retrospect, it must have seemed to Colonel du Boulay that Hawker was rubbing salt into his already sore wounds when, on 7 December 1953, du Boulay wrote to Hawker regarding a telephone conversation he had received with news of the company's intention to base aircraft on the south side of the airfield adjacent to his property. One may imagine the dismay with which this news was received. In the event, these would not be Hawker's aircraft at all, but would be under the control of Airwork Ltd. Hawker's Mr Jeffery assured du Boulay that they would speak to the Airwork team when they arrived and reiterate that engines were not to be tested in this area although quite where they were to be tested was left hanging.

One last note on the noise problem, which would follow Hawker and its successors through to closure, must come from the very top. In the House of Commons on 13 July 1955, the Under Secretary of State for Air stood to answer a question tabled by the opposition of the day. Mr Gough had asked:

> if the Ministry of Supply was aware of the distress and shock caused, particularly to elderly people living in the proximity of Dunsfold Aerodrome, of the noise of jet fighter planes landing and taking off from that aerodrome; and what steps he proposes to take to minimise this trouble.

While the minister's response was bland and reassuring, investigation had shown that the likely complainant, far from living close by, in fact resided in Horsham, over eight miles away and had no idea where the distressful aircraft actually originated. Further digging showed that in fact an RAF

Hawker test pilots at Dunsfold in the 1950s. From left, Frank Bullen, Bill Bedford, Duncan Simpson, Hugh Merewether and David Lockspeiser. (BAE Systems, courtesy of Brooklands Museum)

low-flying zone extended over Horsham and so the answer was likely to lie there rather than with Mr Duke and his colleagues.[10]

As the last of the Mk 1 Hunters continued to clear finals at Dunsfold in 1954, the aircraft were in various stages of modification and still awaiting CA release. Without this, the aircraft could not be despatched to squadron service and started to accumulate on the airfield. To bring them under cover, two large Bessoneau hangars were erected on the dispersals to the east of the Compasses gate and the brand-new Hunters stored for the duration. Eventually, with the airbrake position decided and the modification being embodied on airframes already completed as well as those aircraft still on the production line, a limited CA Release was issued to the Hunter and deliveries could begin to squadrons.

The test-pilot team at this time comprised Neville Duke and his number two, Bill Bedford, responsible for experimental testing, and Frank Murphy, Frank Bullen, Don Lucey, Hugh Merewether and Duncan Simpson undertaking production testing, joined in 1955 by David Lockspeiser. Duke had moved into Primemeads Farmhouse just inside the Compasses gate in 1952, his wife Gwen finding it rather dilapidated after years of hard use during the war and after. Frank Murphy and his wife drew the short straw and moved into Broadmeads Cottage, also known as Canada House, which was on the south side of the airfield adjacent to Benbow Lane. As is well known, the cottage had been moved from its original location on the north side of the airfield in the earliest days of the aerodrome's construction and therefore did not have the convenience of water or waste facilities for a while. Murphy would give up test flying in 1955 and move into Hawker's Technical Sales department based at Kingston.

As the Hunter started to be tested by the squadrons, it became apparent that there were instances of the engine surging when the guns were fired. Initially this was thought to be connected to individual engines but it soon became apparent that all Avon engines were similarly affected. At first this was a mystery for gun firing had been one of many tests undertaken by the pilots at Boscombe Down, who had cleared the test point satisfactorily. Then the penny dropped; the testing had been conducted on Sapphire-powered Hunters with no problems; it was the Avon-powered machines that were experiencing the problem. Added to this, the aircraft were found to be prone to fuel shortages and several were lost on fairly short flights because of it. Work on producing modifications to deal with this continued, but the surging of the Avon could only be cured with a new engine and that would have to await subsequent marks of the aircraft.

On squadron airfields and at MUs, as well as at Dunsfold, the new modifications were feverishly introduced to existing aircraft where possible, including a new surge-free Avon RA.21 engine. These modifications brought the aircraft up to something approaching F.4 standard and these were joined by a further eighty-five new-build F.4 which went through the flight sheds at Dunsfold between October 1954 and April 1955, followed soon after by a further eighty-five aircraft, completed by September 1955. After this F.4 production was transferred from Kingston, Langley and Dunsfold to Blackpool and in total some 368 F.4s were built plus a further ninety-five F.4s built under licence by Fokker for the Royal Netherlands Air Force and 142 aircraft by SABCA and Avions Fairey from kits manufactured by Fokker. The F.4 Hunter was followed by the F.5, the Sapphire-powered updated F.2 which had been constructed by Armstrong Whitworth at Coventry and Bitteswell. Kingston and Dunsfold's lines would take on the Hunter F.6.

But first, the opportunity was taken to construct further F.4 aircraft for the valuable export market. Sweden had ordered 120 Hunters (Mk 50) and Denmark a further thirty (Mk 51), together with two T.53 trainers. Sweden's order was dated 29 June 1954 and the first twenty-four aircraft were built at Kingston/Langley and assembled and flown from Dunsfold. Thereafter, the order was transferred to Blackpool for completion. The Danish order was signed on 3 July 1954 and built at Kingston and Dunsfold with completion by September 1956. These were followed by a small order for Peru consisting of sixteen RAF F.4 aircraft returned to Dunsfold and prepared for the Peruvian Air Force, becoming Mk 52s. These aircraft were completed during 1956, the work taking place in the newly-extended 'Black' hangar rather than in the production bays and delivered by sea. A small team of Hawker engineers was sent to Peru and quickly reassembled the aircraft for flight testing by Duncan Simpson.

With the jigs clear of Hunter F.4s, Hawker could turn to production of the F.6. This mark included all the various modifications which had belatedly been introduced into the earlier marks but with the addition of a new engine, the Avon Mk 203 rated at 10,000lb. Wing leading-edge extensions to deal with the pitch up problem were also introduced some way down the line and retrospectively installed on some of the earlier F.6s.

Hawker's first order for the F.6 had incredibly been signed as far back as 19 July 1951 for seven essentially pre-production aircraft but had been delayed by the lack of a suitable engine and the need to bring the earlier marks up to scratch. To this must be added the prototype airframe XF833, constructed in part from the remains of the cancelled P.1083. This batch was

Dutch Hunter T.7 trainers awaiting delivery at Dunsfold 1958. Note the Bessoneau hangar and engine-running pen in the background. (BAE Systems, courtesy of Brooklands Museum)

followed by a further order dated 24 August 1953 for another 100 aircraft to be built by Hawker Aircraft at Kingston/Dunsfold and Armstrong Whitworth at Coventry/Bitteswell. Again, none of the aircraft were built with leading-edge extensions, these being fitted later at Dunsfold during 1957/58 on a return-to-work basis. This was followed by a third batch of 110 F.6s, again split between Kingston/Dunsfold and Coventry with further batches for forty-five and 153 aircraft being ordered and constructed at Kingston/Dunsfold.

The first Hunter F.6, WW592, flew at Dunsfold on 23 May 1955 with Bedford at the controls and was retained by Hawker for various trials work at Dunsfold and Boscombe Down. On 10 January 1957 the aircraft suffered brake failure on landing and ran off the end of the runway into the western overshoot but without severe damage to pilot or aircraft, the Hunter being removed from the mud next day. A further near accident was recalled by John Parrott who happened to be on the then flight-line outside the armoury dealing with some US pilots flying the Hunter, no doubt as part of the MDAP funding for NATO procurement. Having tried to move away with the chocks still under the wheels, the American on his return landed some 100 yards short of the runway and skidded along through the mud until reaching the runway and correcting his somewhat aberrant trajectory.

Following closely on the heels of the F.6 contracts came an order for fifty-five T.7 two-seat trainer aircraft, two prototypes of which had been ordered in 1954 under project P.1101. Production was relatively straightforward and involved the fitting of a side-by-side seating front fuselage unit, the remaining airframe being a standard Hunter. The first of these two prototypes had flown on 8 June 1955 in the hands of Duke. Early flights showed airflow buffet around the canopy and so the lines of the canopy were eventually faired into the centre fuselage with an elegant fairing, this curing the problem. With receipt of the production order in 1956, the first flight of the first production example occurred in October 1957 at Dunsfold with the remaining forty-five for the RAF following through to completion in January 1959. The remaining ten aircraft of this order were re-allocated to the Admiralty and designated T.8. The order for these aircraft had been placed with Hawker (Blackpool) Ltd but, due to political considerations, the order had been transferred to Kingston. These aircraft were completed between May and December 1958.

So it was that, by the end of 1958, Hawker had completed an incredible 1,501 Hunters for the RAF comprising seven prototypes, 139 Mk 1, forty-five Mk 2, 367 Mk 4, 105 Mk 5 and 377 Mk 6 aircraft, of which 919 had been produced by the Kingston/Langley/Dunsfold unit. They had also produced a further ten for the Admiralty and 150 for export, producing a welcome profit for the company and the country's flagging coffers.

In retrospect it is clear that in the haste to get a transonic aircraft into operation in an effort to counter the Soviet threat in the early Cold War years, insufficient prototypes were ordered to allow proper testing to be carried out and the aircraft pressed into service in too short a timescale. Stan Lawson, who began working at Dunsfold in 1954, recalled that problems with directional control meant that fins and rudders and sometimes whole

Early testing of the four-gun pack for the Hunter in the butts at Dunsfold. (BAE Systems, courtesy of Brooklands Museum)

rear fuselage sections were regularly being swapped in an effort to make aircraft that would fly straight. That said, eventually the Hunter turned into a world-beating design which still flew regularly seventy years after design began.

It need not be stated that the test pilots engaged on the testing of the many aircraft completed at Dunsfold were consummate professionals and needed to be when things did not go according to plan. Both Duke and Murphy suffered severe accidents in the course of their work, two examples showing just what they faced. Murphy was the first to test a Hunter to destruction in an F.4, WT707, on 25 January 1955. Writing up the incident in his log-book later he described it thus:

> Crash landed RNAS Ford – wheels up. Flame out 44,000 feet above 8/8 stratus at 1,500ft. Relight circuit U/S then radio U/S whilst still above cloud. Unable to lower emergency flaps so aircraft of necessity belly landed at high speed – initial impact 240mph – 19 bounces then aircraft slewed port went through caravan site – 3 fatalities, 2 injured – hit sunken road sideways still about 80mph – Aircraft broke up and self in cockpit tumbled further 100 yards. Sustained cracked vertebrae severely torn back muscles superficial cuts and abrasions and deceleration bruising. Royal West Sussex Hospital and RAF MRU Headley Court. Discharged 11/5/55.[11]

Then, in early August 1955, Duke flying Hunter F.1 WT562 suffered an engine failure and carried out a forced landing at RNAS Ford. The aircraft engine was replaced and on its next flight on 6 August the engine again failed, this time after take-off at 1,000 feet. A forced landing was attempted at RAF Thorney Island but the aircraft, landing fast, bounced to destruction whilst crossing the airfield boundary and came to an abrupt halt in a ground depression. The aircraft was destroyed and Duke severely injured with a fractured back. Although flying again within a month, the injury probably weakened his back so that when, on 9 May 1956, while flying the P.1099 prototype XF833 modified with a P.1121-type cockpit layout, he made a heavy landing at Dunsfold he suffered further injury to his back, described in his log as 'slipped disc – fractured back'. Despite attempting to regain his ability by flying a Hunter in October, the writing was on the wall, Duke having to accept that his fast jet testing days were over.[12]

HUNTER INTO PRODUCTION

Who were the engineers tasked with producing Great Britain's great new hope – the Hunter? They came from a disparate background. John Parrott had started as a 15-year-old 'shop-boy' in the Flight Shed on the last of the F.4 Hunters; his father worked in the armoury. He recalled that in 1954, production was arranged so that new aircraft firstly entered Bay 1 as a fuselage and set of wings on a Queen Mary trailer, from Langley. The aircraft would be erected in this bay, wings attached and all the necessary functions carried out. Once complete the aircraft would move into Bay 2 and be prepared for its '1090', a full inspection by company and ministry inspectors prior to engine run. Once engine running tests were complete, the aircraft would come back and be sited in Bay 3, the flight shed, from where all subsequent testing would take place. Occasionally, a trip to the Experimental Hangar might be required, which entailed passing through the security gate and signing in before gaining entry to this wondrous place. 'I was in awe of the Hunter really; it was THE aeroplane.' John recalled seeing some exotic Hunters there, including one with rear airbrakes (WB188) and another with wing-tip tanks (XG131). Also there were kept the older aircraft – the Hurricane, Hart and Cygnet.

Norman Hayler had also joined as a shop boy, but at Kingston in 1951, later taking up an apprenticeship. As part of his studies, Norman and other apprentices were sent to Langley to assist on the structural test rig, which was then testing the Hunter. During one test, the wing tips had been stretched upwards by a remarkable three feet before one of the wings failed catastrophically, shaking the whole structure and surrounding area. Following his transfer to Dunsfold, Norman worked in the instrument test lab within Experimental and recounted some, at times, worrying incidents. During the extended gun-firing trials being undertaken between Boscombe Down and Dunsfold, one Hunter was inadvertently brought into the hangar with ammunition still in the guns. During pre-flight inspection, the gun trigger was tested and the gun fired off at least one round, across the hangar, through the wall and last seen heading for the canteen. The carriage of underwing stores could also catch out the unwary. One day, a service pilot had been given the task of evaluating the carriage of four bombs on a Hunter and had completed his handling trial and was returning to the runway when, as the aircraft touched down, all four bombs detached in unison and proceeded to plough and tumble their way down the airfield. Later, one Hunter had its hydraulic/pneumatic emergency accumulator pressurised with oxygen instead of nitrogen, which, given the explosive potential of mixing oil and oxygen, resulted in the accumulator exploding through the wing and exiting the hangar through the roof.

Chapter 4

Crisis at Hawker

The cancellation of the P.1083 Hunter with 50-degree swept wing, which would have provided the UK with a supersonic fighter at least five years before the advent of the P.1B Lightning, meant that Hunter development would now be directed at producing the aircraft less as an interceptor and more as a strike weapon, with an emphasis on ground attack. While this work had been going on as a matter of course, what really mattered to Camm were fighters – this was Hawker's real forte and so designs began to be schemed around 1954 for an advanced supersonic strike fighter to replace the Hunter.

As early as 1951 project P.1092/3 had been schemed for a delta-winged supersonic all-weather fighter in twin- and single-seat configurations, followed by P.1096, a highly swept supersonic research vehicle. The following year P.1100 sought to achieve supersonic capability with a reconfigured Hunter powered by an Avon RA.24. In early 1954, following initial information on draft specification OR.329 becoming available to design offices, Hawker produced two designs that they felt would meet this specification – P.1103 and P.1104. These early studies were in the 'developed Hunter' fold, with twin crew requirement seen as necessary for the role, powered by a DH Gyron engine with afterburner. By early 1955, with an official specification F.155T issued, concern about the ever-rising weight and size of the aircraft had seen P.1103 redrawn as a smaller single-seat design with ventral intake, Gyron Junior engine and rockets in the wing roots for additional thrust.[1]

By the summer, in the face of continually changing load-carrying requirements, Hawker's single-seat offering was already looking outmoded and indeed Camm questioned industry's ability to fulfil the requirement. However, a revised issue of F.155T suggested that they were on the right track with changes aimed at reducing weight in the tendered designs and by September Hawker had finalised their submission. The design submitted on 5 October 1955 featured a mid-wing with large ventral intake and

Hunter-type tail plus a 32-inch radar dish in a nose radome. Speed was expected to be Mach 2+ from a 25,000lb-thrust DH Gyron engine. With the requirement continuing to change within the Air Ministry, by December of that year Hawker's submission was out of the race although the company was not officially informed until April 1956. While no submission had been accepted in its entirety, Fairy and Armstrong-Whitworth were selected for further development work, a sure sign that the Air Ministry was still unsure what it wanted.

Far from being put out at this turn of events, Camm – believing he had support for his actions within the Ministry – set about reinventing the P.1103 design to fulfil a strike role for use in more limited war situations. By 16 May 1956 brochures were with the Air Ministry for a revised aircraft design under P.1116 which featured a similar aircraft but with smaller wing and nose more akin to a direct Hunter replacement and two fixed Aden cannon.[2] Following lukewarm responses from the Ministry to this latest submission, design effort reverted to the P.1103 as a single-seat aircraft minus its wingtip missiles, for use in the strike role, a brochure being submitted to the Ministry to this effect under the project code P.1121. Although some departments within the Ministry were averse to any further development of the design, others gave sufficient encouragement for Hawker to continue the

Mock-up of P.1121 in the Experimental Department at Richmond Road, Kingston, probably mid-1956. (BAE Systems, courtesy of Brooklands Museum)

work on a company-funded basis and, by July 1956, work was in hand for the construction of a full-sized mock-up in the Experimental shop at Kingston.

Meanwhile the OR.329 competition for the new interceptor that Hawker had failed to win was withering on the vine due to lack of funding, but was not yet dead. More than ever, it looked as if Hawker's decision to pursue their present course was the right one and, with memories of the private venture background to the Hawker Hurricane still fresh in some minds, the company's stance on the privately-funded P.1121 was noted in the press of the day. In January 1957 two Air Ministry officials visited Kingston to view the now completed P.1121 mock-up. Their response was underwhelming and worryingly, during the subsequent discussion, they informed Hawker that they did not see a requirement for an interceptor after 1960. The import of this was surely not missed by the Hawker team, but the detail of what it all meant would become all too apparent in the following months.

Meanwhile, at Dunsfold, preliminary work to support the P.1121 project had been carried out. As recounted in the previous chapter, Neville Duke

P.1121 front fuselage under construction in the Experimental department, Richmond Road, Kingston, 1956. Note the chin intake and pop-out rocket-pack recess. (BAE Systems, courtesy of Brooklands Museum)

had used the prototype Mk 6 Hunter to simulate the landing behaviour of the P.1121, which had poorer visibility from the cockpit on landing, and had made a very hard landing that exacerbated earlier injuries received in a forced landing in a Hunter leading to his premature retirement from test pilot duties, being replaced in the Chief's role by Bill Bedford. On 11 February 1957, at a meeting between design staff and Bedford, concerns were raised regarding the limited length of Dunsfold's runway and the higher take-off and landing speeds of the new aircraft. Various remedies were discussed including an arrester wire system 200 to 300 yards from the end of the runway and nylon barriers at the extremity of the runway overshoot – as later fitted – but it was considered politic that testing of P.1121 remain at Dunsfold with its short runway to illustrate to potential customers the likely short-field performance being called for in a new requirement – GOR.339 – that Hawker had their eyes on.

The Ministry view was that

> The firm chose to take an optimistic view of the possibilities of developing the new generation of aircraft from a 2,000-yard runway such as exists now at Dunsfold. We were strongly of the view that 2,500 yards was vital. Our decision as to the

Illustration showing proposed P.1121 paint scheme. (BAE Systems, courtesy of Brooklands Museum)

firm for OR.329 must depend, inter-alia, on our view as to the adequacy of their facilities, including runway and production resources. The firm might, however, suggest using the runway at Bedford for development flying which has some merit. We should as the next step sound the Ministry of Housing and Local Government on the possibilities 1) of securing permanent or long-term tenure for Hawker at Dunsfold and 2) of lengthening the runway to 2,500yds.[3]

On 4 April 1957, the notorious White Paper on the future of the UK's defence was announced by the Defence Minister Duncan Sandys which foresaw protection of British airspace by guided missiles and the end of manned interceptors. While the cost-cutting policies that drove the paper would have severe implications for British aircraft manufacturers, especially fighter design houses of which Hawker was the prime example, in terms of its implications for P.1121 the impact was less since the project was privately funded and P.1121 was being offered as a strike rather than interceptor aircraft. It did, however, spell the immediate end to the OR.329 requirement and to government funding of the DH Gyron engine that was being considered as the powerplant for Hawker's aircraft. Although de Havilland agreed to continue development of the Gyron on a private venture basis, more bad news followed when initial engine runs with the P.1121 intake fitted proved disappointing, the engine repeatedly stalling.[4]

Following the news that one of the few aircraft requirements that would continue post-Sandys would be a Canberra replacement under GOR.339, which eventually gave rise to TSR.2, P.1121 would be reinvented as a twin-seat, twin-engined low-level strike aircraft which would become Hawker's submission as the P.1129. In the meantime, in October 1957 the Hawker Board agreed to reduce work on the first prototype by 80 per cent, given the problems with the Gyron engine and lack of any interest from potential customers. While attempts to interest customers in the P.1121 continued, the Hawker Siddeley Group Board agreed to a joint submission to GOR.339 by Hawker and Avro which was submitted in November 1958 and, with no customer in sight, all work on the P.1121 ended the following month. In January 1959 Hawker learned that GOR.339 had been won by English Electric and Vickers, who would go on to construct the ill-fated TSR.2 amid a fog of political interference.[5]

While the thinking behind the Sandys White Paper had had little effect on P.1121, its more immediate impact was felt in the cancellation of the final hundred F.6 Hunters for the RAF in January 1957 and the threat of more cancellations to come. With production lines emptying at an alarming rate and a large gap in its budgeting – after all the company had no other aircraft in manufacture at the time – Hawker, in the person of the General Manager John Lidbury made sure that government ministers understood the reality of this ill-conceived proposal.

Throughout the 1950s, government policy had been to disperse essential industry – including aircraft manufacture – away from the vulnerable south-east to the north and west of the country.[6] This policy was allied to the perceived need to increase employment in the north and had resulted in continuous pressure on Hawker Aircraft to move the Kingston/Dunsfold operation lock, stock and barrel up to Squires Gate in Blackpool, a large wartime airfield which was looking for a new user. Although the constant pressure had resulted in a reluctant Hawker board agreeing to allow some Hunter production at the northern site, there was never any serious consideration within the company of moving their design and development departments north.

At a meeting in March 1955 between Controller Aircraft (CA) and Sir Frank Spriggs, Hawker Aircraft director, regarding the insecure tenure of the company at Dunsfold, CA was clear that he could see no permanent future for the company in the south and strongly urged a move of the entire operation to Squires Gate.[7] A later meeting held out the possibility of production moving to the north and the retention of development only at Dunsfold after 1958. Given the need for Hawker to construct new experimental facilities soon, it was mooted that these could be built at Guildford and the Kingston premises sold. It was concluded that the Ministry of Supply should tell Hawker:

> a) that we are prepared to open negotiations with the local authorities about continued use of Dunsfold for development flying only. b) that we would like them to put up their new experimental facilities in the Guildford area.[8]

The debate rumbled on for the next couple of years with various ploys, such as the impact of the proposed expansion of Gatwick to the east as a civil airport, being thrown into the mix in vain attempts to get Hawker out of Kingston and Dunsfold. In September 1955 an internal MoS note commented:

> It seems that the limitations that Gatwick will impose upon flying at Dunsfold will occur during the winter months only, and since they will depend entirely on the weather,

Danish Hunter T.7 35-272, designated T.53. First flown November 1958. Repurchased by HSA in 1975 for refurbishment. (BAE Systems, courtesy of Brooklands Museum)

> their distribution will be more or less random. I do not know what opinion I can express on this beyond saying that any restriction of development flying is to be deprecated ... . I suggest that we should tell Hawker what the Ministry of Transport and Civil Aviation are proposing (without any indication that we think of asking for concessions) in the hope that this will induce the firm to fall in line with our wishes about their move.[9]

By summer 1956 the Air Ministry had lost interest in Dunsfold and had ceased to maintain the facilities, including the runway, for which they had responsibility, much to the annoyance of Hawker who felt that urgent runway works were required.

However, any chance of the Government seeing Hawker move out of the south-east was dashed by the cancellation of the remaining F.6 Hunter order in January 1957.[10] An internal MoS note spelled out the consequences:

> Mr Lidbury of Hawkers called to see me on 25th January at his request on a matter of extreme urgency. He said that the

decision to cut the Hunter programme by 100 together with the indication given a few days ago by the AM that they still had surplus Hunters in the programme which they might be obliged to cancel when the review of the programme had gone a stage further had faced his company with a situation which called for immediate action. He proposed to go to Blackpool on Monday to tell the company's management and employees, the town clerk and the local press that work would be withdrawn from Blackpool to Kingston. He did not propose to say that this decision would lead to the closure of Blackpool as an operating unit but in response to questions he agreed that this would be the inevitable consequence and that it might happen as quickly as in 6 months' time. His reason for this decision was that Hawker would have to depend upon export sales of the Hunter for a long time and they had to keep an economic production line running for as long as possible in order to maximise these sales. Blackpool was far too large and its overhead costs far too great; if the firm concentrated their work at Blackpool this would break them. Kingston had been tooled up for 30 Hunters a month and could cope with any requirements which were foreseen; it was a much more flexible and less costly unit to operate.[11]

The news threw the Ministry into a predictable flap; the day following Lidbury's visit it was noted:

Since the decision is one which seems likely to lead to the closure of Blackpool within a period which may be as short as 6 months and this will present a major industrial and political problem we should consider whether to put any obstacle in the way of the proposed transfer of work and, if not, what future use to make of the Blackpool factory. The policy of the Ministry has hitherto been to encourage the transfer of Hawkers from the south of England to Blackpool. The objects of this policy were to get one of our most important fighter companies out of old-fashioned facilities into the largest and most modern we have available, to release Dunsfold airfield to the continued use of which there has always been local opposition, on war potential grounds to reduce the concentration of the aircraft industry in London, and on distribution of industry grounds to get part of the aircraft industry to emigrate from London. The future of Hawkers as a fighter company is now clearly much less promising than when our policy was formulated and their need for large modern premises is smaller.[12]

With the cancellation of 100 F.6 Hunters from the Kingston contract in January and a further fifty from the Blackpool contract in February 1957, new Hunter production was quickly transferred from Blackpool to Kingston/Dunsfold, including the T.7 trainers initially scheduled for Blackpool production. Hawker's presence at Blackpool, and also at Langley which was also involved in Hunter production, had largely ceased by 1959.

As if all this was not enough with which to test the mettle of Hawker, in late 1957 the local authority chose this moment to attempt yet again to either remove Hawker from Dunsfold or at least impose tough conditions upon the company. It will be recalled that, although the Ministry of Housing

Indian Hunters. In the foreground BA209 (formerly XK165) and BA220 (formerly XK176) visible behind in 1957. These aircraft began life as F.6s for the RAF but, following cancellation of the order, were completed as Mk 56. Note the Hunter T.7 parked on the gun butts behind. (BAE Systems, courtesy of Brooklands Museum)

and Local Government (later the Ministry of Town and Country Planning) had claimed that Hawker's tenure was limited to five years, in fact they had to later agree that this was not the case and that the company's term was simply for a 'temporary' period. However, the idea that Hawker would need to re-apply for planning consent lingered in official circles and had been agreed by the Ministry of Supply some years earlier. Added to this confusion was the Air Ministry's desire to be rid of several of its airfields, including Dunsfold, since it no longer featured in their plans. They saw a possible means of achieving this by supporting Hawker's continued use of the airfield with a view to inducing the company to purchase the property outright. Failing this, it was hoped that the Ministry of Supply, as the sponsoring ministry could be persuaded to take on the responsibilities currently resident with the Air Ministry.[13]

At a meeting on 17 March 1958 with Surrey County Council, Ministry of Supply and Hawker Aircraft, SCC confirmed that Hawker would need to re-apply for planning permission and it was made clear that, while the local authorities would be prepared to grant an extension on the same basis as heretofore, it would be temporary again with a finite expiry date. The reasoning behind this was that '[SCC] are averse to giving permanent consent lest either Hawkers should nefariously introduce a large nuisance or a worse than Hawker should appear as a new tenant inducted by an unscrupulous ministry'. Such was the trust between the various government ministries and local authorities![14]

With the way clear for Hawker to continue at Dunsfold pending renewal of their planning consent, it fell to the Air Ministry and the Ministry of Supply to finalise future ownership of the airfield. It was agreed that with the closure of Langley and the imminent closure of Squires Gate and the

> concentration of Hawker Aircraft at Kingston, Dunsfold has become their sole airfield for flight testing of production aircraft as well as their centre for testing research and development aircraft ... . It is fair to say however that it is likely that the Hawker Aircraft Co. will need Dunsfold airfield for so long as they stay in the aircraft industry.

As negotiations on future ownership of Dunsfold dragged on, Hawker, wishing to keep all options open, were careful not to appear averse to purchase of the aerodrome although no agreement on price was forthcoming, and the prospect of the company renting for a couple of years was also mooted.

Hunter F.4 WT703, retained at Dunsfold and Boscombe Down for external stores trials, pictured around 1955. Note the Bessoneau hangars erected on the southern dispersals for storage of aircraft awaiting release to service. (BAE Systems, courtesy of Brooklands Museum)

In the event, having secured a renewal of their planning consent on 13 April 1958 for a further period to expire on 30 April 1965, and with a major re-organisation of Hawker Siddeley Group under way, Hawker declined to purchase the airfield and, since a requirement still existed for its use, the Ministry of Supply, now the Ministry of Aviation, conceded that it should pass into their direct care with Hawker leasing at £29,000 per annum (increased to £35,000 per annum in 1963).[15] The transfer was dated 30 June 1960 and comprised 527.24 acres. The Ministry of Aviation also conceded that some £9,000 to £10,000 spent by Hawker on repairs to the main runway might be repaid by the ministry. Also under consideration as part of the transfer of the airfield were two pieces of land which might affect the total extent of land for transfer and the requirement to renew the temporary closure of the three roads across the airfield co-terminous with the planning permission. The first land plot was at the extreme western end of the runway that had been requisitioned for the installation of VHF Homer equipment and the owner, Mrs Nugent, wife of the local MP, was keen to sell to the

Air Ministry. Because the plot in question was close to the centre line of the extended runway, there was concern that, if the Air Ministry or Hawker did not purchase it, a future owner might seek to build there, causing a serious obstruction at the end of the runway. The Air Ministry was relaxed about this since their 'safeguarding' procedures gave them a veto on any development that might cause harm to aircraft operation. The second plot was an area of hardstandings behind Broadmeads Cottage on the south of the airfield comprising some fourteen acres. Hawker's old 'friend' Colonel du Boulay was seeking to purchase this land and the cottage to add to his property, having already purchased a smaller co-terminous piece in 1958. Hawker were sufficiently concerned at someone moving into Broadmeads and making it habitable again that they asked for it to be excluded from any sale of the land behind it and, preferably, demolished. However, since neither MoA nor Hawker were prepared to pay for this, the property was left untouched, although still on Hawker's side of the fence after the rest of the plot was sold.[16]

With the loss of their Hunter replacement project – P.1121 – and the cancellation of a substantial number of Mk 6 Hunters, not to mention the longer-term implications of the *Defence White Paper* of 1957, Hawker had moved swiftly to retrench by announcing the closure of Blackpool and the transfer of the Hunter Repair Scheme to the south as well as new-build T.7 Hunter trainers. The extremely short notice of the Hunter cancellations could have left the company financially embarrassed; the production lines were going at full tilt; long-lead materials would already have been purchased for the cancelled aircraft and unbudgeted redundancy costs would have to be met.

However, little changed immediately because India and Switzerland took the opportunity to avail themselves of the spare capacity. India was first out of the blocks with an order for 160 Mk 6 Hunters, sold as Mk 56s. The first thirty-two aircraft were diverted from the 100 cancelled aircraft for the RAF and a further sixteen were ex-RAF Hunters, thus allowing the Indians to receive their first aircraft almost immediately. The remainder of the order was fulfilled with new-build aircraft built at Kingston/Dunsfold between 1957 and 1960. The order from Switzerland comprised 100 Mk 6 Hunters sold as Mk 58s. The initial twelve aircraft were again diverted from the cancelled RAF order with the remainder new-built at Kingston/Dunsfold between 1958 and 1960. The Hunter had been demonstrated to the Swiss Air Force in competition with French, Canadian and British alternatives and won the day, thanks in large measure to the spirited displays by Bill Bedford

P.1109A Hunter WW594. A modified nose was intended to accommodate an AI Mk 20 radar, while armament would comprise two DH Firestreak infra-red missiles carried under the wing, c. 1956/57. In the far background can be seen two Supermarine Attackers awaiting the attention of Airwork Ltd. (BAE Systems, courtesy of Brooklands Museum)

and David Lockspeiser. Bedford's party piece was to take the aircraft to around 18,000 feet and set up a fast spin down to low level before rounding out into a climbing roll. At a display at Emmen, near Lucerne, as he spun down towards the airfield, Bedford realised that the ground was far closer than it should be. With just a hundred feet to spare, he managed to avoid catastrophe and pulled out in time, producing a quite spectacular display. The error had been caused by a failure to reset the altimeter after leaving Dunsfold to the higher altitude of Emmen, hence the unforgettable image of the ground being VERY close. Bedford kept the story of how he nearly died a secret for eighteen years but eventually revealed it in the hope that others would realise that even the best pilot is fallible.[17]

These orders were followed by another Indian requirement for twenty-two T.7 Hunter trainers, all new-build at Kingston and Dunsfold between 1958 and 1960. The last new-build Hunter was a trainer sold as T.66B to Jordan in 1960. Thus ended production of new Hunter aircraft but the story was far from over; an entirely new lease of life would come for the machine as air forces around the world saw in the Hunter a low-cost solution to their defence requirements. But with Hunter Mk 6 production at an end, where would the airframes come from to fulfil this need? The answer lay in the Hunter Mk 4s produced for the RAF in the mid-1950s and, with the arrival of the Mk 6 Hunter with the larger engine, now languishing at various MUs around the country. Some F.4s had already been reworked as T.7s for the RAF and T.8s for the Admiralty. Hawker also received an order from the Admiralty for conversion of Mk 4s to GA.11 standard, forty airframes passing through Dunsfold in 1962 for rework.

On the basis that there seemed to be plenty of life in the F.4 design yet, in 1961 Hawker bought back from the RAF a further sixty-one F.4 aircraft, forty-five of which were brought to Dunsfold and stored pending resale. Unfortunately, no further requirements existed within the UK armed forces and export customers wanted the F.6 with its 10,000lb thrust engine. At the time it was considered far too expensive an exercise to contemplate rebuilding the F.4 fuselage to take the bigger engine. The F.4s languished at Dunsfold, and at Chilbolton, where Hawker had acquired space in the old Supermarine hangars, until eventually being broken up, fourteen in 1962 and the remaining thirty in 1964.[18] With regard to the F.6 Hunter, Hawker also received contracts to refurbish F.6 airframes and upgrade

Hunter demonstrator G-APUX up from Dunsfold complete with ferry tanks. (BAE Systems, courtesy of Brooklands Museum)

to FGA.9 and FR.10, many of these aircraft passing through Dunsfold between 1960 and 1965 in small batches. Thus ended the second phase of Hunter works for Kingston and Dunsfold. Incredibly, several years after, a further lease of life would see Dunsfold's production hangars full of Hunters again, but that is a story for later. In light of these subsequent events, the scrapping of the F. 4s in the early 1960s must later have had Hawker's management in tears.

With Hunter work now tailing off, Hawker moved to prepare the site for their next, and only, aircraft project, P.1127, and on 24 May 1960 requested permission from the MoA and the local authority to extend the runway at the east end with a 300 x 25-yard extension.

> The position is that during the trials of the VTO design, the machine will need to make traditional landings and, although we have an adequate over-shoot area, we are unwilling to let our new aircraft over-shoot into soft ground and we are therefore proposing a 300-yard extension, 25 yards wide to deal with this eventuality.[19]

One wonders whether the rationale of having to extend the runway for an aircraft that did not need one was lost on the powers that be. In the event, this was approved the following month.[20] At the same time, it was also pointed out that a proposed Royal Observer Corps bunker on the south side, to monitor nuclear explosions in the event of war, could not be higher than three feet above ground level to avoid conflict with flying.[21] On 20 November 1964 the vexed question of Hawker's remaining at Dunsfold raised its head yet again as the company applied to the local authority for another permission to 'Continue to use the above aerodrome as hitherto for a period of at least ten or twenty years'. In the event, they received another five-year extension.[22]

Chapter 5

Sea Fury and Hunter Refurbishments

With the completion of the various Hunter contracts, work at Dunsfold began to slow at the end of the 1950s. The Indian and Swiss new-build contracts had filled part of the gap resulting from the cancellation of the last RAF Hunters but the 1957 White Paper had effectively ruled out any chance of further orders in the UK. However, the closure of Langley and of Squires Gate by 1960 meant that Dunsfold was now the only remaining flight-test centre for Hawker Aircraft Ltd. So, when a requirement arose for modification and upgrade work to the Sea Fury in the hands of the Fleet Air Arm, it was to Dunsfold that all eyes turned.

The Fury had been developed by Hawker at Kingston as a lightweight version of their successful Tempest fighter; indeed, it was initially referred to as the Tempest Light Fighter. Various prototypes were produced fitted with a variety of engines and an order for 200 Furies was placed by the RAF. The Admiralty were also interested and specification N.22/43 was issued for a carrier-borne version, for which an order for 200 aircraft was placed in April 1944. The first production Fury NX798. flew on 1 September 1944 followed by the first navalised Fury SR661, flying in February 1945 but, shortly after, with war in Europe coming to an end, the RAF order was cancelled and the naval order halved. Work continued on the naval order slowly at Langley after the end of the war, the intention being that the 100 aircraft would be split with half designated Sea Fury F.X and the other half Sea Fury FB.XI. As the Royal Navy began to accept the new aircraft, and intensive trials were conducted, it became apparent that Hawker had produced another superlative machine and further orders followed into the early 1950s including for a two-seat trainer version, the T.20. Export orders followed for Canada, the Netherlands, Australia, Iraq and Pakistan. Eventually some 729 aircraft were built, comprising fifty F.10s, 615 FB.11s and sixty-one T.20s which, together with licence-built, brought the total to approximately 860.

Sensing a lucrative market in export sales of the aircraft, in December 1956 Hawker purchased 251 aircraft from the Admiralty as they reached the end of their service life and set about finding customers for them. It was not the first time that Hawker had sought to maximise returns from their older aircraft. In the years immediately following the Second World War, the company had been much involved in the refurbishment of surplus aircraft for Commonwealth and European countries keen to update and replace existing equipment. The scheme had principally revolved around Hurricane and Tempest airframes and had allowed Hawker to retain their workforce in the light of reductions and cancellations in UK government contracts for new equipment.

Concurrent with this new potential revenue stream, when the Sea Furies of the FAA began to be returned to aircraft holding units due to reductions in fleet strength and the introduction of the Sea Hawk jet fighter, the Hawker Board committed to the acquisition of redundant Sea Furies in 1956 for potential resale to interested parties abroad. Of the 251 aircraft purchased, 105 were flown into Hawker's facility at Squires Gate, Blackpool with the remainder arriving by road – another small batch would be purchased in 1962 – and stored where possible under cover, but the remainder were stored in an open-air compound on the airfield. From there, the aircraft in best condition were refurbished and sold to Burma (twenty-one) and Cuba (seventeen), with a further contract for eight T.20 Furies under negotiation

Royal Navy Sea Furies await refurbishment on Dunsfold's eastern dispersals, c.1960. (BAE Systems, courtesy of Brooklands Museum)

for provision as target tugs for West Germany, becoming TT.20s. Further small batches were refurbished and supplied to existing users as attrition replacements. Given the large numbers acquired, and the relatively small number subsequently resold, one is led to the conclusion that the project was not quite the success story that Hawker had hoped for. Added to the difficulty of reselling the aircraft came the rather abrupt decision to terminate the lease on Squires Gate in light of the 1957 Sandys Defence White Paper which had resulted in cancellation of substantial numbers of Hunters for the RAF.

The orders for Burma and Cuba were the last to be completed at the Squires Gate factory. Burma's requirement for eighteen Sea Fury FB.11 and three T.20 aircraft and the option to purchase a further twenty-four was placed in September 1957 with delivery scheduled for December 1957 to May 1958. Dunsfold's pilots carried out the flight testing of these aircraft at Blackpool, using the Hurricane or Anson for the journey north; Lockspeiser and Lucey did most of the work, which ended at the beginning of 1959 with the eventual closure of Squires Gate. The Burmese contract had included the requirement for in-country support and, on this basis, Lockspeiser flew out to Burma to facilitate the entry of the aircraft into the Burmese Air force in October 1959.

While the Burmese order had been completed without fuss, the Cuban order would be anything but; indeed this insignificant contract could be said to have unintentionally helped bring the world to the brink of nuclear war in the early 1960s. The secret contract with the Batista regime for fifteen FB.11 and two T.20 Sea Furies from Hawker's repurchased stock was signed in 1957, twelve of the aircraft arriving in Havana in crates in October 1958 by ship from Liverpool. The regime of Fulgencio Batista was widely unpopular but had the support of the US government, keen to see stability in its backyard and this support had been sufficient for Macmillan's UK government to approve export licences for the aircraft. With the first batch on the quayside in Havana, a Hawker working party under Len Hearsey and Derek MacKay was despatched to re-assemble the Sea Furies, with Don Lucey on hand to test fly the aircraft and carry out some initial training for the pilots. It is likely that the order had been placed to strengthen the defences of the government against the revolutionary intentions of one Fidel Castro, a growing thorn in the government's side. But, no doubt to the intense irritation of Batista, the aircraft had been apparently delivered without armament or ammunition, this forming part of the second batch of aircraft and so were of little use in countering the insurgency.

Sea Fury T.20 G-9-62, formerly VX302, awaits engine run in the Harrier engine pen. This aircraft was subsequently sold to Germany as D-CACY and delivered in April 1963. Note the rudimentary tie-downs at the rear of the fuselage. (Via Peter Amos)

Len Hearsey, of the Repair and Service Department based at Blackpool – later to become the manager of Dunsfold's Experimental Hangar – remembered his time in Cuba thus:

> In September 1958 I arrived in Cuba for the assembly of 17 refurbished Sea Furies which had been crated and shipped to Havana. A colleague, Derek MacKay, and myself, together with Cuban Air Force personnel, started work. This proceeded very well until one evening the manager of our hotel asked if I had heard the news from Venezuela. Naturally I hadn't, and even if I had it probably would have meant nothing to me. He told me that the Freedom Front leader, Senor Castro, had broadcast on Radio Venezuela, quoting my name and room number, holding me responsible for assembling the Sea Furies that were bombing and gunning his troops. He gave me three days to get out of Cuba! That night Derek and I locked ourselves in our room with a bottle of Scotch and the next day moved out of the hotel and into Campo de Columbia,

the Air Force headquarters. We stayed there until our departure after we had more or less completed 12 aircraft, then returned to England.[1]

On New Year's Day 1959 Batista fled the revolutionary onslaught and Castro became the *de facto* leader of Cuba. Subsequently, around September 1959, another team, again led by Don Lucey, arrived in Cuba to erect and test the remaining five aircraft. It appears that the second team comprised Lucey, a local Hawker rep, 'Mr Grupe', and two further Hawker technicians. The situation under Castro was utterly chaotic and the team had an enormous task in trying to erect and test the last five aircraft. Lucey subsequently issued a report in November 1959 to Hawker castigating the Castro regime, the remnants of the air force and the general situation in-country.

Therefore, the Revolutionary Government of Castro came to be possessed of, notionally, seventeen Sea Fury fighter-bombers, although rather fewer were available due to crashes resulting from lack of training for the pilots. An attrition order for a further eleven aircraft was placed but never delivered, being embargoed by the UK government. Just two years

Sea Fury T.20 G-9-50, formerly VZ372, retained at Dunsfold for development. Fitted with towing winch powered by the airscrew mounted on the starboard cockpit wall. Delivered to Germany as D-CAME in July 1960. (BAE Systems, courtesy of Brooklands Museum)

later, when an invasion army of Cuban exiles funded by the CIA arrived in the early morning haze of the Bay of Pigs on 17 April 1961, it was Hawker's Sea Furies that were instrumental in inflicting heavy losses on the ships and men of the invasion force and driving them back into the sea, leading to the ignominious retreat of the invading forces.

As a postscript to the Cuban order, after Castro's accession as leader, the British government was approached with a request that Hawker be allowed to offer Hunter Mk 5 aircraft to Cuba in exchange for the return of the remaining Sea Fury aircraft, the idea being that this would show that Cuba was not intent on increasing its air arm, merely bringing it up to date. In the event, American pressure prevented the order going ahead although not before suitable Hunters had been allocated to the contract.

So it was that Hawker unwittingly shored up Castro's regime which, the following year in the absence of defence equipment being available from elsewhere, would reach agreement with the Soviet Union for aircraft and missiles to be based in Cuba, just ninety miles off the coast of the US, triggering a crisis such as the world had never seen before or since.

Meanwhile, the closure of Squires Gate meant that the large stock of Sea Furies on site had to be found a new home. Those aircraft capable of flying, including the follow-on Cuban order, were flown down to Langley and Dunsfold around the end of 1958, those at Dunsfold being stored in the south-eastern dispersals. Most of the other airframes were moved by road down to Langley in early 1959 but, since Langley had been sold to the Ford Motor Company, they were soon on the move again, this time to the Ministry of Supply airfield at Chilbolton. This airfield had been used by Supermarine and, latterly, by the Flight Test Department of Folland Aircraft, themselves in process of being acquired by the Hawker Siddeley Group, and it was in the former Supermarine hangars that, in late 1959 to early 1960, twenty-three of the Sea Furies found lodging.

In a report accompanying the condition survey dated September 1960, the chief inspector commented that:

> The condition of all Sea Fury aircraft at Chilbolton is very poor, due to the unsatisfactory storage conditions and lack of appropriate protection … . If the aircraft are to be retained and held at Dunsfold, it is apparent that storage there would be in the open, and in this respect, it can be said that open storage would be little worse than in the hangar in question at Chilbolton … . It is suggested that if the likelihood of resale

in the foreseeable future is indeterminate, then only a selected number of aircraft be transferred to Dunsfold and adequately protected before storage.[2]

In light of this report and future plans for the airfield impinging on further storage, together with the decision to move the Folland Aircraft Flight Test facility to Dunsfold in February 1961, it was decided to move the best of the remaining airframes up to Dunsfold where they arrived in late 1960, joining the earlier batch in the dispersals to await their fate. The remaining Sea Furies at Chilbolton would be scrapped on site.

In the event, the only further contract to be completed, begun at Squires Gate but completed at Dunsfold, was for the TT.20 target-towing version for West Germany, the best T.20s being selected for this contract. The first ten were delivered in 1960 with the remaining six delivered in 1963, despatched from Dunsfold with one further aircraft, an FB.11, being supplied later although not before it had almost despatched Duncan Simpson, innocently carrying out the last manoeuvre of the flight test schedule. On 1 August 1963, he had taken WG599 (D-CACY) up for a last check flight before delivery. On looping at around 6,000 feet, Simpson found himself pointing at the ground with the ailerons locked and immovable. Quickly finding

Sea Fury T.20 D-CABU, formerly VZ353, prior to delivery to Germany May 1960. (BAE Systems, courtesy of Brooklands Museum)

himself at between 2,000 and 3,000 feet and unable to bale out, a last-ditch roll-under released the restriction, allowing Simpson to regain control and make a straight-in approach to Dunsfold, where the aircraft was left on the ORP for inspection, a loose article being suspected.

A final batch of eight Sea Fury FB.11s arrived at Dunsfold between February and April 1963, flown in from Lossiemouth, Scotland, by the company pilots; these included one aircraft that had a lucky escape, TF956, an FB.11 flown into Dunsfold on 6 March 1963 by David Lockspeiser and initially stored in a hangar awaiting resale. However, on 9 April 1964, with no offers forthcoming, the aircraft was moved to open storage on the eastern dispersals. Some digging through the documentation revealed that this Sea Fury was the first production FB.11, as well as a Korean War veteran and worthy of preservation and possible addition to Dunsfold's fleet of historic aircraft and it was therefore returned to storage in the back of Production Bay 3, the flight shed, on 12 June 1964. There it stayed awaiting officialdom's decision. In the meantime, a couple of engineers – Colin Balchin and Don Russell – started their own small renovation project of this aircraft, assisted unofficially by several others and soon pretty much everything that could be replaced or repaired on the aircraft was complete. With just a new engine remaining on the requirement list, officialdom belatedly sat up and took notice, stopping further work on the aircraft.[3] The aircraft thus remained until moves to dispose of the historic aircraft fleet began to gather pace, the Sea Fury becoming part of this process. Simpson, who had been instrumental in saving TF956, fought to obtain approval from the Hawker Board for the aircraft to be rebuilt to flying status rather than have it languish in a museum, and eventually agreement was reached that the aircraft would go to RNAS Yeovilton for rebuild to flight status and to be retained there for display duties. Another of this batch, WJ288, was rescued at the last moment and towed behind a car all the way to Biggin Hill for preservation. This aircraft is still airworthy in the US at time of writing.

For the other Sea Furies, however, the story was not so rosy. By 1964 they were a sorry sight and ready only for R.J. Coley and Son's, scrap merchants, attentions. Yet even in this state they still had a valuable role to play. At about this time Hawker was keen to acquire redundant Hunter airframes to further its export business, the original production jigs having been long dismantled. Thus it was that news reached the company of the intention of the Netherlands authorities to destroy twenty-two Hunters in fire-fighting experiments. Quickly, a deal was done which saw eighteen Sea Furies, including the remaining erstwhile Cuban aircraft, being taken by road to Holland between February and June 1964 to be burnt in exchange for twenty-two Hunters later flown in for refurbishment. Quite what the transport drivers made of the idea of transporting the aircraft all the way to Holland just to be burnt can only be imagined. What remained were ultimately scrapped by Coley's on site and, by 1965, the dispersals were empty of Sea Furies. In all, thirty-five Sea Fury FB.11 and twenty T.20 aircraft passed through Dunsfold, providing an interesting diversion from Hunters for the workforce.

Hunter Refurbishment

As the decade ended, Hawker was still trading on the enormous success of the Hunter, no longer as a pure fighter but as a combined interceptor and ground attack aircraft. It was a significant blow to the company that the P.1121 project had not been taken up by either the UK armed forces or NATO nations and this had left the future order book looking patchy at best. However, there was still plenty of life in the Hunter and Hawker concentrated on securing further orders, both from home and overseas, to keep Kingston and Dunsfold in operation while new projects were developed in the wings.

As the Hunter F.6 entered service with the RAF squadrons, the F.4 aircraft were slowly withdrawn and placed into storage at MUs around the country. With the success of the 'big engine' Hunter, the requirement to retain the old F.4 and F.5 Hunters receded and thoughts turned to their scrapping. In the event, many of those Hunters did indeed fall to the scrapman but Hawker, as ever intent on future sales, purchased from RAF stocks a number of F.4 aircraft for possible refurbishment and resale in 1961. Through 1962 the sixty-three airframes acquired were taken by road and placed into Hawker storage, thirty-one aircraft coming to Dunsfold and a further thirty-two being stored at Chilbolton. Later in 1962 fourteen of the aircraft at Chilbolton were transported to Dunsfold by road. While at first this acquisition had seemed to be good business practice, for a number of reasons the airframes thus acquired were deemed uneconomical for refurbishment and, having sat in the dispersals for several years, began to keep appointments with Coley's. In 1962 fourteen aircraft were scrapped followed by another ten in 1964. By 1966 all were gone, as were the Chilbolton examples.

Yet slowly it emerged that the F.4 Hunter could have a new life and the scrapping programmes were stopped as new orders emerged from the Admiralty and the RAF for Hunters upgraded to Fighter Ground

Dunsfold Production Hangar. Hunters undergoing refurbishment in the middle bay. These aircraft were mainly destined for Switzerland (left of picture) and Chile (right of picture), August 1972. (BAE Systems, courtesy of Brooklands Museum)

Attack (FGA). Further Hunter F.4s were procured to fulfil these orders, firstly for forty single-seat Hunter ground-attack weapons trainers to be designated GA.11 for the FAA in 1962. Those Hunter F.4 airframes started to arrive at Dunsfold for refurbishment and upgrade in 1962, the work taking approximately three months to complete per aircraft. All were delivered by July 1963. A similar requirement was behind an order for the RAF for dedicated ground-attack aircraft to be known as the Hunter FGA.9. For those, redundant F.6 airframes would be used, upgraded to allow the aircraft to operate in hot and high environments, particularly the Middle East which was fast becoming a patchwork of minor wars and skirmishes. Aircraft to fulfil this requirement were flown into Dunsfold, mainly from No. 5 MU at Kemble, thirty-two aircraft arriving between August and October 1957. Many of the aircraft would return to Dunsfold in the 1970s to be reworked for further customers. While the initial batch was completed at Dunsfold, later batches were shared between Dunsfold and working parties at RAF bases. Eventually 130 aircraft were modified up to FGA.9 standard. In late 1957 sixteen aircraft flew in for conversion to Indian F.56s and a further twelve arrived by air in early 1958 to be converted to Swiss Hunter

Hunter T.7 70-617, formerly XL620, for the Royal Saudi Air Force taxis past the Harrier engine pen. Note the original detuners from this pen lying discarded in the background. (BAE Systems, courtesy of Brooklands Museum)

F.58s, these aircraft being delivered through 1958. These were followed by six Hunter F.4s for conversion to T.7 trainers, this work being shared with the Bitteswell site.

As noted above, former Dutch Hunters had been acquired by the company in exchange for redundant Sea Fury airframes; twenty-one were F.6s with one a T.7 aircraft. Between February and April 1964 the flightworthy Hunters were flown into Dunsfold by Dutch Air Force pilots in full Dutch colours. Around the same time, some ninety-seven ex-Belgian Air Force Hunter F.6s were acquired, thirty-two of these being flown into Dunsfold by the company pilots; those aircraft had the service markings removed prior to delivery to Dunsfold. This was followed by a second batch of sixty-four Belgian Hunters, this time flown in by Belgian Air Force pilots who took the opportunity to show Dunsfold staff their display credentials while arriving at the airfield in 1964 and 1965. Peter Amos described the spectacle thus:

> their arrival was usually heralded by a noise like a clap of thunder as they descended on the airfield! I shall never forget the sight of the last three Hunters as they came in from the western end of the airfield, with literally nothing on the clock

'but the makers' name' (but definitely much more than that on the ASI) and then executing THE most perfect break UPWARDS for landing in fast stream. Phew![4]

Those aircraft would form the beginnings of a very lucrative trade for Hawker, or Hawker Siddeley Aviation as they had become by then, as the world was scoured for redundant aircraft with which to supply a seemingly endless appetite for inexpensive Hunters around the world, but particularly in the Middle East and South America.

Those Dutch and Belgian Hunters were used to fulfil orders from a variety of Middle Eastern nations; Kuwait ordered four aircraft brought up to FGA.9 standard and designated FGA.57, plus a further two in 1967, together with a further five T.67 trainers, delivered by 1965. An order from Iraq in 1964 comprised twenty-four aircraft, again brought up to FGA.9 standard and designated FGA.59 with further orders for twenty-two single-seat (FGA.59A & FR.59B) and five T.7 aircraft (T.69) in 1965, making Iraq the largest user of Hunters in the Middle East. Lebanon had received six F.6 Hunters as part of an aid package in 1958 and ordered a further four FGA.9s plus three T.7 aircraft in 1965 while Saudi Arabia purchased four F.6 Hunters, designated F.60, and two T.7s in 1966. Jordan had acquired

Hunter F.56A outside the Flight Shed. This Indian Air Force aircraft was temporarily painted in Jordanian colours for the 1966 Farnborough Air Show. Delivered November 1966. (BAE Systems, courtesy of Brooklands Museum)

ex-RAF Hunter F.6 aircraft in 1958 and received further aircraft in early 1960. Almost the entire strength was subsequently destroyed by Israel in the Six Day War of 1967, a further eighteen aircraft being acquired in the late 1960s and early 1970s.

South America also proved to be fertile ground for refurbished Hunter sales; Peru had received sixteen F.52s in 1956 from ex-RAF F.4 stock and acquired a T.7 (T.62) in 1960. Chile had ordered fifteen Hunter FGA.71s in 1966, these being delivered through 1968. A further order was for three former RAF F.6s to FR.10 standard (FR.71A) aircraft and three trainers (T.72) for delivery in 1968. On the African continent, Rhodesia ordered twelve FGA.9 Hunters in 1963 although the imposition of sanctions after the Declaration of Independence precluded any more orders. In the Far East, in 1969 Singapore placed an order for sixteen ex-RAF F.6 Hunters, twelve upgraded to FGA.9 (FGA.74) and four to FR.10 (FR.74A) standard; these would begin deliveries in 1970.

Meanwhile, two of Hawker's older customers returned to the company seeking attrition batches for earlier losses. India ordered a further fifty-three F.56A aircraft in 1966, these being delivered over the next four years. Switzerland would also return for further aircraft but that is a story for later.

While many of the Hunters returned to Hawker for onward sale were in need of a complete refurbishment, others could be in surprisingly good condition, some of them with very few flying hours accrued. But whatever the condition of the aircraft on receipt, after its overhaul and return to flight, its systems would be thoroughly checked out before delivery to its new customer. Sometimes, disaster was just a moment's inattention away as Andy Jones found out one day. Jones was aloft in a single-seat Hunter carrying out a straightforward engine check requiring a full-throttle climb to 50,000 feet. For that height, Jones would be relying on his oxygen system to be working to its optimum. As he passed 40,000 feet, things did not seem to be quite right. An oxygen system check showed everything working as normal but a little later, feeling distinctly unwell, he selected 100 per cent oxygen instead of the air mixture. Now feeling that he was going to pass out, he descended as quickly as possible and, passing 10,000 feet, began to recover. Having managed to land, a check of the oxygen system showed it to have been inadvertently filled with air instead of gaseous oxygen: a lucky escape for a great pilot.

As for the erstwhile Cuban Hunter F.5s, they never made it to Dunsfold. The aircraft were initially stored at Langley until closure when some were moved to Kingston for use in the fatigue frame while the rest were scrapped around 1963.

With the advent of the early 1970s, the Kingston and Dunsfold sites were once again in full flood with orders for some seventy-eight Harrier GR.1s and fourteen T.2 trainers, plus G-VTOL, passing through the shops together with another thirty AV-8A Mk 50 Harriers from the first two allocations of US funding for the project and another eighty-four expected through over the next few years. Although the years of the late 1960s had been lean, work on Hunter refurbishment had enabled the workforce to be retained with no requirement for largescale redundancies. In all, something like 184 Hunter conversions for national and foreign air arms had been completed at Kingston/Dunsfold in the 1960s and, now, as the shops and hangars were full of aircraft came news that, far from tailing off, requirements for the previous generation Hunter were if anything threatening to overtake sales of HSA's latest V/STOL strike aircraft. Talk about an embarrassment of riches!

Orders for provision of Hunter aircraft to existing customers and smaller air arms continued to flow into the Kingston sales office throughout the 1970s. This could have been wonderful news for Hawker Siddeley but was complicated by two rather crucial factors. Firstly, the jigs and lines for production of new-build aircraft had long ago been cleared from the shops to make way for quantity production of Harrier and, secondly, there was the most extraordinary famine of available second-hand airframes to be had for refurbishment; all the aircraft purchased back by HSA had been either converted and resold, or delivered to the scrapman.

With requirements for additional aircraft already received from Switzerland and India, both existing customers of large numbers of Hunters in the 1950s, as well as orders from potential new customers, particularly in the Middle East, HSA cast about for any airframes that might usefully be procured and converted. That search was to lead the company into some unusual negotiations.

On 14 January 1971, the requirement was summarised as follows:

As well as the existing allocation of 8 x FR.10 aircraft for India in March ...
1) A number of Mk.66 (large engine) trainers for India – 12
2) Fighter Recce aircraft for India. Revised quotation under preparation – 8
3) FGA.9 for Jordan. Will be urged by King Hussain end of January – 21
4) FGA.9 for Iraq. Awaiting finance – 16
5) FGA.9 for Chile. Requirement stated by C-in-C Lord Aldenham and likely to be pursued politically – 16

6) FGA.9 for Singapore – 16. Mk 7 trainers for Singapore – 4 (Likely to be raised with Mr Heath).
7) FGA.9 for Switzerland. (The Swiss might take up to 50 aircraft) – 50
8) FGA.9 for Abu Dhabi. (We have been advised they would like another squadron) – 12
9) Mk 7 trainers for the RAF. The RAF are apparently concerned about a pending lack of training capacity – ?
10) There is a market for 30-40 OCU aircraft in Saudi Arabia and for various types of Hunter in other countries which have not been approached as no surplus aircraft are available - ?
11) The Kuwait Government have enquired whether any Hunters could be supplied direct from the RAF in 3-4 months. On being told this was not possible they asked to be advised of the earliest delivery they could obtain – 12?[5]

Neatly summarising the shortage of airframes, the *aide memoire* noted the following potentially available to HSA, but for the Singapore contract only:

Immediately – 7 x Mk 4 carcasses from Training Schools, 2 x GA.9, 3 x FR.10, 1 x GA.11.
In six months – 5 x Mk 4 carcasses from Training Schools.
End of 1971 – 7 x GA.9 ex-Bahrain.[6]

By June 1971 things were a little clearer with a number of Mk 4 airframes being available, again mainly from RAF Training Schools such as Halton and Cranwell, although with a requirement in some circumstances for other airframes, possibly available from Naval sources, Sea Vixens or Sea Hawks, to replace them. As the search widened for other airframes, a lucky break was facilitated during a visit to the MoD at Harrogate when twenty Mk 4 airframes were offered at a cost of £1,800 for each that was subsequently refurbished and resold, together with the possible acquisition of airframes or wings from sources as diverse as ATC squadrons and a motley collection of twelve aircraft stored at 32 MU, RAF St Athan. A survey of the latter revealed that, of the twelve aircraft inspected, 'The flying hours are all low ... but all have suffered, as the aircraft at RAF Halton, from spanner wear and boot adjustment and not from actual functional wear.[7]

In considering timescales for delivery of refurbished aircraft, John Glasscock, Executive Director and General Manager, noted that the current estimate was around twenty-two months for whoever placed their order first, with even longer lead times for subsequent orders, but this was inevitable with the current load and capacity. It was perhaps with an eye to reducing this timescale, and with HS.1182 work likely to be ramping up, that a plan was hatched to off-load the Hunter refurbishment programme from Dunsfold onto the HSA factory at Chester.

As the requirement for ever more Hunters for export kept the Sales and Contracts staff busy at Kingston, in July 1972 Colin Chandler, Commercial Manager, wrote to the Defence Sales Organisation within the MoD with a view to acquiring yet more Hunters from RAF or FAA sources, making the point that further sales of Hunters to foreign air arms 'provide not only useful work in their own right but also provide the opportunity to maintain a British Industry presence, thus keeping out the competition and laying the foundations for eventual sales of Harrier and HS.1182'.[8] A further forty to fifty Hunters were being sought by the company from the MoD with a view to servicing a likely requirement for them, pending a firm order from Switzerland. Chandler noted that, as well as potential stocks held by the RAF, a further area of study might be 'the Royal Navy to whom we supplied some 68 Mk 8 and Mk 11 Hunters some years ago' as well as further Mk 4 Hunters from the RAF. The reply to this enquiry was not long in coming and was all bad news, a telegram confirming that 'Plans re Hunters have been completely revised extending holding time both RN and RAF'.[9] In short, the services were expecting to hang on to their Hunters into the late 1970s and early 1980s. No further releases were expected from the RAF until the HS.1182 entered service around 1976 at the earliest.

With the door closed on acquisition of large numbers of airframes from the services, the contracts department returned in September 1972 to its hand-to-mouth policy of identifying individual airframes, spotting a Mk 4 'Gate Guard' at RAF Spitalgate and six instructional airframes at RAF St Athan, including four Mk 1s and another on the fire dump! Sweden also proved to be a happy hunting ground, four fuselages and six pairs of wings being located and acquired. As each aircraft was located and purchased, its remains were roaded back to Dunsfold to join the varied store of Hunters awaiting return to flight status. Many of the returns were filthy inside and out, the unfortunate engineers tasked with the refurbishments being readily identifiable by the state of their overalls.

While attempts continued to satisfy the various governments around the world in their search for supplies of Hunters, yet another enquiry was received in February 1973, from a private company trading as the 'Intercontinental Armament Corporation' based in Florida, USA, for supply of a number of Hunters for an unspecified South American client. With the prospect of the Hunter becoming the weapon of choice for nascent air forces in the Americas, Glasscock was clear that no airframes were available with which to satisfy their mystery client and would be unlikely to become available anytime soon. Not one to give up so easily, the IAC retained ex-Group Captain Hamish Mahaddie, latterly the brains behind the formation of the private air force that had constituted the many vintage aircraft assembled for the epic film *The Battle of Britain* and then working as an aviation consultant, and again approached HSA. In identifying the likely cost to their client of such aircraft (£350,000 for each FGA.9 and £400,000 for trainers), Glasscock was clear in the need to sooner or later identify both Mahaddie's client and the end user.[10] Hard on the heels of this enquiry came another, from a company based in Tolworth, requesting HSA to supply Hunter parts for resale to unspecified customers; subsequent enquiry revealed these customers to be located in … South America. The identity of the customer is unknown to the author but may be related to the supply of numbers of aircraft to the government of Chile and concerns from neighbouring nations; Peru had similarly acquired Hunters in the 1950s and 1960s and Venezuela was also seeking to obtain the aircraft.

Hunter T.72 for Chile, fitted with 230-gallon drop tanks, makes a low pass along Dunsfold's runway. (BAE Systems, courtesy of Brooklands Museum)

With all this interest in the acquisition of refurbished Hunters and the heavy workload at Kingston/Dunsfold, concern was aroused as to how best to accommodate the programme within the capacity of HSA Group's holdings. Attention soon turned to Bitteswell, a former RAF station near Lutterworth in Leicestershire. The aerodrome had been part of Armstrong Whitworth's holdings and had therefore become available to the HSA Group in the 1930s. Following production of most of the Sea Hawk family of aircraft at Armstrong Whitworth's Coventry factory, and subsequent flight testing at Bitteswell, the aerodrome had been used for testing of the Sapphire-powered Mk 2 and Mk 5 (and some F.6) Hunters, as well as servicing and updates of a variety of different HSA Group aircraft. It seemed natural, therefore, to look to Bitteswell to pick up some of the Hunter refurbishment work and steps were taken to make it so. With the Bitteswell staff eventually getting to grips with the multiplicity of problems incumbent in any attempt to turn old aircraft into new marks, HSA looked to a capacity shortfall at the Chester site which was experiencing slow sales of their HS.125 executive jet. Following a suggestion that some Hunter work be moved to Chester, the Executive Director Production raised concerns at the likely implications of such a move, including increased costs, delays in production and increased man hours, due to the learning curve involved in acquiring the new skills necessary for the task. However, notwithstanding these concerns, some work was indeed moved to Chester and eventually the fuss died down.[11]

Mostly the refurbishment of the Hunters went very smoothly but occasionally there were problems. In November 1967 a Chilean Hunter T.72 trainer, serialled G-9-218, piloted by a Chilean pilot suffered a brake failure on landing at Dunsfold and called for the barrier at the end of runway 07 to be raised. The aircraft ran off the end of the runway but was successfully stopped on the grass overshoot with minimal damage, and delivered three weeks later.

Eventually, by the mid-1970s, diligent enquiries by HSA staff had resulted in the unearthing and acquisition of sufficient airframes both here and abroad to service most of the orders received. These included:

India: a further five T.66Es for delivery in 1973.

Switzerland: a further fifty-two Mk 58As for delivery between 1971 and 1975 and eight T.68s for delivery in 1974-5. To be delivered from Dunsfold broken down for re-assembly in Emmen, Switzerland.

Jordan: a further nine FGA.73As and three FGA.73Bs for delivery in 1971.

Chile: a further four T.72 for delivery in 1970-71, eleven FGA.71s for delivery in 1971-74 and three FR.71As for delivery in 1974. The work split between Bitteswell and Dunsfold. There would be a further delivery of Hunters to Chile after the Falklands War, in recognition of assistance provided to the UK by Chile during that conflict, but these were not routed through Dunsfold and publicity was not encouraged.

Singapore: Having received an initial batch of twelve FGA.74 and four T.75 Hunters in 1970-71, a further order was received for four FR.74As, twenty-two FGA.74Bs and five T.75As for delivery between 1970 and 1973. The single-seat aircraft being refurbished at Bitteswell and the trainers at Dunsfold.

Abu Dhabi: A new order for seven FGA.76s and three FR.76As together with two T.77s for delivery in 1970-71.

Qatar: A new order for three FGA.78s and one T.79 for delivery in 1971. The aircraft were refurbished at Bitteswell but delivered from Dunsfold.

Kenya: A new order for four FGA.80s and two T.81s for delivery in 1974.

In 1970 Switzerland was in the throes of seeking a replacement for the Hunter in the air interception and strike roles and among the submissions received was one from Hawker Siddeley which was promoting the 'Super Hunter', designated by the Swiss the Hunter 'S.2-minus'. Building on the basic Mk 58 in service with the Swiss Air Force, the proposed replacement Hunter promised additional hardpoints for underwing stores carriage, including sidewinder AAM to allow double the payload of the Mk 58, improved fuel capacity, improved weapon-aiming via a laser-ranging unit, updated communications and flight instruments, and improved thrust from an Avon 801 engine. After a prolonged evaluation period, the Swiss opted to purchase additional Mk 58 Hunters and would retain the aircraft in their inventory until the early 1990s, a quite remarkable vote of confidence in an aircraft which was by then over forty years old.[12]

In all, some 162 refurbished Hunters were provided by HSA bringing the total of refurbishments provided over the period 1957 to 1975 to something like 553, of which 390 were for export, a quite remarkable record for an aircraft designed in the late 1940s. As a postscript, it was ironic that, just as further orders for Hunters dwindled away around 1975, a cache of a dozen or so Danish Hunters became available; they were flown into Dunsfold some twenty years after they had left the airfield for their homeland and were parked on the northern dispersal awaiting customers. Five years later they were still there, slowly deteriorating until the decision was made to dispose of the aircraft to whoever could offer a home. Several went to museums while others kept an appointment with the scrapman. Two found their way to Brooklands Museum where they joined Hurricane IIa and Harrier G-VTOL as representatives of Hawker's achievements.

So it was that Dunsfold bade farewell to the Hunter, a mainstay of the airfield for nearly twenty-five years. But not quite. In the late 1970s, a new shape appeared at Dunsfold, another Hunter, XL602,– a two-seat aircraft upgraded to T.8M standard to be used in the development of the avionics for the soon-to-fly Sea Harrier FRS.1. Delivered to the Royal Navy in 1958 from Dunsfold, XL602 was modified at Brough along with two others and remained at Dunsfold, both as a systems trainer and chase aircraft, until 1994 when it was delivered to RNAS Yeovilton. As a postscript to the long years of Hunter manufacture at Dunsfold, in 1995, as the Swiss parted with their long-serving Hunters to new owners, four aircraft piloted by Swiss Air Force pilots and acquired by the Jet Heritage Charitable Foundation flew across from the continent bound for Bournemouth Airport. However, prior to landing, they were joined by Hunters G-BOOM and G-HHUN, the six-ship formation overflying Dunsfold as a salute to their birthplace. Quite a sight for those lucky enough to be able to watch them sweep through.

In all the years of Hunter operations at Dunsfold, no fatalities or serious injuries had been recorded, yet ironically, it would be a Hunter that would claim the last fatality at the aerodrome, as late as 1998.

On 5 June 1998 a pair of Hunters, F.4 G-HHUN and T.7 G-VETA, part of the Jet Heritage fleet based at Bournemouth, had flown into Dunsfold to prepare for the following day's displays at Biggin Hill and Dunsfold Families Day. G-HHUN was a former Blackpool-built RAF Hunter F.4 registered XE677, which, on retirement, had returned to Dunsfold for refurbishment prior to being presented as an instructional airframe to Loughborough University of Technology in 1962. It had been acquired by Jet Heritage in 1989 and restored to flight in 1994. G-VETA, formally XL600, had a rather dark past. While undertaking aerobatics in 1963, the second pilot fell from the aircraft whilst inverted and died, due to his seat not being locked correctly.[13]

In the afternoon the pair departed Dunsfold to carry out a practice display at Biggin Hill but, advised of poor weather at this location, opted to return to Dunsfold and carry out a practice display over the airfield. This was approved and the display flown, following which it was decided to fly the routine again. Halfway through the display, the pilot of G-HHUN transmitted 'Mayday Mayday Mayday engine failure heading for the field,' answered by Dunsfold ATC, 'You're cleared to land'. With the aircraft at approximately 500 to 700 feet and a flame some 10-feet long issuing from the rear and another coming from the side, forward of the tailplane, the aircraft was very low as it was pulled round for runway 25 before striking the ground short of the runway, bouncing back into the air and landing again in a heavy roll akin to a cartwheel and sliding across the runway before coming to rest. The pilot, John Davies, was found dead at the scene. An investigation by the AAIB at Farnborough concluded that the aircraft had suffered damage to the engine caused by an uncontained turbine explosion and fire, probably caused by massive over-fuelling as a result of incorrect use of the fuel pump isolation switch.[14]

Chapter 6

Skyways, Airwork, Folland and GQ

Before Hawker obtained access to Dunsfold, another company had been able to use the aerodrome for the conduct of their business; this was Skyways Ltd, an air charter company, whose story is summarised below. Also making use of the airfield was an outstation of Airwork Ltd, GQ Parachute Company Ltd and, until the name was swallowed in the jaws of the Hawker Siddeley Group, Folland Aircraft Ltd.

Skyways Ltd

The cessation of the Second World War in the summer of 1945 resulted in a glut of former RAF transport aircraft being available on the open market and a requirement for short- and long-range transport and freight operations to and from the countries of Europe and the Empire with few companies in a position to exploit the opportunities thus presented. Into this vacuum stepped several entrepreneurs who quickly acquired aircraft and began to offer their services to businesses and government agencies to fulfil aviation-related needs.

One such company was Skyways Ltd. Originally set up in 1929, the company name remained dormant until, in May 1946, it was relaunched as an air charter company under Brigadier General A.C. Critchley, a former BOAC director, as chairman, Sir Alan Cobham, founder of Flight Refuelling Ltd, as deputy chairman and Captain R.J. Ashley as managing director. Initially the new company operated from Hawker's Langley airfield due to concerns with access to Northolt. The first aircraft on strength were an eclectic mix, including two Avro Lancastrians, two Avro Yorks, both types developed from the Lancaster bomber, a DH.104 Dove and a DH Dragon Rapide. On 18 June the company, under the sponsorship of the Ministry of Civil Aviation and with the consent of the Air Ministry, moved their maintenance activities down to the now redundant Dunsfold Aerodrome,

92

and took over T2A hangar for aircraft overhauls and a number of Nissen huts for use as technical workshops for the servicing of instruments, radio and navigation equipment and engine overhaul.

By the end of the year Skyways had five Lancastrians, three Yorks, three DC-3s, a DH Rapide and a DH Dove based at Dunsfold, with another seven Doves and a Bristol Freighter on order. That same month one of the Lancastrians was severely damaged when it caught fire in the T2A hangar resulting in the eventual scrapping of the aircraft and remedial works to the hangar. By the end of 1947 Skyways had added to their fleet five Douglas DC-4 Freighters, also known as C-54 Skymasters, and had a staff at Dunsfold of over 1,300 people, of whom some 500 were housed in the camps to the north of the airfield, and appear to have also obtained the use of hangar T2B, A being used for C of A overhauls and B for other routine servicing. The business expanded quickly on the back of transport contracts, of which the most important was for the Anglo-Iranian Oil Company and various other quasi-government charters including sub-contracted routes from BOAC that Skyways covered using the Skymasters.

Skyways Lancastrian 'Skylane' G-AGLV undergoes maintenance in front of the Technical site at Dunsfold c.1949. (Author's collection)

During the period between 1947 and 1948, Skyways was involved in the transport of a number of Hurricanes and Spitfires to the Portuguese Air Force, and many of these are believed to have staged through Dunsfold. At least one aircraft never left the aerodrome; Hurricane IIc LF383 was still sitting in a blister on the southern dispersals in 1950 slowly rotting, eventually becoming a derelict in a nearby hedge until the remains of the frame were extracted in the 1970s and disappeared from the airfield.[1]

One fly in the otherwise profitable ointment for Skyways was the number of complaints generated from the local population regarding the incessant noise of engines being tuned and aircraft taking off and landing, often throughout the night. Complaints to the Air Ministry and to Skyways themselves became particularly intense in 1947 as the pace of work built up and were more often than not from Major Hugh Rowcliffe, the former owner of the land upon which the airfield had been built. On 5 September 1947 Major Rowcliffe was moved to report that 'On Friday August 29th a large machine rose from the aerodrome and passed very low over Mill Farm at 11.45am causing my oldest and quietest cart-horse to bolt' and 'the noise caused this morning at 4.50; the furniture in my room was rattling from it'. The situation had not improved by the following year, when Rowcliffe, in a blast at the Air Ministry noted 'the racing of aeroplane engines continues between midnight and 7am on many nights. The noise was particularly bad at 03.15 hours on Sunday (the day of rest!)... .'[2]

Moved to look into the complaints, the Air Ministry despatched one of their number to Dunsfold to interview Skyways Managing Director Captain Ashley, who was not in an expansive mood, blaming the complaints on Rowcliffe's desire to have the company purchase his estate at a 'fancy price'. Clearly any concessions from Skyways would be minimal.[3]

The year 1948 saw Skyways seeking charter work between the UK and Argentina, Critchley flying out to have discussions with likely sources. Out of this came a contract for Skyways to take on the maintenance at Dunsfold of the DC-4 aircraft of the Flota Aérea Mercante Argentina (FAMA). Later that year Skyways was called upon to assist in the re-supply by air of West Berlin after Soviet forces closed the land routes into the city. Skyways initially placed two Lancastrians and three Yorks onto this work, beginning on 16 November, later losing York G-AHFI in a crash at Berlin's Gatow Airfield on 15 March 1949. Staff numbers rocketed to handle the additional work, many being based in Germany. By the end of the airlift Skyways aircraft had flown some 2,730 sorties.

Hurricane IIc LF383 abandoned in one of the blister hangars adjacent to Canada House 1950. Allocated to the Portuguese Air Force, it was left to rot at Dunsfold following faults which prevented delivery by Skyways. (Phil Jarrett via Peter Amos)

By the beginning of 1949 Skyways was the largest charter airline in Europe, with a fleet comprising a mix of Lancastrian, York, DC-3, DC-4 Skymaster, Dove and Rapide, and was set fair to continue expansion into the next few years. However, its maintenance base at Dunsfold was proving to be an expensive operation and the company made it known that it would be happy to share the airfield with another tenant, possibly a Royal Auxiliary Air Force squadron, in an effort to cut costs. The end of the Berlin blockade and the associated charter work was a significant financial blow to the company which quickly moved to retrench; in September 1949 Skyways announced ninety redundancies at Dunsfold, bringing job losses to 310 since the end of the Berlin Airlift, although *The Aeroplane* had reported redundancies of 400 at Dunsfold on 8 July. In November 1949 the company lost the BOAC contract and the Skymasters joined the Lancastrians and York at Dunsfold awaiting further work. In February 1950 the company put the three surviving Douglas DC-4 Skymaster aircraft up for sale; these were later bought by Air France.[4]

In March 1950 Skyways Ltd was placed into voluntary liquidation by its owners, followed by the registration of a new company, also called Skyways, which took on the DC-3s, still operating out of Dunsfold, but left the old Lancastrians and surviving York with the former company for disposal. On 2 June one of the company's DC-3s was hired out to Crewsair Ltd, a rival charter company, and later purchased outright by them. By 1951 Skyways was down to just two DC-3s. operating mainly in Kuwait, but, by the following January, those two aircraft had also been sold and the company became dormant before being bought out by the Lancashire Aircraft Corporation and moving the Skyways operation to Bovingdon Aerodrome in Hertfordshire.

As Hawker moved into the aerodrome in 1951, remnants of Skyways tenure remained in T2A hangar and a number of airframes dispersed on the airfield but by the end of the year all was gone; Hawker had the aerodrome to themselves and Major Rowcliffe a short period of relative peace.

Airwork

As was noted earlier, Airwork had been allowed tenure at Dunsfold on the southern dispersals. Airwork Ltd, or Airwork General Trading Ltd, was a private company supplying aviation services to the armed forces, aircraft industry and the post-war nascent airlines. They operated in the main as lodgers at RAF and RNAS bases and other companies' properties, undertaking a range of maintenance and upgrade works to any aircraft requiring their services. One of the many airfields from which these services were carried out in the post-war period was Hawker's at Langley, Slough, where Hawker would have become familiar with their activities.

Before the Second World War Gatwick airfield had become the location of Airwork's principal repair and maintenance division in the south, at that time still a grass airfield with no hard runways. In 1950 the company had received a large Ministry of Supply order for the refurbishment of Spitfires and Seafires for supply to overseas air arms, the work being carried out between 1951 and 1953. The post-refurbishment testing of the aircraft, with their Rolls Royce Griffon 61 engines, appears to have been trying in the wet winter conditions that were Gatwick in 1952 because Airwork took to bringing aircraft over to Dunsfold for testing from the metalled runways. On 12 February Supermarine test pilot John 'Peewee' Judge travelled over to the aerodrome to take Spitfire Mk 22s, including PK515, PK604 and PK485, through their initial tests for Airwork. The following day he flew over from Gatwick in PK613 and tested it, plus PK485 and PK604 again.

The tests continued to 5 March, twelve Spitfires being tested in that period. Judge was back the following year with another Spitfire 22 carrying the 'B' serial G-15-244 on 21 and 24 August and this appears to have been the last of Airwork's Spitfires to use Dunsfold.[5]

Then, in 1953, Airwork received a contract for the refurbishment of 145 Supermarine Attackers comprising sixty F.1s and FB.1s, and subsequent orders for twenty-four, thirty and thirty FB.2 aircraft. The Attacker, powered by a Rolls Royce Nene 101 engine of some 5,000lb thrust, had been Supermarine's first production jet aircraft for the Royal Navy's Fleet Air Arm. Although not possessed of particularly sparkling performance, it did allow the Royal Navy to get used to jet operations at sea prior to the arrival of the Hawker Sea Hawk a couple of years later. As the Sea Hawk was issued to the FAA so the Attackers were withdrawn from service with the front-line squadrons, although retained for use by RNVR squadrons for another few years. Again this refurbishment work was based at Gatwick with its grass flying field and, while this had been suitable for the Spitfire and Hornet contracts, the Attacker's performance from such a surface was marginal due to the requirement for longer take-off and landing runs and because the ground attitude of the aircraft, designed as a 'tail-dragger', resulted in severe ground erosion problems. In the event, it appears that aircraft were flown into Gatwick for refurbishment and then flown out to Dunsfold for their flight testing and subsequent delivery back to the Fleet Air Arm. Those Attackers which were not airworthy were transported by road direct to Gatwick of course.[6]

Colonel du Boulay, the landowner on the south side of Dunsfold airfield, had been told in December 1953 to expect works to begin adjacent to his property shortly so it seems likely that the Attackers began to pass through Dunsfold in early 1954. Space to work was allocated on some of the southern dispersals and a Bessonneau temporary hangar was lent by the Air Ministry to afford some cover for the works and, once the operation took shape, a blister hangar nearby was also brought into use, but creature comforts were obviously going to be in short supply and, in the event, much of the work was undertaken in the open.[7] There was a certain irony in the arrival of the RNAS Attackers on the southern dispersals at Dunsfold as the aircraft that had supplanted them in FAA service, the Hawker Sea Hawk, was erected and test flown from the northern side of the aerodrome.

The first Attacker at Dunsfold appears to have been WA520 which 'Peewee' Judge brought over on 12 and 24 January 1954, this incidentally being the last time that Judge's name occurs in connection with Dunsfold.

He later joined the Beagle Aircraft Company and, when that collapsed, joined Airmark Ltd, for whom he was displaying a modified Wallis autogyro at the SBAC show at Farnborough in 1970 when the aircraft crashed with fatal results; he was 48.

As the Attacker refurbishment got into gear, the first aircraft, other than the example above, arrived at Dunsfold for its initial flight testing, WA516 being flown over from Gatwick on 18 January 1955 and despatched to the Aircraft Handling Unit at Abbotsinch on 8 February by a Short Brothers' pilot. This would form the pattern for most of the Attacker aircraft refurbishments; at least twenty-six F.1 and twelve FB.2 aircraft are known to have passed through Dunsfold between January 1955 and April 1956. In this way, the time and expense of transport by road could be avoided. The last Attacker to be delivered from Dunsfold appears to have been WA474, which left on 19 April 1956.[8]

As the first Attackers started to arrive at Gatwick in 1954, Airwork received another contract, this time for RCAF F-86E Sabres in service with the RAF, to whom it was known as the Sabre F.4, to be refurbished and passed on to foreign air arms. Again the irony of the situation was probably not lost on the more enlightened at Hawker, for the Sabres had been acquired in 1952 and 1953 as a stop-gap answer to the lack of a transonic aircraft in Fighter Command and was now to be supplanted by ... the Hawker Hunters from Dunsfold. The procurement of the CL-13 F-86 Sabre for the RAF had been the result of protracted negotiations between the US, Canada and the UK. Production by the manufacturer, North American, was already fully committed to fulfilment of USAF requirements but Canadair had obtained a licence to build the F-86E and was thus able to supply some 431 Sabre F.4 aircraft, funded through the Mutual Defence Assistance Programme (MDAP). Most of these were supplied to eleven squadrons of the 2nd Tactical Air Force in West Germany with another two squadrons equipped for the defence of the UK. The Sabre F.4 was supplied complete with a General Electric J47 engine developing some 5,200lb thrust. Given its swept wing and flying tail, it was in advance of anything that the UK possessed until the advent of the Hunter.[9]

For the refurbishment operations at Gatwick, Dunsfold could be used for receipt of airworthy airframes, the aircraft being disassembled sufficiently to allow them to be transported by road to Gatwick. This process could then be reversed and the aircraft roaded back to Dunsfold for final flight test and delivery post-modification but work was also undertaken at Speke and Ringway.

The first Sabre movements noted in the Airwork log were in November 1954, those being deliveries of refurbished aircraft back to the RAF; information on earlier movements is missing due to the absence of Dunsfold ATC logs. From early 1955 Sabres can be seen arriving at Dunsfold to be broken down for transport to Gatwick, thirty aircraft arriving during 1955, a further thirty-six during 1956. As the Sabres for refurbishment tailed off at the end of 1956, the following year saw a glut of post-refurbishment aircraft returning from Gatwick by road; 1957 saw over sixty-five aircraft return to Dunsfold in this way. At the same time Sabres refurbished at Speke in Liverpool were flown into Dunsfold for their test flights and onward delivery to USAF bases, twenty-five aircraft arriving during 1957.[10]

Refurbished aircraft were initially flown out by RAF pilots to maintenance units in England, sixteen deliveries occurring in 1955. In 1956 there were just four deliveries back to RAF MUs while a further forty-one were delivered to locations abroad – to Chambley-Bussières and Marseilles, or Marignane, air bases, both in France, and to Munich, Spangdahlem, Bitburg and Fürstenfeldbruck in West Germany by USAF pilots. The deliveries were to USAF air bases established under the control of NATO. By 1957 deliveries abroad accounted for sixty-two of those made, principally to Châteauroux-Déols, Marseilles, Toul-Rosières in France and to the West German air bases noted above. Those deliveries also included those to Ypenburg in the Netherlands. A further six deliveries to UK bases included to RAF Burtonwood Cheshire, used as a major maintenance facility by the USAF in the 1950s. A few aircraft were flown from Dunsfold over to Lasham for what appear to be minor works, the aircraft returning to Dunsfold by air for subsequent test flights and delivery.

Once the aircraft arrived back at Dunsfold from refurbishment at Gatwick and had been re-assembled, flight testing could be completed in as little as three flights if all was found to be well. However, some aircraft languished at Dunsfold for several months before all the flight snags were cleared and the aircraft could be delivered.

The aircraft received from the RAF were upgraded by Airwork to F-86E (M) standard before being forwarded under the auspices of NATO to other deserving nations such as Italy (179 aircraft) and Yugoslavia (121 aircraft) under MDAP. On receipt of the post-refurbishment aircraft at Dunsfold, it would go straight into its flight-test schedule if it had flown in or would be re-assembled and ground tested before entering the flight-test phase. Flight testing was carried out by an Airwork pilot, often their chief test pilot – from 1953 Joe Tyszko. Any deliveries within the UK would latterly be undertaken by an Airwork pilot although, as seen earlier, the deliveries back to RAF bases in 1954 and 1955 were undertaken by RAF pilots. Once the aircraft was ready for despatch abroad, a USAF pilot would carry out a check flight to ensure that the aircraft was acceptable and then a delivery flight to the continent would be arranged, often flown by Gary Sparks, a major in the USAF. His first delivery from Dunsfold was to Pratica di Mare airbase near Rome, another forty-three deliveries following over the next three years. The aircraft carried USAF markings and RCAF serials for the delivery flights. Altogether, over 170 Sabres passed through the small Airwork facility at Dunsfold, typical annual movements being forty-six in 1955, along with twenty-six Attackers, eighty-one in 1956, together with ten Attackers, and ninety-seven in 1957.[11]

By early 1958 the work at Dunsfold was drying up for the Airwork team, only eight aircraft passing through Dunsfold's Airwork facility. The last flight took place on 13 January 1958 when Sabre 19795 was flown out to Manston by Clark. In late June, with deliveries to Italy and Yugoslavia complete, work ceased fairly suddenly and the work force was laid off. Around sixteen aircraft were still in the dispersals behind Canada House when this happened; a few had been languishing at Dunsfold for some time and had likely suffered cannibalisation to furnish parts for other aircraft. Eventually, during August and September 1958, those were broken down for transport to Airwork's premises at Lasham, later finding their way to Staravia at Church Crookham for scrapping. By 1959 Airwork had been encouraged to vacate the burgeoning civil airport at Gatwick and relocate their operations to Hurn.[12]

An interesting postscript to Airwork's tenure at Dunsfold occurred in 1954. When Reginald Cantello of Airwork was asked to explain how the company had come to be occupying space at Dunsfold at that time, his riposte was that they had never left! He explained that they had been on the airfield since the middle of the last war repairing Liberators and had stayed on all through Skyways' tenure and neither Hawkers nor any other operator received, or indeed asked for, any payment for this presence. While this explanation stretched credulity somewhat, it seemed that in fact it was quite right. In 1946 some Liberators had been parked on the southern dispersals and indeed their presence had attracted the attentions of some of the younger locals, who had ended up in court accused of breaking into the aircraft in a fit of boyish enthusiasm.[13]

Reg Dennis had been one of the Airwork team at Dunsfold. He had joined that company in 1951 at Gatwick and moved to Dunsfold in 1954 to work on the Attackers and, from 1956, on the Sabres. Reg remembered that the blister hangar could accommodate two aircraft and the Bessonneau hangar a further four. Those were located roughly where the later DH hangar was built in the 1980s. Much of the work was very hands-on but there was an old crane available to assist in the mating of the wings to the fuselage although later they were permitted to do this work over on the north side by the armoury to save time. Once the aircraft were complete, they would be taken over to the north side and positioned in the engine detuners for their engine runs but were delivered from the south side in full camouflage with USAF markings and drop tanks fitted.

Reg was able to join Hawkers in early July 1958 and moved across the aerodrome to work on Indian and Swiss Hunters in the Black Hangar, closely followed by his work colleagues Ron Cooper, Bill Brown, Joe Cree, Charlie Mellins and 'Spud' Taylor.[14]

Folland

Folland Aircraft Ltd was acquired by the Hawker Siddeley Group in 1959. The company had previously traded as British Marine Aircraft but, following financial woes, was re-organised and changed its name to Folland Aircraft in 1937 with Henry Folland himself in charge. In 1950 W.E.W. Petter joined the company as Folland's deputy and, later that year, became managing director and technical director – and later chief designer – due to Folland's ailing health. Petter had formerly been with Westland and English Electric where he had been instrumental in the design of the Westland Whirlwind, Welkin and Wyvern and the English Electric Canberra and P1A, the Lightning prototype.

Petter was not alone among his peers in being concerned at the ever-increasing weight of military aircraft and, in particular, fighters, and had for some time been scheming a truly lightweight fighter as an alternative to the leviathans that would culminate in the P1B Lightning. Through a series of design specifications, the company had arrived at the Folland Fo.139 Midge, a private venture aircraft first flown on 11 August 1954. While only an aerodynamic test aircraft, it did highlight the possibilities that could be achieved when weight was the governing factor in design from the outset.

From the Midge came forth a developed aircraft proposal – the Folland Fo.140 single-seat fighter, followed by the Fo.141 Gnat F. 1 fighter,

The only Folland Gnat F.1 to come to Dunsfold, XK741, is seen here on Dunsfold's western flight line c. 1961. The aircraft was used for stores-handling trials before being sent to Boscombe Down for trainer development in 1962. (BAE Systems, via Peter Amos)

of which a single example was built and made its first flight on 18 July 1955 as G-39-2 at Boscombe Down powered by a Bristol Orpheus of 3,285lb thrust. In March 1955 an order for six development aircraft was received from the Ministry of Supply. The Gnat fighter was truly diminutive, having a wingspan of just 22 feet and a length of 28 feet 6 inches. Basic weight was only 4,604lb which, with its developed engine's maximum thrust of 4,850lb, gave the aircraft a sparkling performance. Armed with two 30mm Aden cannon in the intake lips, the Gnat promised much as a point defence fighter although its relatively short 'legs' meant that, in common with many other aircraft of the time, drop tanks would be required to increase fuel capacity.[15]

Throughout its brief life the Gnat fighter failed to win any production orders from the RAF but did succeed in gaining orders from Finland for thirteen aircraft and from Yugoslavia for a further two. India showed more promise by ordering forty aircraft in September 1957, twenty-five complete from Folland together with another fifteen as major assembly kits. A further fifty-two aircraft were to be built under licence by Hindustan Aircraft Ltd in India.

By the mid-1950s a replacement for the obsolete Vampire trainer aircraft in RAF service was well overdue. While the weapon-training requirement would be covered by T.7 Hunters, there was a need for an aircraft able to allow *ab-initio* training on jets for new pilots entering the RAF. Folland looked to their Gnat as the basis for an airframe capable of fulfilling the trainer requirement and schemed an enlarged aircraft with tandem seating, the resulting aircraft being just nine inches longer than the fighter variant but with a wing of greater span. The resulting design met with favour at the Air Ministry and an order for a batch of fourteen Fo.144 Gnat trainers – eight development and six pre-production aircraft – was received in March 1958. But a production order was not forthcoming, rumour and speculation at Folland equating this with presumed pressure from government to persuade the company of the sense in being absorbed into the Hawker Siddeley Group as part of HM Government's then current craze for rationalisation in the aircraft industry. While this was partly correct, in fact the company's financial position was not strong and Petter, realising that changes would have to be made, entered negotiations with the Hawker Siddeley Group which resulted in the company becoming a member of that group while Petter retired to Switzerland.

Folland Gnat T.1 XP509 arrives at Dunsfold from Hamble for flight testing and delivery. First flown 16 November 1962 and delivered to 4 FTS Valley 13 February 1963. (BAE Systems, via Peter Image Amos)

Eventually, with the takeover of Folland Aircraft agreed, an order for thirty Gnat T.1 aircraft powered by a single Orpheus engine rated at 4,400lb thrust was received in February 1960 with further orders for twenty aircraft in July 1961 and forty-one in 1962. While this was good news for Hamble where the aircraft would be constructed, it meant the closure of Folland's flight development centre at Chilbolton, the work being transferred to Dunsfold where the majority of the flight testing and future development work would take place.

The first of the development batch aircraft – XM691 – made its maiden flight from Chilbolton on 31 August 1959, followed by the other thirteen development Gnat trainers over the next sixteen months. While preparations were in hand at Dunsfold to receive the production aircraft from Hamble, design and development staff started to transfer to the aerodrome and Kingston, soon followed by the first of the Gnat development batch. On 20 February 1961 development Gnat trainers XM691, XM692 and XM696 were flown into Dunsfold and later that day were joined by XK741, as far as is known, the only Gnat F.1 to make it to Dunsfold. Also brought over from Chilbolton were Folland's two modified Meteor T.7s, used for trials of the Folland lightweight ejector seat, later joined by the company Percival Proctor hack, sold in September 1961. On 24 February development batch aircraft XM694 flew into Dunsfold to be joined later in the year by XM697 and XM698, together with pre-production aircraft XM704 and XM709 in early 1962. Thus the majority of the development aircraft and two of the pre-production batch were relocated to their new home and with them came test pilots Squadron Leader 'Ted' Tennant, Squadron Leader Leslie 'Dick' Whittington and Mike Oliver.[16]

For the production Gnat trainers a system of transporting the aircraft by road to Dunsfold was instituted, as had already been the case for Hunters from Kingston and Langley. The Gnats would be assembled and tested as far as possible at Hamble and then loaded onto low-loaders with the wingtips removed and the aircraft canted at an angle to reduce the width of the load – one advantage of the aircraft's diminutive size. However, later aircraft were transported with the wings removed from the fuselage, making a more compact load. The first Gnat T.1 erected at Dunsfold made its maiden flight on 25 June 1962, the other 103 aircraft tracking through the Production Hangar over the next three years in company with various refurbished Hunters and the occasional Sea Fury. The last Gnat, XS111, first flew on 9 April 1965.

One of many tasks required of the Flight Test team at Dunsfold was the clearance of the Gnat for spinning in service. Given the somewhat

Later aircraft deliveries from Hamble came with the wing removed. Here John Parrott assists with the refitting of the wing. (BAE Systems, via John Parrot)

risky nature of the trial, it was to be carried out above the aerodrome with the aircraft in contact with a mobile ground station which could display the flight data being produced by the aircraft during the various spinning manoeuvres. Given the unstable nature of the Gnat in a spin, at times the pilot or flight test engineer on the ground would need to advise the pilot in the aircraft of which way up he actually was! After an extended series of test flights of a highly dubious nature, it was clear that a predictable spin could not be produced, a most important aspect for a trainer aircraft, and the decision was finally taken to release the aircraft to service with a prohibition on spinning.

The sole Gnat F.1 to relocate to Dunsfold, XK741, appears to have taken part in some store clearance trials, photographic imagery showing it fitted with Matra rocket pods, but very little is known of the flight trials on this aircraft. It ended its days at Dunsfold wingless behind the Production Hangar but, remarkably, the fuselage survives, last seen at the Midland Air Museum, Coventry.

Given the somewhat sustained criticism of the Gnat over the years, one might be forgiven for considering its acquisition by the RAF as a mistake, but what was it like to fly for the student pilots who would train on the aircraft? Chris Roberts, former RAF pilot and later Chief Test Pilot at Dunsfold, transitioned from the Jet Provost onto the Gnat at RAF Valley as part of his fast-jet training, graduating top of his course and later becoming a Gnat Qualified Flying Instructor (QFI). His view on the trainer?

> I can still remember my first Gnat flight in 1965, it was just Wow – this is what it's all about! I think it was an excellent trainer because it made me what I was. It was not too difficult for the students – it turned me from a below average pilot to above average. You had to work hard to do well on the Gnat.

The Folland Gnat is perhaps best remembered by the public as the mount of the Red Arrows display team: painted in a vivid red scheme and trailing coloured smoke, they became the best known of the various RAF display teams in the 1960s. The origin of this particular team was to be found at No. 4 Flying Training School at RAF Valley on Anglesey whose flying instructors formed the core of the first team and who presented their

Folland Gnat T.1 XM693 being towed to the flight line. This was the third development aircraft, first flown 8 March 1960, retained for trials at Boscombe Down and other facilities. Note the original detuner arrangement for the Harrier engine pen in left background. (BAE Systems, via Peter Amos)

first display at RNAS Culdrose in July 1964 using five Gnats painted in high-visibility yellow, the team taking the title 'Yellowjacks'. Following the successful first season, it was decided to have a combined formation aerobatic team display at Farnborough in 1964 using the 'Yellowjacks' and 'Red Pelicans' from CFS. The clear superiority of the Gnat in the role resulted in the RAF deciding to pass the mantle of the RAF Aerobatic Team to a new team formed on the Gnat. In April 1965 the Red Arrows became the first fulltime team, using nine Gnats painted red, going on to perform 1,292 displays across the country for the next fifteen years until the replacement of the Gnat by the BAe Hawk T.1 in 1980.

As mentioned above, one trademark of the team was the use of different-coloured smoke. This was achieved by pumping diesel fuel and coloured dye into the jet exhaust of the aircraft, the different colours being selected by cockpit switching. The development work for this system was carried out at Dunsfold, mainly on Gnat XR540, using a variety of pipework schemes before the optimum arrangement was confirmed. The ground tests involved much pumping of coloured smoke over the airfield, later followed by air tests to bring the system to its final form.

In 1970 Chris Roberts was successful in joining the Red Arrows, at that time flying the Gnat. How did the aircraft compare to the Hawk which supplanted the Gnat as the mount for the team?

> It was a better aeroplane for the Arrows than the Hawk from a pure flying point of view, but not from a role point of view. The flying characteristics were more typically 'swept wing', the Gnat flew much more like a Hunter or a Lightning and the visual image of the shape of the formation would give better formation pictures than the Hawk. So from a pure flying point of view the Gnat was a better aeroplane for formation aerobatics but from a role point of view – maintenance, engine changes etc., the Hawk has always been a better aircraft, both in the training role and in the Red Arrows.[17]

Work was also continued on the Folland lightweight ejector seat with which the Gnat trainer was to be fitted. This had resulted from an approach from the Ministry of Supply in 1952 for such a device and chimed well with Petter's weight-saving philosophy. The move to Dunsfold had brought with it the Meteor T.7 aircraft used by the company for air-testing the designs, the rear cockpit glazing having been removed to allow repeated

Meteor T.7, modified WF877, used to develop the Folland lightweight ejector seat, shown here prior to carrying out a high-level test ejection over Larkhill Range, February 1964. (BAE Systems, via Peter Amos)

firings from that cockpit. Folland had used two Meteor T.7s for the seat trials, WT690 and WF877, both of which were flown up to join the team at Dunsfold on 20 February 1961. Thereafter, WA690 was not used for the seat trials from Dunsfold and on 12 May of that year departed to Boscombe Down for their use, possibly with ETPS. That left WF877 to carry out the remaining flight tests on the seats.

Those comprised the final tests required to clear the seat for ejection at high altitude. As far as can be discerned, the first 'live' seat trial from Dunsfold was around 1 August 1963; the first trial of the seat had occurred at Netheravon airfield in December 1956. Prior to this various 'dummy' drops had been carried out over Dunsfold's runway much to ATC's chagrin. This live drop was to be courtesy of Arthur Harrison, then employed by GQ Parachute Company Ltd of Woking (more of them later) and consisted of ejection at 20,000 feet over Larkhill range on Salisbury Plain, followed by a free-fall of 160 seconds to 5,000 feet and then auto-separation and parachute deployment to a hopefully smooth landing. All appears to have gone smoothly, for Harrison was still available to be the subject of the last drop. However, this test would be the first with a fully-instrumented seat, designed to cover all aspects of the ejection, timing and accelerations, and required the 'ejectee' to complete a series of selections in his cockpit prior to being shot at velocity into the ether by the pilot. For whatever reason, Harrison suddenly went off the idea, leaving the Folland team with an important trial but no 'jumper'.

Shortly after this setback, Peter Amos, one of the Folland team, stumbled upon a solution. He recalled:

> I was in A Squadron hangar at Boscombe Down with the Gnat Trainer and was talking with one of the staff about our predicament when an RAF chap came across and apologised for having heard what we'd been talking about but said that he was an RAF Parachute Jumping Instructor and that, if we could arrange it, he would be more than willing to undertake it for us – manna from heaven! On my return to Dunsfold I immediately put the wheels in motion and Sergeant Russ Sawyer, as he was the one who had volunteered, duly became our willing and very able live subject!
>
> Russ was really up for it and he duly came up to Dunsfold to be introduced to all the idiosyncrasies of the Folland Ejector Seat. But our troubles were not yet over as, just as things were, at long last, beginning to come together (the Ministry were, by this time, also getting more than a little impatient with us as they wanted to clear the Gnat Trainer into service), 'Dick' Whittington (our normal and only pilot cleared to fly the Meteor) went and got mumps! What else could go wrong?
>
> I was in the pilot's office in the ground floor of the tower the following morning talking to David Lockspeiser and bemoaning the fact that our long-awaited seat trial was in jeopardy yet again when he said, 'I can fly the Meteor. You get me clearance and I'll do it for you' – luck had struck again! Following a couple of familiarisation flights for Lockspeiser, the live test was scheduled for 15 July 1964.
>
> Well, it all finally came together late one glorious summer's evening and everything went off like a dream. I had waited in the tower at Dunsfold and had seen them off and stayed there until word came through that the ejection had been the success that we had all been hoping for and that Russ was having a medical check before going to our pre-arranged meeting place, the nearby pub called 'The Pheasant' on the A30 (now a private dwelling), for a celebratory drink! I then took off rapidly in the

Folland Gnat T.1s lined up at Dunsfold prior to departure. The two with numbered fins have probably brought pilots from RAF Valley to pick up these deliveries. (BAE Systems, via Peter Amos)

car with Russ's civilian clothes and David said he would come down after he'd put the Meteor away and changed!

It seemed that I had no sooner arrived at the pub, when David walked in! He must have had some drive down as it was 62 miles by road and it regularly took me about an hour and a half – but not David that evening! What an evening that was! The ejector seat team from Hamble were also there (they'd been watching from the range) but it must have been a good evening as I can remember little of it.[18]

GQ Parachutes

Another of the disparate companies that found Dunsfold a convenient location for their particular niche business was the GQ Parachute Company Ltd. The company was founded in 1932 by James Gregory and Sir Raymond Quilter and incorporated in 1934, operating firstly from rented space in RFD's premises in Stoke Road, Guildford, before moving to more spacious surroundings in Portugal Road, Woking. The company had expanded rapidly during the Second World War, producing both emergency parachutes for aircrew and paratrooper assemblies for airborne forces. Postwar, GQ became involved in the development and production of braking and anti-spin parachutes for the new generation of fast-jet aircraft, as well as those for the ejector seats that were now mandatory on military aircraft, mainly produced by Martin-Baker, ML and Folland.

Testing of the parachutes proved to be somewhat tricky at first until a solution was found in the mid-1950s in the use of a high-powered racing car, the one-off Napier-Railton fitted with a 24-litre Napier engine derived from a high-powered aero-engine. This was driven at suitably high speeds up and down Dunsfold's runway in March 1955, usually at the weekend, to test the deployment of the various drogues and chutes then in development. The company even developed a braking parachute that could

Publicity image for GQ Parachute Company featuring the Napier Railton racer on Dunsfold's runway, 1954. This vehicle is now preserved at Brooklands Museum. (The Aeroplane, via Peter Amos)

be automatically re-stowed after landing, although it does not appear to have gone into production. The Napier Railton still exists, is held at Brooklands Museum at Weybridge and occasionally brought out for a run.

In 1963 GQ Parachutes was acquired by its old stablemate RFD, founded by Reginald Foster Dagnall. This company had started in the First World War manufacturing balloons and kites for the British Army. Postwar, the company moved to Stoke Road, Guildford, producing aircrew dinghies and kite balloons as well as gliders. By the mid-1930s RFD had expanded into new premises in Catteshall Lane, Godalming. In 1963 it acquired GQ Parachutes and, in 1968, the Mills Equipment Company, reconstituting in 1970 under the RFD-GQ banner, still producing aircraft safety equipment. For many years the fuselage of a Canberra bomber rested in front of the Godalming premises for use in developing some of the company products which included inflatable liferafts, life-jackets, aircraft escape slides and parachutes. Other products required rather more substantial airframes and, for the testing of what the company termed 'pneumatic elevators' or lifting bags to assist in raising crashed aircraft, a redundant HS Trident airliner was acquired and flown into Dunsfold to perform this function in the 1980s. Based on one of the south-eastern dispersals, the Trident ended its days on its belly, becoming part of the landscape until removed prior to closure.

Chapter 7

Vertical Take Off

With the renewal of planning authority under their belt and the transfer of the aerodrome to the Ministry of Aviation, Hawker moved to prepare the site for their next major aircraft project and, on 24 May 1960, requested permission from the MoA and the local authority to extend the runway at the east end with a 300 x 25-yard extension.

It was something of a truism, and often used in a pejorative sense, that Camm and Hawker never produced anything truly innovative, preferring to move forward in tried and tested steps where the technology had already passed the rigours of actual flight. Thus an untested engine would not be coupled with a new airframe, at least initially, if at all possible. Of course, it was this very conservatism that had allowed Hawker Aircraft to produce some of the world's superlative aircraft and reap a healthy profit into the bargain. Yet, when the company produced what at the time was THE truly innovative aircraft of the 1960s, their detractors were quickly busy claiming that the design was too innovative and not sufficiently conservative, was too radical for operational use and, anyway, would never carry a useful load or amount to anything. History was to prove the detractors spectacularly wrong, yet the Harrier – for that is of what we speak – had to suffer such slurs throughout almost its entire life, quite often from within the services and government ministries, where one would have hoped Hawker might find support for this home-grown and unique aircraft. Sadly that was not to be.

Dunsfold has become synonymous with the Harrier. It was, after all, where the first hovers of what would become the world's first VTOL operational aircraft occurred and from whence almost every Harrier first flew, yet this is to ignore its history as the location from which many of the world's Hunters took flight and also the Gnat T.1s, not to mention the first production Sea Hawks and later the British Aerospace Hawk. Be that as it may, it was Dunsfold where the culmination of the expertise of the Kingston and Bristol Design Offices first took to the air and which would ever more be known as the 'home of the Harrier'.

How did it all start? As previously discussed, Hawker's great hope of a large Mach 2 strike fighter – P.1121 – had failed to find favour with a government intent on pursuing a philosophy which saw the end of manned interceptors as part of its national defence and an Air Ministry intent on an 'all things to all men' approach to aircraft design which would culminate in TSR.2. As work on P.1121 tailed off, the design office was left with concepts based on an advanced Hunter and even a Hunter-based passenger jet. Such was the paucity of ideas that Camm was even prepared to tolerate a design for a research aircraft, something that was anathema to him if it did not lead to a production aircraft. The P.1122 was basically a P.1121 with a steel wing and turbo-rocket propulsion capable of Mach 3-4.

However, one of the few ideas kicking around the design office was in response to early thoughts on vertical take-off. This concept had been around for a long time, its most prolific manifestation being in boys' comics and books about the future where aircraft would replace the car, take off and land vertically, and even enter space.

Somewhere closer to earth, in the 1950s the RAE at Farnborough had instigated a rather more prosaic research project that sought to define just how such a vehicle could be controlled in hovering flight. Rolls Royce was given the job of developing a Thrust Measuring Rig, more popularly known as the 'Flying Bedstead', which used two Nene centrifugal engines mounted back-to-back on a basic frame with the main jet exhaust directed downwards for jet lift and pipework which ducted part of the engine thrust to the extremities of the rig for reaction control. The rig had aroused immense interest with the general public and even more so when the research was applied to an actual aircraft design funded by the government in 1953 and built by Short Brothers – the Short SC.1. This stubby little design had four dedicated lift engines and a further engine for cruising flight. Its unveiling to the public at Farnborough had raised expectations within both the public and indeed the Air Ministry that the vision of aircraft that had no need of runways might soon become a reality.

More importantly, it was dawning on the defence staffs of various countries that military aircraft tied to miles of concrete runway were uniquely compromised. If the enemy could knock holes in those runways before the aircraft could take off, there was no need to destroy the fighters and bombers in the air since they had no way of leaving the ground to join the fray. Indeed it had been explicit in NATO defence doctrine since 1954 that surprise attack on airfields to immobilise aerial forces would be the *first* act of any future war.

> We must particularly guard our air forces against such (surprise) attack by basing them on as many different airfields as possible, by dispersing them to the maximum extent possible on these airfields, and by improving their ability to redeploy to operate from alternate bases at immediate notice.[1]

An aircraft capable of operating from dispersed locations thus became the holy grail of military thinking in the 1950s.

So it was that several research establishments and aircraft companies across the developed world began to take an interest in 'vertical take-off' machines as a way of avoiding the embarrassment of having an air force that could not take off in time of war and which could be dispersed away from main airfields at short notice. Research aircraft were produced in Europe and the USA to explore different lifting configurations since there was no bible to follow. In this sense, Hawker Aircraft and Bristol Engines certainly did not 'invent' vertical take-off and landing, but theirs was the only project in the West that would come to fruition as an operational military aircraft.

Ralph Hooper, P.1127 Project Engineer from 1957 to 1963 and later executive director and chief engineer at Hawker Siddeley from 1968, recalled

> a residual 'race memory' ... which suggests that the HSA board in discussing the Sandys paper had reviewed alternatives, if fighters were to become extinct, and had noted VTOL progress as something to watch. It is possible that Sir Sydney (Camm) (and perhaps others) had been asked (encouraged?) to follow up this line.[2]

Hooper again: 'We know that HSA HQ had documents relating to BE.53 (the early Bristol VTO engine project) dated as early as March '57 ... . Perhaps news of this had reached Sir Sydney for on 17th May 1957 he wrote to Stanley Hooker, Technical Director at Bristol Engines.' Camm had written:

> I recently saw a film of the Ryan VTO aircraft [a US research aircraft] and it started me wondering whether we ought to give more attention to this possible development (i.e. to VTOL). I have also heard that you have given some consideration to it and I should very much like to hear your views ... . Perhaps you could drop me a line about it.[3]

In the event, it appears that Hooker omitted to respond to Camm's enquiry and only later did a copy of the BE.53 brochure (PS.17) reach Camm himself, who passed it on to the project office at Kingston for consideration but no action was called for. Hooper recalls that 'It was passed on, perused and discarded and then picked up by someone who found it more interesting than test rigs or spinning models or weapon systems.' In other words Hooper himself![4]

Hooper quickly schemed several possible designs around the strange engine, which was unlike anything that had been seen before. Originating from a patented design by French aeronautical engineer and entrepreneur Michel Wibault in 1956, his 'Gyropter' (*Gyroptere* in French) comprised a Bristol Orion engine driving four centrifugal blowers arranged on the sides of the aircraft to exhaust either down for vertical manoeuvring or aft for conventional flight. As a favour to the MWDP office, who had made funding available for development of the Orpheus engine for the NATO Light Strike Fighter project – won by the Fiat G.91, Hooker had agreed to look at Wibault's idea to see whether it possessed any merit. The job had landed in the in-tray of a young designer named Gordon Lewis, earlier responsible for the design of the Olympus engine for the Vulcan bomber.

Lewis carried out work on Wibault's concept which resulted in an engine designated BE.48, later BE.52, where the cold train from the low-pressure (LP) compressor exhausted through two side-mounted vectorable nozzles and the hot train conventionally aft but it was still very much a 'paper' engine when the brochure found its way onto Hooper's desk at Kingston in May 1957. Camm's reaction to his initial sketches is not recorded, but it was no doubt scathing. However, with Sir Arnold Hall, Chief Executive of the Hawker Siddeley Group, arriving at Camm's door to discuss, among other things, 'our VTOL studies which are being investigated around the Bristol engine', he was not best placed to prevent work continuing on the idea.[5]

At this point, Hooper proposed two changes vital to the future of the project; one was to split the hot gasses from the turbine area by bifurcating the jet-pipe as per the Sea Hawk, resulting in the engine's total thrust now being capable of vectoring through four nozzles rather than two. The other, slightly later, innovation was to suggest to Bristol Engines the counter-rotation of LP fan and high-pressure (HP) compressor to eliminate gyroscopic coupling. Ironically, both innovations had already featured in the joint Wibault/Lewis patent submitted by Bristol in 1957, but Lewis had not highlighted them to Hooper, knowing that each would bring with it further problems to be resolved. By July 1957 the proposal, to be powered by the

BE.53 engine, was sufficiently developed to be given a project number – P.1127 – and a simple brochure was produced for the benefit of MWDP and other interested parties including HM Government. The Mutual Weapons Development Agency (MWDA) was a US-funded NATO office whose aim was to provide funding to European countries for military programmes which might be of benefit to NATO as a whole and also known as MWDP (Mutual Weapons Development Programme). As such, they were crucial to the re-armament of Europe in the early years of the Cold War period.

At a meeting in October 1957 with Colonel Chapman of MWDP in Paris, Hawker was informed that Supreme Headquarters Allied Powers Europe (SHAPE) finance, if forthcoming, could only amount to 50 per cent and that HM Government or Hawker would need to fund the rest of the development costs; the government quickly responded that no funding would be available from them.

By March 1958 Chapman had confirmed that MWDP would be prepared to fund the development costs of the engine up to 75 per cent; Bristol had confirmed that the compressors could counter-rotate and an engine thrust of some 13,000lb was possible without water injection. That left the undercarriage to be finalised. Early studies had shown carriage of a nuclear bomb on the centreline with a conventional undercarriage attached to the wings. Unfortunately, the jet efflux passing over the wheels would have caused undesirable pitching moments during the transition and therefore the nuclear bomb was ditched and the undercarriage moved to the centreline. While this was good for the main and nose legs, with a high-mounted wing, the outriggers required to balance the aircraft would be vulnerable to snapping due to their inordinate length. The solution was found by applying some 10 degrees of anhedral to the wing, allowing the outriggers to be shorter and supplying much needed lateral stability and control characteristics to the airframe.

Hooper knew that Camm would hate the new design and so conspired to avoid his having sight of it prior to the next meeting in Chapman's office in late-March 1958. At the meeting the result of this little conspiracy played out; Hooper:

> It was a close-run thing, at one point, with Col Chapman trying to unroll the drawing while Sir Syd tried to roll up the other end! But all was well because Col Chapman's reaction was so positive. The official diary records 'the chief designer returned from the meeting with high hopes'.

Finally, Chapman asked Camm to submit costings and a manufacturing programme for seven prototypes.[6]

Meanwhile the Ministry of Supply suggested that, 'as a result of Air Staff interest', they were considering an order for two P.1127 prototypes although MWDP were still of the opinion that offshore funding for a production aircraft via their office would be difficult, given that they were already supporting the BE.53 engine development. However, all was not lost; various US facilities including NASA were able to offer assistance on likely aircraft behaviour by flying models in their wind tunnels which greatly added to Hawker confidence in their design. So it was that work on the project continued as a private venture and, in March 1959, preliminary construction and parts manufacture was authorised, confirmed on 1 July with an instruction that maximum effort was to be expended to achieve a first flight date of the end of July 1960.

The first BE.53/2 engine, No. 901, had its first run on 2 September 1959 in test cell 12E at Bristol's Patchway site and recorded some 9,000lb thrust before fan-blade vibration led to a decision to throttle back; not bad for such a radical design. However, back at Hawker, it had become apparent that using bleed air from the fan stage of the low-pressure compressor for the reaction control system would result in overly large ducting to achieve the level of controllability required. Hooper duly notified his Bristol colleagues of this and asked whether the bleed take-off could utilise the high-pressure compressor instead. The inevitable delay that this caused was used to good effect and led to the engine being upgraded with an additional stage to the HP compressor, the designation changing to BE.53/3. This new engine was successfully tested in April 1960; six BE.53/3 engines would be built for the initial engine runs and flight trials at Dunsfold.

Meanwhile, with concerns both at Bristol and Kingston regarding the thrust that would be available from the first engines, it now being obvious that this would be marginal given an aircraft weight of around 10,000lb, in May 1960 the Project Office at Bristol produced a brochure proposing a wingless short-range freighter for battlefield use, the BE.53 engine being used for both VTO and (slow) cruise. At Bristol it quickly gained the moniker 'Flying Pig' and did not proceed. Another study suggested a P.1127 type airframe with very small wings, in order to reduce the aircraft weight. Camm noted in a letter to Hooker, 'Your wingless aircraft proposals will require a great deal of thought,' no doubt 'Camm speak' for 'leave aircraft design to us,' but nonetheless passed it to Chris Hansford in Hawker's project office who looked at the idea and schemed some initial thoughts

Roll out of the first P.1127 XP831 prior to initial engine run, July 1960. (BAE Systems, courtesy of Brooklands Museum)

on how such an aircraft would compare to the P.1127 in terms of range and payload.[7] While VTO range was improved, STO range was roughly halved. As far as is known, the proposal went no further but was just one of many red herrings current at the time, as was to be expected, VTO was a completely new concept for the industry and fertile minds everywhere were looking at how it could best be applied to aircraft and tactics.

In May 1960 the first BE.53/3 Pegasus 2 engine, No. 905, was ready to leave Bristol for delivery to Hawker. Andrew Dow in *Pegasus – The Heart of the Harrier*, has this delivery going to Dunsfold 'for ground running in the prototype airframe XP831'. However, since the aircraft would not arrive at Dunsfold until July, it is more likely that it was sent to Kingston for trial installation in the aircraft. The designation of Bristol engines as 'BE' would shortly change to 'BS' to reflect the amalgamation of Bristol Aero-Engines Ltd and Armstrong Siddeley Motors to create Bristol Siddeley Engines Limited (BSEL) on 1 February 1959, with its first managing director being Sir Arnold Hall, late technical director of Hawker Siddeley Group; in 1964 Hall would return to Hawker Siddeley Aviation as chairman and managing director. The merger that created BSEL would be further enhanced in April 1962 when the engine interests of the de

Havilland Engine Company and Blackburn Engines Ltd joined with Bristol Siddeley, the aircraft-manufacturing components of these two companies being merged with Hawker Aircraft as part of the Hawker Siddeley Aviation Group. In June 1960 firm funding for the first two aircraft was received from the ministry; finally Hawker could move forward with the project with confidence. In July 1960 the first airframe, XP831, was delivered to Dunsfold and late that month the completed aircraft rolled out of the Experimental Hangar for official photographs. The first engine run followed, using engine No. 905, in the new ground-running pen. Some minor problems asserted themselves, including a small fire in the engine at one point, quickly dealt with by the site fire brigade.

To accommodate the new aircraft project, various works had been required at Dunsfold. As seen at the beginning of the chapter, a 300-yard extension at the eastern end of the runway had been called for to allow the maximum run for the P.1127 when landing in the conventional manner. To this were now added alterations to one of the three ground-running pens which, in their current design, for Hunters, were unsuitable for the new aircraft. The aircraft's relocated jet exhausts required the removal of the central detuner from the pen and the installation of a gridded platform, over trenches cut into the floor, to allow limited vectoring of the nozzles during testing. The efflux from the exhaust nozzles could then be ducted away under the floor of the pen to two new detuners constructed behind the pen and angled out at approximately 45 degrees to the vertical. Coupled with this, portable steel covers were designed to be pushed up against the body of the fuselage to contain and direct the efflux down into the detuner trenches. Also constructed at this time was a new installation comprising a pit let into the surface of the western ORP some 4-feet deep and 88-feet long by 40-feet wide, overlaid partly with a gridded platform to allow exhaust gasses to be ducted away via cascades from the aircraft while in the hover and prevent hot gas recirculation by the engine which would decrease the thrust available and, in the centre, a solid platform constructed of steel plates. The pit grid included shackles to allow the aircraft to be restrained for ground-running tests of the engine away from the confines of the running pen. This tie-down arrangement was supplemented in late-1965 with additional shackling points on the adjacent concrete hardstanding. Also trialled at this time were clamps to reduce the vibration induced in the tailplane by the jet efflux when ground running.

The following weeks covered further ground runs both in the pen and shackled on the gridded platform on the western ORP. It was found that

P.1127 XP831 being prepared for the first engine run, July 1960. Note the exhaust collector shrouds at the side of the fuselage, soon discarded, and the early arrangement of gridded troughs to channel the exhaust into twin detuners. (BAE Systems, courtesy of Brooklands Museum)

the exhaust collector shrouds used to contain the hot gasses within the running-pen tended to encourage heating of the rear fuselage and in time these would be deleted and the running-pen redesigned.

October saw the first flight engine, No. 906/7, delivered to Dunsfold for installation in XP831 and further checks in the running-pen and on the platform confirmed that the engine was delivering close to 11,000lb thrust; the 11,300lb thrust quoted by Bristol was its uninstalled value. (Losses from the aircraft intake and reaction control bleed would result in rather less being available for hovering.) It was evident that, when the weight of pilot and fuel was added to the airframe weight, any attempt at vertical take off using this early engine would be marginal at best. Therefore, everything that could safely be stripped from the aircraft was removed, including the undercarriage doors, pitot boom and even the radio. With all extraneous equipment removed, some 700lb, the aircraft weight was calculated at approximately 9,750lb with fuel and the engineers adjudged that sufficient thrust over weight existed to allow for the first hovers to be performed. These would be within strict confines of engine RPM and JPT and airframe restriction by weighted tethers secured beneath the grid.

Finally, on 21 October 1960, in the hands of Chief Test Pilot Bill Bedford, XP831 started up on the grid and after fourteen minutes, with RPM increased to 89 per cent, rose uncertainly in the first ever hover, of some eighteen inches, by what would become the Harrier. History was made that day by Bill Bedford, XP831, Hawker Aircraft Ltd and Dunsfold.

Tests continued for the next month with XP831 performing twenty hovers over the grid as the tethers were slowly lengthened to allow greater heights in the hover. Some concerns were raised regarding high temperatures suffered by the main gear wheels and by the lateral 'skipping' about the tethers but, all in all, surprisingly few major concerns presented themselves. Eventually the day dawned on 19 December which saw the removal of the tethers and the completion of flight No. 21, the first 'free' hover. It was then apparent that at least some of the problems seen in the early hovers had been caused by the tethers.

With the completion of flight No. 21, XP831 returned to the Experimental Hangar for extended service and maintenance and for the short-life engine

Early tethered hover by P.1127 XP831 over the pit. The aircraft has had all non-essential equipment removed to save weight. October 1960. (BAE Systems, courtesy of Brooklands Museum)

to be replaced with No. 905. Alterations to allow for the start of conventional flights were also made, including the removal of the bulbous intake lips and replacement with thinner profiles optimised for conventional flight. In early March 1961 the aircraft was roaded to RAE Bedford and prepared for a series of conventional flights from the extended runway at Thurleigh starting on the 13th. Ten flights were completed with the aircraft returning by air to Dunsfold on the 24th. There, in May 1961, with a further new engine fitted, XP831 resumed hovers, all from the grid and mostly untethered. The flight experience was then extended to occasional VTOs from the grid, followed by a landing on the solid platform and later to translations down the runway at slow speed and back to a vertical landing, the piloting being shared by Bedford and Merewether. Also in May 1961 it was announced that the BE.53 engine would be named Pegasus, in line with Bristol's use of classical mythological nomenclature, after the winged horse that could rise vertically into the air. Henceforth the BE.53/3 became the Pegasus 2.

The months up to November 1961 saw some 155 flights made by XP831 as the flight envelope was gradually opened up and including short take offs (STOs) which would allow greater weight to be carried by the aircraft once it entered service. Again the short life of the early engines

P.1127 XP831 in free hover with equipment removed for the early flights replaced. (BAE Systems, courtesy of Brooklands Museum)

required several replacements over the first year of flying, six engine changes being required. However, by the anniversary of the first flight, immense gains had been achieved. The aircraft had demonstrated successful vertical take off and landing, transition from vertical to low speed forward flight, conventional flight up to 30,000 feet and the ability to do all this with no auto-stabilisation.

On 7 July 1961 the second prototype, XP836, made its first flight and quickly joined the test programme, concentrating on partially jet-borne flight down to 95 knots, to investigate the 'other end' of full transitions from normal flight to vertical landing, and the expansion of the flight envelope to supersonic speed, achieved on 12 December by Bedford in a shallow dive. Unfortunately, two days later, the aircraft was lost at Yeovilton when the port cold nozzle detached, causing uncontrollable roll at slow speed when the flaps were lowered. Bedford escaped at low level without serious injury. The use of reinforced fibre-glass for such an essential area of the engine might in retrospect appear strange but dated from intense efforts to keep the weight of the engine to a minimum. Earlier manifestations of the engine had included fibre-glass ducts on the external casing of the engine to carry the fan air to the cold nozzles. Although these had been designed out of the later engines prior to flight, the nozzles remained in fibre-glass for the simple reason that they saved weight over steel versions.[8]

Notwithstanding the loss of the second prototype, full accelerating and decelerating transitions had been achieved in September 1961. Indeed, so remarkable was the ability of the aircraft to achieve such transitions, essential for any proper service use to be considered, so quickly that Robert 'Bob' Marsh from Kingston's design department noted to Stanley Hooker that 'Our pilots have just completed landing transitions using the forward tilt of the nozzles and have been "shaken rigid" by the deceleration – the complete manoeuvre from wing-borne to touchdown now takes place in about 600 yds.'[9] Luckily, in the interim, the Ministry of Aviation had belatedly ordered a further four prototypes and the first of these, XP972, was available for a first flight on 5 April 1962. This aircraft was used for various handling trials, lift boundary and flutter clearance of the fourth wing shape, and trials with an anhedral tailplane. In September this aircraft, together with XP831, had been shown to great advantage to the world's aviation community at Farnborough; this was really the first time that most people had had the chance to see this amazing new technology in action. In the crowd that day was none other than Michel Wibault, the originator of the vectored-thrust principle. Unluckily, on its forty-ninth flight, on 30 October,

Three P.1127s: from left, XP831, XP976 and XP980. All appear to have had the rubber inflatable intake lips fitted. (BAE Systems, courtesy of Brooklands Museum)

XP972 suffered a complete engine failure after high 'g' manoeuvres. Following a 6.5g turn at 550 knots, the aircraft suffered buffeting before the engine flamed out. With limited height and no power, Merewether was able to get the aircraft down into RAF Tangmere for a successful forced landing. It was found that the engine compressor casing had deformed under the high 'g' loading and caused the titanium blades to rub against the casing resulting in a titanium fire.[10]

On 12 July 1962 the fourth prototype, XP976, took to the air for its first flight, the aircraft being used, on its early flights, on handling and flutter clearance of the third wing design. So it was that, despite this being the fourth aircraft, it would shortly become just one of two prototypes available to Hawkers to continue with the immense amount of work required to bring the P.1127 design to a standard that could be presented to the services as a viable military fighting vehicle. The last two prototypes – XP980 and XP984 – were first flown at Dunsfold in May and October 1963 respectively. Each new aircraft introduced new features as the design matured so that

XP984 was most representative of the aircraft that would become the Kestrel and the P.1127 (RAF).

Be that as it may, ministerial and service interest in a developed P.1127 was noticeable by its absence. The ability to move away from entrenched thinking wedded to massive concrete runways and airfields, the location of which were known to every Warsaw Pact country, while accepted by those whose job it was to explore such game-changing possibilities, was not believed to be possible with the current state of play as represented by P.1127. Interest in VTOL did not equate to interest in P.1127 as a service aircraft. What instead they were focused on was the chance to get an aircraft with Phantom-like capability that could also take off and land vertically, although the full implications of VTO capability in terms of the whole concept of dispersal of assets was not being given too much thought. The Royal Air Force was looking for an aircraft to replace the Hunter and Javelin while the Royal Navy was looking for an aircraft to replace its Scimitars and Sea Vixens. As will be seen, both of these requirements would be linked to a potential VTOL solution, a proposal that would descend into farce a few years later.

Meanwhile, on the continent within the ambit of NATO, a search was on for an aircraft to replace the Fiat G.91 lightweight fighter that could be manufactured by the European countries. For reasons explained earlier, all these requirements were now looking for a VTOL aspect to be implicit in the responses from industry. The Fiat G.91 replacement competition was gathered under the title NATO Basic Military Requirement No. 3 (NBMR-3). This was first identified in draft format in 1959, i.e. before P.1127 had even flown, and called for an aircraft with subsonic speed at low level but later this was changed to Mach 2 ability at altitude. The aircraft was to have VTOL capability and was expected to be purchased by many NATO air forces. In November 1961 Hawker and Bristol Siddeley, as those with the greatest expertise in VTOL operations, were briefed by the government on NBMR-3. Hawker duly unveiled their thinking on such a requirement in the shape of P.1150, again schemed by Hooper, which could meet a possible RAF requirement and, with further development, should also be capable of satisfying the NBMR-3 requirement. Both designs would come with supersonic performance around Mach 2 achieved by a new engine from Bristol Siddeley – the BS.53/6 – with plenum chamber burning (PCB), a means of introducing reheat into the exhaust from the front nozzles.

With the large carrot that NBMR-3 represented before them, Bristol Siddeley began the task of getting to grips with the design and construction of the new engine, by now designated BS.100, and particularly the tricky matter of plenum chamber burning to give a Mach 2 performance to the aircraft; in essence this would require a reheat system built around a corner in order for the efflux to be capable of exhausting via the front nozzles. In the event, although started as a privately-funded project, Bristol were able to call on financial assistance via MWDP and practical assistance from the National Gas Turbine Establishment (NGTE) at Pyestock. The final specification settled on for P.1150 defined in September 1962 was the BS.100/8 version offering 33,640lb thrust via a 52-inch fan.

As it became clearer that both NBMR-3 and a UK requirement for replacement of RAF and RN aircraft could be fulfilled with a common design, the P.1150/3 became the P.1154. Meanwhile work continued to get the BS.100 concept into a workable form and, in January 1962, P.1154 was formally submitted to the NBMR-3 competition. The prize was well worth having; the projected requirement for NATO was in the order of some 1,000 airframes with another 300 for British forces and Hawker and Bristol could point to several years of practical V/STOL experience that none of the other tenders could offer. The principal opposition to P.1154 was the Dassault/ Sud Mirage IIIV, for which Rolls Royce would supply the lift engines. Also in the running were Breguet/Fiat with G95/4 and Fokker/Republic with the D-24, both entries planning to use BS.100 engines. The Dassault project was seen to be turning into a very expensive programme and hope was expressed in Whitehall that the French would reject it, leaving the Germans to plump for the P.1154 proposal. Eventually, the Hawker P.1154 was announced the technical winner of NBMR-3; technical because it ignored the political aspect of multinational collaboration that the other designs offered, both airframe and engine being UK projects. To address this, Hawker sought collaborative agreements with several of the continental aviation companies, particularly those in West Germany, but, in the face of French intransigence insisting that they would have nothing further to do with the project but would pursue their own path, NBMR-3 was withdrawn by NATO.

Having failed to secure an order for the new technology on the continent, Hawker Siddeley reverted to opportunities to replace aircraft in UK service. The RAF had a requirement to replace the Hunter but did not see a P.1127 derivative as fulfilling that role; they wanted supersonic dash capability, while the Royal Navy was seeking to replace the Sea Vixen and, later, the Buccaneer, this being formalised in an Operational Requirement – OR.356 – and the then Minister of Defence Harold Watkinson, issuing instructions that both service requirements were to be met with a common aircraft. With the demise of NBMR-3, it is clear that Hawker Siddeley concentrated on getting the P.1154 into the UK inventory, the company considering this vital to the future of VTOL and indeed the future of the company, resources being concentrated on achieving a firm order for the aircraft. At the same time, as P.1154 moved into focus, P.1127 diminished in importance, other than as a means of collecting research data that would feed into refinement of the P.1154 concept.

While the NATO competition had dragged through its many iterations, Britain's services had been quietly compiling their own requirements for a P.1154-type aircraft with the RAF initially accepting that the NBMR-3 proposal would suit their own requirements for a Hunter replacement. With one eye on the *diktat* from MoD regarding a common aircraft for both services, the RAF and RN now sought to define a common requirement for such an aircraft. This was unlikely to succeed: the RAF sought a single-seat, terrain-following aircraft with supersonic dash capability while the Royal Navy was seeking a twin-seat airframe with sustained supersonic performance at altitude *and* carrier capable. At Hawker in Kingston, John Fozard was given design lead on P.1154, leaving Ralph Hooper to run with development of P.1127. To Fozard

Model of the two-seat P.1154 proposed for the Royal Navy, 1964. (BAE Systems, courtesy of Brooklands Museum)

then would fall the task of producing one aircraft from two disparate specifications to suit the requirements of the RAF and the Royal Navy.

Perhaps surprisingly, a design was formulated by March 1963 which would provide broadly a single aircraft to fulfil both requirements, albeit with both a single-seat and a twin-seat version and significant pressure was brought to bear on HM Government by senior Hawker Siddeley board members to move quickly into a development contract to maintain the momentum thus achieved and forestall any backsliding by ministers. It should be emphasised here that, with P.1127 now unlikely to be more than a development programme, P.1154 was the only game in town for Hawker Siddeley and continued employment for its staff and indeed the continued existence of the company was now riding on the project.

It was at this point that Rolls Royce, seeing the way the wind was blowing for its lift engines which had yet to find a role in anything other than experimental aircraft, put forward a proposal to use two of their Spey engines in P.1154 on the dubious basis that, since it was already available, it would need less development finance than the paper engine that BS.100 then was. Though this ignored the costs that would be associated with the introduction of vectoring and PCB into the engine and the inevitable licence payments to Bristol, it nonetheless muddied the waters for Bristol Siddeley to the extent that, with Rolls Royce approaching the Admiralty with the proposal and suggesting that Hawker were not averse to the switch, Hawker felt bound to explore the concept and its implications and the programme started to drift.

Finally, having discarded the twin-Spey idea, Hawker and Bristol moved forward, with the project receiving approval to proceed in 1963 and work started at Kingston on the single- and twin-seat prototypes early in 1964. Similarly, Bristol obtained approval for BS.100 development to begin in April 1964, some four engines eventually being produced for development trials.

At this crucial point in the project, the Admiralty dropped a bombshell in the form of cancellation of its entire requirement for P.1154 in February 1964, opting instead for McDonnell F-4 Phantoms powered by Rolls Royce Speys. As work continued on the single-seat prototype at Kingston, concerns were mounting both on the board and at shop-floor level about the future of the project. Surely things could not get any worse? Things did indeed get worse with the arrival in October 1964 of a Labour administration antagonistic to Britain's defence industry intent on using MoD funding to support its social care programmes. Something would have to give and the new government quickly focused on three major defence projects that were under threat: the BAC TSR.2 strike fighter, the AW.681 VTOL transport and P.1154.

Two of the aircraft were Hawker Siddeley Group projects while TSR.2 was the major project for the British Aircraft Corporation, a grouping of smaller companies forced together by the previous administration using TSR.2 as the carrot for amalgamation. Two of these would have to go to save the third and, on 2 February 1965, Dennis Healey, Minister of Defence, cancelled both Hawker Siddeley projects. The shock of the decision at Kingston was palpable, although unofficial word had been passed to Kingston in January. With no other work coming through the factory, workers were looking at almost immediate unemployment through the actions of a government that numbers of them had no doubt only recently voted into power.

To heap further ignominy on the government's parlous handling of the affair, just two months later, the final project, TSR.2 – for which allegedly the other two had been sacrificed – was itself cancelled, leading inevitably to Britain losing its place as one of the foremost aviation producers in the world, a position it would never recover. Some 70,000 high-skilled jobs would be lost over the next year or two as engineering excellence drifted away from aviation into other roles. Bizarrely, the government decided to replace the cancelled projects with aircraft imported from the US; the Royal Navy P.1154 would be replaced by the McDonald F-4 Phantom and the AW.681 with the Lockheed C-130 Hercules. TSR.2 would henceforth be replaced by … another US import, the F-111 variable-geometry strike aircraft. No sooner had the contracts been signed for the purchase of F-111 than the Labour government summarily cancelled, incurring swingeing penalty clauses for breach of contract. Quite what the government thought this would do to Britain's ability to export its own technology and thus bolster the balance of payments for the UK is not known, but it is hard to ignore the feeling that ideological considerations had obscured the reality of Britain's need for export success. A farce indeed.

Meanwhile, back at the Air Staff, with the loss of their entire aircraft replacement programme for the next decade, P.1127 was really the only option left and slowly the RAF warmed to the idea. But before this happened, work to trial a developed P.1127 had been quietly moving forward behind the scenes. It was back in December 1961 that a proposal came from the USA to form a trials squadron to formulate operational concepts for a P.1127 development. It was further suggested that funding would be shared between the US, UK and West Germany. The German interest in V/STOL had been fairly constant throughout the proposals that eventually became NBMR-3 and, whereas France was expected to select a national product to fulfil the requirement, Germany had remained open to all the proposals on the table at that time and, appreciating the advantages that vectored thrust offered over lift jets as proposed by the French and Rolls Royce, were looking at Bristol engines for their own proposal from Focke Wulf. With US encouragement, an agreement was formed in February 1962 between America, West Germany and the UK that would lead to the formation of a squadron of nine new-build aircraft, as distinct from inclusion of the P.1127 prototypes, and fourteen new BS.53 engines. In this way, funding to continue development of both aircraft and engine was confirmed and the final Tripartite Agreement was signed in Paris in January 1963.

That the agreement was officially signed at all was perhaps surprising; Frank Wood at the Ministry of Aviation noted that, of the signatory governments, 'None of them is now very enthusiastic about it'. He expanded this point by stating that:

a) The Americans say they are prepared to co-operate for the sake of stimulating interdependence in NATO but profess little operational interest in the outcome of the evaluation.
b) The Air Ministry have no interest in the P.1127 as an operational aircraft and are nervous that if they spend money on this programme there will be less available for the P.1154.
c) The Germans are interested only in developing satisfactory successors to the G.91 and F-104G.[11]

Hawker Siddeley had received an Instruction to Proceed for nine aircraft for what was now called the Tripartite Evaluation Squadron (TES) in May 1962, before the final documentation had been signed. The aircraft would be powered by the Pegasus 5 engine offering some 15,200lb thrust and was test flown in the sixth P.1127, XP984, in February 1964. This aircraft later made a forced landing at Thorney Island in March 1965 while carrying out strain gauge work on the new engine but was subsequently repaired.

The first of the new aircraft, now named Kestrel FGA.1, XS688, arrived at Dunsfold from Kingston on 24 February 1964 and made its first, conventional, flight on 7 March in the hands of Bill Bedford, followed by a first hover on 2 April with Hugh Merewether. This was followed by XS689 arriving at Dunsfold on 6 May and five further Kestrels that year, the last two having arrived by February 1965. Meanwhile, at the Central Fighter Establishment at West Raynham in Norfolk, the Tripartite Evaluation Squadron was formally commissioned on 15 October 1964 comprising seventeen officers and 173 other ranks under Wing Commander David Scrimgeour,

Kestrel FGA.1 XS691 bogged down while undergoing soft ground trials at Dunsfold, February 1965. (BAE Systems, courtesy of Brooklands Museum)

What might have been – BS100 engine at Bristol Siddeley Engines. Proposed for P.1154, the engine would have had PCB in the front nozzles to allow supersonic speed. The burners can be seen inside the right exhaust opening. (BAE Systems, courtesy of Brooklands Museum)

the flying officers being made up of three from the RAF, two from the Luftwaffe, one from the US Navy, two US Army pilots and one from the USAF.

Initially all work on conversion to the aircraft for both pilots and ground crew was undertaken at Dunsfold, pilot conversion being in the capable hands of Duncan Simpson, using the early Kestrels and XP984, some 730 flights being accrued in this way. The aircraft to which they were introduced differed from the earlier P.1127s in a number of ways. One of the modifications trialled on the prototypes had been variable geometry air intake lips in an attempt to cater for the requirement for blunt bulbous lips for hovering and low-speed flight and the sharp lip edge necessary for faster conventional flight. This was achieved by having inflatable bags forming the intake lip which could be blown up for hovering and sucked down for high-speed flight. Although this was not particularly successful, the modification was also introduced on the Kestrels although, following the failure of the bags on two aircraft while still based at Dunsfold, the modification was removed from the Kestrels and replaced with solid intake lips of a profile somewhere between the two extremes. Also introduced was a fully-swept wing, trialled on XP984, taller fin, to improve weathercock stability, and a longer fuselage to accommodate the new engine and correct the thrust centre relative to the aircraft CG, plus provision to carry two drop tanks. A nose-mounted camera was now included and, later, an extended tailplane to improve longitudinal stability. The Kestrels also introduced a cartridge-start system as a first stage to making the aircraft more self-sufficient; previously the P.1127 engines had used an air trolley for starting.

Prior to the start of the trials, pilots from A&AEE had converted to the P.1127 at Dunsfold to conduct preliminary service evaluation. The results were pretty much in line with Hawker's own thinking and produced no surprises.

In March 1965 the aircraft began to be transferred to West Raynham, often by the service pilots following their successful conversions at Dunsfold. By May sufficient Kestrels were present at West Raynham for the main trials to commence on the 10th and these were complete by 30 November, the aircraft achieving over 1,367 flights to and from a wide variety of surfaces and locations positioned away from West Raynham and including rough field and wooded environments together with representative 'damaged' runways, of which Norfolk offered plenty of examples. One of the aircraft, XS696, was lost early in the trials at West Raynham when the US Army pilot attempted to take off with the brakes on, the aircraft being written off.

Kestrel FGA.1 XS690, the third aircraft, first flown August 1964. The aircraft was one of several shipped to the USA after completion of TES trials. It was used to conduct trials aboard the USS *Guam* in 1968 before being dumped into the Virginia river on completion of trials. (BAE Systems, courtesy of Brooklands Museum)

Also damaged towards the end of the trials was XS689, on 13 October 1965, when the German pilot, Oberst Barkhorn, made a heavy landing at a dispersed site that damaged the undercarriage.

The rest of the Kestrels proved to be exceptionally reliable, especially given the rough and unprepared locations from which much of the flying was carried out. It should also be remembered that the pilots were in many cases ordinary service pilots and, in the case of the US Army pilots, had limited fixed-wing experience. The trials were adjudged a success and many of the lessons learnt would be used when eventually the developed aircraft made it into squadron use.

At the completion of the TES trials, the aircraft were used in a number of tests and investigations by the participating governments, the original agreement stipulating that the aircraft would be shared between the three nations for their own use although, in the event, Germany declined to take their aircraft, these being added to the three aircraft allocated to the US. So it was that XS688, XS689, XS690, XS691, XS692 and XS694 left

West Raynham for delivery to test and evaluation establishments in North America, being known there as the XV-6A. XS693 returned to Dunsfold on 7 February 1966 where it was broken down and transferred to Hawker Siddeley's Brough factory for works to allow installation of the Pegasus 6 engine and revision of the intakes to improve airflow.

This aircraft had its first flight with the new engine from Holme-on-Spalding-Moor on 10 February 1967 and was then transferred to Bristol Siddeley's facility at Bristol. Subsequently, while flying out of Filton on 21 September 1967, Squadron Leader Hugh Rigg, brother of actress Diana Rigg, a pilot attached to Boscombe Down A Squadron, suffered an engine surge at high altitude near Boscombe Down and ejected over High Post, the aircraft being destroyed. The other aircraft retained in the UK was XS695. This aircraft had had an inauspicious start to the TES trials when the undercarriage collapsed while under tow at West Raynham although no damage was caused. The aircraft was returned to Dunsfold on 11 January 1966 and next day was with AVFR before returning to West Raynham on the 13th. It then returned to Dunsfold from Boscombe Down on 21 April to be prepared for display at the Hanover Air show, returning from Germany on 3 May and being transferred back to Boscombe until August when it was again at Dunsfold for display at that year's Farnborough Air show. On 1 March 1967 the aircraft was badly damaged at Boscombe Down when it landed short of the runway.

So it was that, by 1965, Kingston and Dunsfold had become the world's leading exponents of VTOL flight although without any production order to secure its future. Refurbishment work on Hunters provided employment for the workforce at Dunsfold in the short-term, but clearly such a situation could not long endure.

Chapter 8

Troubled Times

Before moving on to the fall-out from the cancellation of P.1154, it would be helpful to return to the early 1960s and review what had been happening both within the Hawker Siddeley Group of companies and the Flight Test Team at Dunsfold.

We have seen that, in the 1930s, Hawker Aircraft Ltd had been able to purchase a number of other aviation related concerns and build a strong industrial base called the Hawker Siddeley Aircraft Company Ltd within which the Kingston-based company continued to trade as Hawker Aircraft Ltd. This situation remained until 1959 when Folland Aircraft Ltd was purchased and brought into the group of companies. Folland had been a sub-contractor for Hawker for a number of years producing Hunter tailplanes at their Hamble facility. In the early 1960s further acquisitions were added to the group in the form of the Blackburn Aircraft and de Havilland Aircraft groups of companies. On 1 July 1963, a major re-organisation of the group saw the creation of two new concerns under the titles Hawker Siddeley Aviation Ltd and Hawker Siddeley Dynamics Holdings Ltd. Henceforth, Kingston and Dunsfold would form part of the Hawker-Blackburn Division of Hawker Siddeley Aviation Ltd.

Thus, by 1963, Hawker Siddeley was the largest aviation concern in the UK and Europe, able to exert influence at the highest levels of government, a situation which was not always appreciated at Westminster. But HSA did not have it all their own way for competition existed in the shape of the Vickers Armstrong Group of companies, headquartered at Weybridge, and English Electric Ltd at Warton in Lancashire. These two companies, encouraged by HM Government, had formed a working alliance on the back of the large TSR-2 project in the late 1950s and formalised the arrangement in 1960 with a joint holding known as the British Aircraft Corporation (BAC), later confirmed, in January 1964, by formation of a new group – British Aircraft Corporation (Operating) Ltd. Thus it was that, by 1965, the UK aircraft industry was effectively in the hands of just two major players; smaller concerns still ran independent operations such as Hunting Aircraft at Luton, and Handley Page at Radlett although Hunting would later join with BAC and Handley Page would cease trading in 1970.

While the Hawker Siddeley Group was in a sound financial position, the same could not be said for BAC, with large capital sums committed to development of aircraft that attracted only small orders. Sensing their weakened position, Wilson's government had attempted to coerce the two groups (HSA and BAC) into a merger, with BAC very much the minor player, a move vigorously opposed by both concerns. Thus the situation would remain until the 1970s when, once again, the political machinations of the Labour administration would force a marriage of convenience upon the British aircraft industry.

Meanwhile, at Dunsfold in 1963, the flight test team of pilots and engineers had undergone many changes. The team of pilots who had taken the Hunter from sleek prototype to service thoroughbred had retired or otherwise moved on. Throughout this period flight testing had been in the

Experimental hangar, c. 1965, showing an eclectic mix of aircraft including the company Hart and Hurricane, two Gnat T.1s, a Kestrel FGA.1 and wings of two others. (BAE Systems via Peter Amos)

hands of Neville Duke and, later, Bill Bedford. Under Duke, the test team had comprised Bedford, Frank Murphy, Frank Bullen, Don Lucey, Duncan Simpson and Hugh Merewether but, following a damaging forced landing in 1955 in which he had sustained chronic injury to his back, Duke had handed over the position of Chief Test Pilot to Bedford in 1956. Under Bedford, the team had seen Murphy leave to take up a commercial role in the company and his replacement by David Lockspeiser. With the arrival of the P.1127 in 1960, Bedford and Merewether concentrated on the complex task of bringing the aircraft to a condition whereby it could be safely flown by squadron level pilots, leaving the Hunter work to the rest of the team. In 1962 Simpson was converted onto the aircraft and began to assist with the many and various test flights required.

With the requirement for the P.1127 to be assessed by the government's scientific community, there was a need for the aircraft to operate from RAE Bedford and, on 17 November 1964, the P.1127 project pilot from Bedford – one Flight Lieutenant J.F. Farley – duly reported to Dunsfold for conversion training on XP831. It was probably Simpson who steered the young flight lieutenant through the various flights, both conventional and VTOL, before returning to RAE Bedford to await an aircraft upon which to begin his trials of this new machine. XP831 was duly delivered to Bedford, by Bill Bedford, on 2 February 1965 for Farley to assess more fully. It would be some years later that plain John Farley – ex-RAF – would return to Dunsfold as a test pilot to undertake production testing of the new HS Harrier GR.1 aircraft and in the process forge a career and fame as 'Mr Harrier'.

However, that first flight in November 1964 was anything but a pleasant experience for Farley. Having got the machine into the air from a vertical take off, he intended to move forward away from the grid preparatory to his first landing:

> The translation forward finished up faster and went on for longer than I wanted. At this stage I got very confused with the throttle and found I was making instinctive backwards movements with it to try and stop the aircraft moving forward ... . While all this was going on the nose wandered in yaw, probably up to 20-30 degrees ... . When the aircraft translation was finally sorted out ... I was left with the feeling of 'Well, having stopped it don't be stupid enough to move the thing again – land it while the going is good.'

Finally established in a rather jerky descent, Farley continued:

> I felt very close to the ground and was afraid that my increase in
> power was going to make the aircraft balloon and I instinctively
> took off a large handful of throttle…The aircraft sank several
> feet and landed very firmly on all four wheels, there was no
> bounce, no jarring sensation, just a terrible feeling of squelch.

His final thoughts summed up his experience: 'I make no apologies for writing this in the first person. It was a very first person sort of event.'[1]

Despite the potential ramifications of the cancellations of the three major aircraft projects in the UK, it seems that Kingston's exposed position, and particularly that of the design team, was on the government's radar, if only because its closure would frustrate grandiose plans to further impose consolidation on an already struggling industry and would likely result in the loss of the UK's current lead on VTOL technology. Out of this came the idea that a small purchase of developed P.1127s might suffice to tide the company, and the government, over the immediate crisis.[2]

On 2 February 1965, as Healey stood in the House of Commons to announce the end of P.1154, Robert Lickley, Chief Executive and Director of Hawker Siddeley Aviation, Blackburn Division, wrote to staff explaining that:

> The cancellation of the P.1154 represents a serious blow to the
> Division. Until the intentions of the government regarding an
> alternative aircraft to fill the role of P.1154 are more clearly
> known, it is regretted that no further details can be given at
> this moment relating to employment within the Division. The
> Management are pressing the Government for an immediate
> order for P.1127s so that the minimum disruption is caused.[3]

In the meantime, Hawker Siddeley started laying off workers, as did Bristol Siddeley where 1,900 went quickly. At Kingston plans put in place in 1963 to bring in sub-contract work to fill the near-empty production lines resulted in work being carried out on components for Avro (Vulcan and 748), Armstrong Whitworth (Argosy), Blackburn (Beverley) and Gloster (Javelin). At Dunsfold workers were sensing thin times ahead and exploring potential moves to BAC at Weybridge. In truth, there had been a small two-way traffic between Hawkers at Kingston and Dunsfold and Vickers at Weybridge; as the companies' fortunes waxed and waned, so labour would flow from one to the other. Other Dunsfold staff were seconded to RAF stations to assist in modification work. John Parrott, not long out of apprenticeship, recalled joining one such party and travelling to Suffolk to work on F-100 Super Sabres at Woodbridge and North Luffenham.[4] At Dunsfold itself, work continued on Hunter and Sea Fury refurbishment, together with Gnat T. 1 production.

Notwithstanding the government's decision to axe P.1154, staff at Hawkers was reminded that the project's high security classification remained in force: 'As a result, if it is desired to dispose of documents, such documents should be destroyed by shredding.'[5] Within the industry, further grief was created by the problem that the aircraft and engine companies were finding in attempting to get contractual payments approved from government departments paid to them and decisions affecting future supplies of parts and aircraft cleared by the relevant departments. In November 1965 the Bristol Siddeley board heard that 650 contracts were awaiting government clearance! It sometimes appeared that no stone was left unturned in an effort to frustrate the industry although, in truth, such was the dire state of the country's finances under the Labour administration that any payment that could be deferred, was.[6]

In 1966 Rolls Royce, having got clearance from the government, took over Bristol Siddeley. After 1967 the name of Bristol Siddeley ceased to be used; any Pegasus engines produced would carry the name of their arch rival Rolls Royce. Whether the takeover was wise for Rolls is a moot point. In paying some £61.65m for Bristol-Siddeley the company was laying out cash that it could ill-afford to spend. But seeing the future of Bristol overtaking Rolls Royce, in the words of an anonymous Rolls Royce Director, 'We panicked'.[7] In the event, within five years, on 4 February 1971, Rolls Royce would declare bankruptcy, the day before the second AV-8A was to have been delivered to the US Marine Corps, startling the US into a series of worried phone calls.

In the midst of the clamour over the headline cancellations, came proposals to buy a developed P.1127, as a Hunter replacement and to assist in the retention of the Kingston design team; such a decision being made at least in draft form as early as 29 January 1965, with the aircraft entering service around 1968. Should such a decision be confirmed, it was fortunate that Hawker's decision to design an aircraft as close to an operational vehicle as possible, and the earlier decision to test the concept of VTOL and dispersed operation that had been the raison d'être of the Kestrel Evaluation Squadron, meant that such a telescoped development schedule should be possible.

A new requirement, ASR 384, written around the P.1127, was quickly issued by the Air Staff for a developed aircraft to be known as P.1127 (RAF). Approval to proceed with airframe development followed. The new aircraft, picked up by John Fozard, since Hooper was still busy with Kestrel, although broadly based on Kestrel – itself the result of years of development work on the prototypes – was comprehensively redesigned, resulting in major changes to airframe and equipment. To accommodate a new, more powerful engine, new features included a revised fixed intake lip and six blow-in doors, later increased to eight, introduced into the intake walls to increase mass flow through the engine in the hover. Fatigue life was extended to 3,000 hours while undercarriage load and bird-strike resistance was improved, including strengthening of the intake lip and replacement of the curved centre windscreen with an optically flat, bulletproof section. The wing was the result of numerous trials to improve performance and featured leading-edge extensions, fences and vortex generators, together with slight increases in area and span, all tested on various P.1127 aircraft.

Operational equipment would now include elements of the axed P.1154 project with addition of a Smiths Industries head-up display and Ferranti 541 inertial navigation system together with a head-down moving map display. Reconnaissance was covered by the inclusion of an oblique camera installation in the nose and weapon carriage accommodated via twin 30mm Aden guns in pods on the belly, four underwing stores positions and another on the fuselage centreline. The undercarriage doors were comprehensively redesigned; the main undercarriage door had previously doubled as a crude airbrake. This was discarded, new doors were fitted which were sequenced to the closed position once the main and nose leg were extended, and a new airbrake installed aft of the main undercarriage leg. The wisdom of including, in an aircraft specifically designed for short duration sorties at very short notice, a complex inertial navigation suite that would require several minutes to complete alignment on the ground might be questioned, and was at the time. In its early life the system suffered from indifferent reliability, particularly since the radar to which it would have been coupled in the P1154 (RAF) and which would have generated terrain avoidance information, was omitted from the P.1127 (RAF).

Meanwhile, by March 1965, Bristol had begun work on uprating the Pegasus 5 to Pegasus 6 standard with a thrust of initially some 18,000lb, later increased to 19,000lb while water injection would be re-introduced, allowing for hotter running temperatures. Nozzle appearance was altered from five-vane to two-vane, giving greater exhaust flow, the LP fan was re-engineered with titanium blades and cooling introduced to both HP turbine stages. Engine start would now be by gas turbine starter (GTS), mounted above the engine and replacing the cartridge start of the Kestrel which had been found to be less than reliable, and overcame the requirement for cartridges to be available at dispersed sites. On later aircraft the GTS could also function as an auxiliary power unit (APU) to allow the aircraft systems to be powered up without running the main engine, for example, to align the Ferranti 541 inertial navigation unit.

With the requirement to bring the aircraft into operational use as soon as possible, a contract was awarded in 1965 for construction of six development batch aircraft, rather than prototypes, to allow for the various trials to go ahead without waiting for full production standard aircraft to be available. The first of these 'DB' aircraft, XV276, had its first flight at Dunsfold on 31 August 1966, joined later in the year by XV277 and XV278. By June 1967 all six were available and intensive flying became the order of the day to clear the many test points required for clearance of new aircraft including handling, stores clearance, systems checks and engine handling with the new Pegasus 6, known to the RAF as the Mk 101. However, such was the need to push these aircraft through quickly that, according to Hooper, 'the first was really a quasi-Kestrel – having Kestrel flying surfaces (with bodged-on wing tip and leading-edge mods) and a Pegasus 5 engine. The next two DBs had Pegasus 5(a) engines'.[8]

The remaining prototypes were also utilised at this time to push forward the various trials required to refine the P.1127 (RAF) design, XP984 in particular being kept busy at Dunsfold with flights by company and Boscombe Down pilots, although not without hitches. On a flight on 31 March 1966 'a sudden jolt was felt and the chase aircraft advised that the tail parachute had streamed and jettisoned'.[9] Three months later on 16 June, Flight Lieutenant D.J. Parry from Boscombe Down lost the starboard outrigger wheel in an asymmetric landing. Remarkably, the aircraft had, the previous year on 19 March, been involved in a serious accident at the hands of Hugh Merewether when, following a full throttle supersonic dive, the engine failed at 25,000 feet but Merewether had managed to put it down on the grass at Thorney Island with surprisingly little damage to himself or the airframe. Examination revealed a substantial part of the engine casing protruding from the starboard cold nozzle.[10] In another close call, XP984 had, in January 1968, been involved in what could have been a fatal accident while undergoing testing in Dunsfold's engine pen. Whilst at full throttle, the hold-down equipment failed, sending the aircraft rocketing forward and shearing the nose leg completely off. The Rolls Royce engineer, Bill Robson, in the cockpit managed to close the throttle and shut the engine down before being helped from the cockpit, severely shaken. Not surprisingly, he declined to ever run another Harrier at Dunsfold.[11] A draft contract received by Hawker Siddeley Aviation in 1966 for sixty aircraft against ASR 384, was confirmed in early 1967, the new aircraft to be named Harrier GR.1 (ground attack, reconnaissance), the first production aircraft making its first flight at Dunsfold in the hands of Duncan Simpson on 28 December. As the first aircraft completed their initial flight tests, they joined the DB Harriers at the various government test and evaluation establishments and at Dunsfold itself in clearing the many and varied tests and trials required to obtain CA release for the Harrier to enter squadron use. Dunsfold's Experimental Hangar became a very busy place as the numerous development aircraft were put through the multitude of test flights required to examine the entire flight envelope before the aircraft could be released for squadron service.

P.1127 XP984 after tie-down shackles failed during engine run, shearing the nose-leg off. January 1968. (BAE Systems, courtesy of Brooklands Museum)

As part of the development of new equipment for the Harrier, work was carried out in 1966 to integrate the Ferranti 541 inertial navigation system into the aircraft. Trials to prepare the system for installation into Harrier were first carried out using Dunsfold's faithful DH Dove transport, since no aircraft/IN combination was available. A circular route of approximately 325 miles was planned around the south of England with various prominent landmarks chosen as waypoints in order to check that the route would be suitable for the Harrier to fly during extended testing of the INS, the first course being flown in October 1966.

Peter Amos recalls:

> The Dove was used ... to survey, visually check and photograph the marker points selected by yours truly from 1" OS maps, to see how they compared with the Ferranti nav system. We had the maps all spread out on a long table in the rear Nissen hut and I spent a considerable time working on these routes, which had to be West-East and East-West and provide good objects for the pilot to be able to see and fly over while flying at high speed. He then had to press a button as he flew over the marker to put a mark on the tape so that we could then check to see how accurate the system was! We also took photographs from the Dove of the points, and others, for later possible use as we flew the courses. I flew on all of them and thoroughly enjoyed the experience! The Eastern one caused a stir when Hugh Merewether decided to do a rate 9 turn round Canterbury Cathedral, which must have raised a few eyebrows on the ground – it did in the air also and I took a near vertical photo of it through the cabin side window![12]

On 4 January 1968, with the first Harrier GR.1 airframe available, Hawker Siddeley mounted a major press onslaught to 'sell' Harrier to potential customers abroad and to the public who would be paying for the Harrier in the UK. With the world's aviation press on hand, seven Harriers, including the first production machine, were presented on the southern perimeter track, followed by flying displays by four aircraft including vertical and short take offs from dispersed sites. The event was also used to announce plans for the construction of a two-seat trainer version to be known as Harrier T. 2, it being understood that ten would be ordered for the RAF.

The flying display, always a strong point for the aircraft, was described by *Flight*'s correspondent:

> In an ear-splitting maelstrom of whirling leaves and the pungent fumes of burned kerosene, four Harriers mounted what was certainly the most intimate and one of the most impressive flying displays the writer has ever seen. Dunsfold's runways are largely redundant these days – this display was based upon a short length of peri-track, on the inside edge of which stood the crowd. The entire display took place between them and the airfield fence only a short distance away.[13]

Press Day at Dunsfold to unveil the Harrier to the public. Shown here are a variety of aircraft in varying modification states. Leading the line-up is XV280, the fifth DB Harrier. January 1968. (BAE Systems, via Martin Mace)

Hopes were high that evidence from the recent Arab-Israeli war, in which Egyptian aircraft had been marooned on their airfields following bombing of the runways by Israeli aircraft, would lead to increasing appreciation of Harrier's unique benefits. When questioned as to potential Harrier export customers, 'HSA officials rigidly declined to name any country as a hot prospect for export sales; one said that the first export order was quite likely to be for a navy ...'. Having thus titillated the world's press, the official sensibly left it at that. Given the delicate and extended negotiations that would be required to achieve this first sale, it was a wise move as will be seen in the next chapter.

In the event, a momentous milestone was reached on 18 April 1969 when Harrier GR.1 XV746 became the first to be released to the RAF, joining No. 1 Fighter Squadron at RAF Wittering, just under ten years since the first of its breed had taken uncertainly to the air at a damp Dunsfold in November 1960. Thus did the UK become the first nation in the world to include jet V/STOL in its order of battle, a move that Hawker hoped would stimulate interest and orders from other air arms. Much of the delay in achieving this milestone was reflected not by any particular complexity of the aircraft and its systems but rather by the lack of interest in the entire

Failure of nose undercarriage after flight of Harrier GR.1 XV280. This accident in March 1969 resulted in the pilot, Squadron Leader Mike Adams, being injured and withdrawn from the forthcoming *Daily Mail* Transatlantic Air Race. (BAE Systems, courtesy of Brooklands Museum)

Development batch Harrier GR.1 XV279 in a posed image capturing the rural environment in which Harrier would come to be based. (BAE Systems, courtesy of Brooklands Museum)

concept exhibited by the various government ministries and by its eventual first customer, the RAF. The mania for all things bigger, faster, flashier that had been the dominant emotion in the RAF and Air Ministry was curtailed, not by realisation that V/STOL flexibility would vastly improve battlefield survivability but that the big toys were no longer available thanks to the change of priorities within central government.

The transition to Harrier flying for squadron pilots was facilitated by the establishment of a Harrier Conversion Team at Dunsfold in January 1969 under the tutelage of the Dunsfold test pilots, led by Duncan Simpson. Those first pilots went on to form 233 Operational Conversion Unit at Wittering, the UK base for Harrier operations and, by mid-1971, over 100 pilots had successfully converted, without a trainer version being available. Hawker Siddeley had been well ahead of any Air Ministry requirement for such an aircraft and had drawn initial schemes for a trainer version even before the P.1127 had taken to the air. It was clear that weight and centre of gravity constraints would need to be carefully handled but a tandem layout for the pilots with compensatory changes to the rear had resulted in a design which, if not attractive, was certainly not ugly enough for Camm to order major changes. With no immediate requirement being forthcoming and work on P.1154 increasing, the design had been mothballed. However, following cancellation of P.1154 (RAF) and the resurrection of P.1127 (RAF), requirement ASR386 was formulated calling for a two-seat version of the aircraft and the following year a contract for two trainers was received.

Work on the two-seat version proceeded in tandem with the single-seater with the additional requirement that the trainer should be capable of carrying out the same operational sorties as the single-seat version. To accommodate the second pilot, the front cockpit and nose were moved forward four feet and another cockpit constructed in the resulting gap. At the rear of the aircraft, the fin was moved aft by thirty-three inches and the ventral fin enlarged. The rear reaction control valves were also moved aft in an elongated 'sting'. Just a few days after handover of the first Harrier, on 22 April 1969, the first Harrier T. 2, XW174, took to the air piloted by Duncan Simpson. The second T. 2 followed on 14 July.

So it was that Hawker Aircraft's dream of supplying up to 500 to 1000 VTOL aircraft to NATO under the NBMR-3 competition had been replaced by the potential of equipping the UK services with 300 aircraft

First development two-seat Harrier T.2, XW174, up from Dunsfold. Note original fin shape and anti-spin parachute fairing at rear, May 1969. The aircraft would crash a month later. (BAE Systems, courtesy of Brooklands Museum)

DH Rapides used by Hawker Siddeley as communication aircraft, seen shortly before their replacement by DH-104 Doves, Dunsfold, July 1965. (Alan Gettings via Peter Amos)

Hurricane IIc PZ865 (G-AMAU) at Dunsfold c.1965. (Peter Amos)

Hart G-ABMR, July 1965. (Peter Amos)

Tom Tit G-AFTA, April 1967. (Peter Amos)

Hunter MK.73s for Jordan awaiting delivery, August 1966. (Alan Gettings via Peter Amos)

Hunter T.75 G-9-290 for Singapore outside the Production hangar, delivered July 1970. (Alan Gettings via Peter Amos)

DB Harrier XV277 on the hover pit c.1967. (Peter Amos)

P.1127 XP831 up from Bedford, fitted with anti-spin parachute. (BAE Systems via Peter Amos)

Gnat T.1 in "trainer yellow" scheme, adopted by the Yellowjacks Aerobatic Team, 1964. (via Peter Amos)

Gnat T.1 XS111 for Red Arrows Aerobatic Team, 1965. Note the Rapide and Hunters in the background. (via Peter Amos)

Hawk T.1 XX258 carrying Sea Eagle anti-shipping missile on the centre-line pylon. Hawk was never cleared into service in this configuration. (BAE Systems courtesy of Brooklands Museum)

Hawk Mk.53 LL5318, the last of the first batch in hi-vis colour scheme. (BAE Systems via Heinz Frick)

Sea Harrier FRS.51s for India overfly Dunsfold on their delivery flight, May 1991.
(BAE Systems via Heinz Frick)

Harrier GR.7 in
front of Canada
House whilst
participating
in armament
trials. The
eclectic stores fit
includes AIM-9L
Sidewinder and
Paveway 3 LGB.
This aircraft
is fitted with
100% LERX.
(BAE Systems
courtesy of
Brooklands
Museum)

Harrier Mk.52 G-VTOL piloted by Heinz Frick performs a close hover while demonstrating the Sky Hook concept. (BAE Systems via Heinz Frick)

under the P.1154 umbrella and ended with VTOL finally entering the RAF inventory with a 'mere' sixty Harrier aircraft, plus a further order for twenty in January 1969.

As Hawker Siddeley geared up to deliver on the new contracts and the lines filled with work again, 1969 brought yet more grief for the company. In October that year the entire Harrier fleet was grounded following engine failures linked to fan blade faults. This potentially disastrous turn of events reflected changes made to the Pegasus 6 (Mk 101) to increase engine efficiency and resulted from blade failures on the first stage fan caused by a manufacturing defect. Although the grounding was lifted in December 1969, it had not helped the aircraft's reputation. This setback appeared to be presaged in the summer of 1969 when, on 4 June, Simpson had ejected from the first Harrier T. 2 over Salisbury Plain following engine problems. The late ejection resulted in severe injuries for Simpson, and complete destruction of XW174. Later investigation suggested that fuel system failure had been the cause rather than engine faults. The loss of the first development T. 2 was mirrored a year later by an almost carbon-copy loss of the first production T. 2, XW264, this time with Barry Tonkinson at the controls on 11 July 1970. Again the aircraft was over Salisbury Plain when the engine ran down due to fuel system fault but Tonkinson elected to stay with the aircraft and brought it in to Boscombe Down for a forced landing. The aircraft was badly damaged but both Tonkinson and, crucially, the engine core survived. The engine was stripped by Rolls Royce and a bevel gear, part of the engine that provided motive power for the fuel pump, was found to be fractured.

Considering such hair-raising escapes as detailed in these pages, it is remarkable that the journey to the long-sought position of placing VTOL aircraft into the RAF inventory had been achieved with no loss of life within the test pilot or service community, a quite remarkable achievement which underscored the inherent reliability of the concept. Sadly, just three months before its entry into service, Hawker Siddeley experienced the loss of a pilot at Dunsfold, the first fatality at the aerodrome since Hawker Aircraft's arrival and the first death since the loss of Wade in 1951.

The aircraft was being flown by an American pilot, Major Charles Rosburg USAF, attached to Edwards Air Force Base in California, on 27 January 1969, who, with Major K.J. Mason USAF, was at Dunsfold to carry out an evaluation of the Harrier on behalf of the United States Air Force. Following several evaluation flights in the aircraft, Major Rosburg had landed the aircraft in Dunsfold's 'restricted site' on the temporary

Development Harrier GR.1 XV279 being prepared for its first navigation exercise, linked to Ferranti's mobile ground station coach. (BAE Systems, courtesy of Brooklands Museum)

MEXE pad enclosed by trees on the southern reaches of the airfield. At 15.24 GMT a vertical take off was initiated from there and a transition to normal forward flight commenced during which a roll was seen to develop after a number of seconds. Some twelve seconds after take off, at approximately 90 knots, the roll to starboard quickly increased and Rosburg ejected with the aircraft rolled approximately 90 degrees to the vertical. With the aircraft still only eighty feet above ground the ejection resulted in a very heavy landing, causing severe injuries to the pilot. The aircraft crashed in this attitude about ninety yards north of Canada House, directly in front of the fire tenders which very quickly moved to render assistance to Rosburg and to contain the fire which had engulfed XV743 when the wing was torn from the fuselage. The pilot was headed for hospital in the airfield ambulance within eleven minutes but died of his injuries shortly after reaching Guildford.

The airfield fire brigade, assisted by external appliances, continued to fight to contain the 'metal fire' (titanium) in the engine bay of the aircraft into the evening, this proving very difficult to bring under control but eventually being achieved. At this point the wreckage was placed under RAF guard through the night, awaiting the convening of a board of enquiry the next day under Wing Commander 'Jock' Henderson, who, together with D.N. Stanfield USAF, attached Andrews AFB, and Squadron Leader T.L. Lecky-Thompson RAF would determine the cause of the crash. On 7 February the aircraft remains were removed to Farnborough for detailed analysis.

Crash site of Harrier GR.1 XV743 on 27 January 1969 in which Major Charles Rosburg USAF was fatally injured. (BAE Systems, courtesy of Brooklands Museum)

Arrangements for the USAF to carry out an evaluation of the Harrier had begun in November 1968. Mason and Rosburg were nominated for the task; both had flown the AV-6A Kestrel in the US. XV743 was the sixth production Harrier and had arrived at Dunsfold on 6 October 1968. First flight from the production flight shed was carried out on 19 December but, following a serious fuel leak, it was transferred to Experimental and flown subsequently from there. Most flights had been for conversion training of USMC, USN and USAF pilots. The pilots had arrived at Dunsfold on the 14th to undertake the standard conversion training to Harrier under Duncan Simpson.

The enquiry concluded that:

> lateral control of the aircraft was lost because left sideslip developed to a value which, combined with the effective incidence, generated aerodynamic rolling moments to the right which were greater than the total available roll control power.

151

In layman's terms, the aircraft had developed side-slip and a roll from which the pilot could not recover. This phenomenon, known as 'intake momentum drag', was well known to Hawker Siddeley and indeed to the wider aviation community, and meant that aircraft at low forward speed could be seriously affected by crosswind which would tend to cause it to roll out of control. Following the accident, sensors and equipment were added to the Harrier to alert the pilot to such a situation and what action to take.[14]

It was perhaps ironic that, even if the ejection had been successful, Rosburg would likely still have died due to a very deep gash to his throat caused by the flailing oxygen-mask connection which should have been restrained by his flight clothing and by the ill-fitting helmet, borrowed from Mason, which he could not fasten under his chin.

Following the provisioning of No. 1 Fighter Squadron in the UK, two further squadrons were equipped and based in Germany, Nos. 4 and 20 Fighter Squadrons at Wildenrath; later another squadron, No. 3. was established, also at Wildenrath. In the early 1970s the Harrier GR.1 aircraft were upgraded with the Pegasus Mk 102 engine developing 20,000lb thrust, thus becoming Harrier GR.1A. Later improvements in engine performance resulted in the Pegasus Mk 103 producing 21,500lb thrust and these began to be fitted to Harriers in 1973. Also included in this upgrade was the installation of Ferranti laser-ranging and marked target-seeker equipment (LRMTS) in the nose of the aircraft to give greatly improved accuracy of weapons delivery, and installation of a radar warning system in the rear of the aircraft to alert the pilot to illumination by enemy radar utilised by missile and AAA systems. With these modifications in place the aircraft designation changed to Harrier GR.3, this status remaining for the life of the aircraft, save for minor modifications and changes to stores carriage etc. When these modifications were subsequently applied to the T.2 trainer, these upgraded aircraft became known as Harrier T.4s.

As part of the work carried out to improve the Harrier's weapon-aiming capability, work began in early 1972 on clearing the Laser Ranging and Marked Target Seeking equipment (LRMTS) into the Harrier. A small team was assembled at Dunsfold in Portacabins located to the west of the Experimental hangar and overseen by Phil Wheatley as Trials Controller and Dick Wise as his deputy. The early trials utilised an LM Ericsson laser slaved to the Ferranti 541 navigation system, which Dick Wise recalled meant 'We were working on the edges of technology then.' The laser equipment was installed in the 'Nav-Attack' coach which, for the purposes of the trials, was positioned at the east end of runway 07. A target was erected at the

Harrier GR.3 XZ999 in the Flight Shed with hydraulic rig connected, June 1982. (Author's collection)

western end of the runway, backed by hay bales giving a sighting distance of 1.3 miles and minimising risk to traffic on the A281 road at the east end of the aerodrome; the owner of the bales asked if his cows could have laser-protection goggles! Trials started in early 1972. Later trials with the definitive Ferranti LRMTS equipment used a target erected on the southern boundary giving a 1.1-kilometre range, allowing the laser head to be located more conveniently in the Portacabin on the north side.[15]

While the second half of the 1960s had seen Hawker Siddeley at Kingston and Dunsfold experience their fair share of problems and disappointments, there was some justice in the fact that Sydney Camm was alive to witness the announcement that what would become the Harrier was finally to enter the RAF as an operational aircraft. Sadly, he would not be there to see the first aircraft handed over, Camm passing away on the golf course at Richmond on 12 March 1966 at the age of 73. And neither would he see the signing of the first export order for the Harrier, a quite momentous occasion that saw the aircraft enter the order of battle of the most powerful nation on earth.

Chapter 9

The Yanks are Coming

As seen earlier, the USA had been involved in one way or another in the Harrier story from its very inception. Indeed, it had been Colonel Chapman at MWDP who had first brought the Wibault engine concept to the attention of Hooker at Bristol Engines in 1957. As the design of the engine and airframe progressed at Kingston and Bristol, American finance was made available through MWDP for funding of 75 per cent of the engine development programme. For Hawker Aircraft, some help was forthcoming via NASA Langley with testing of model concepts in their wind tunnels. Following the successful VTOs at Dunsfold by Bedford and Merewether in 1960, two NASA test pilots quietly arrived at the aerodrome to acquaint themselves, and their organisation, with progress in the VTOL concept.

On 13 June 1962 John 'Jack' Reeder and Fred Drinkwater made their first hovers and conventional flights in XP831 at Dunsfold. Reeder wrote later:

> The P.1127 is not a testbed aircraft in the usual sense. It is advanced well beyond this stage and is actually an operational prototype. With which it is now possible to study the V/STOL concept in relation to military requirements by actual operation in the field.[1]

Quite how far up the chain of procurement the report went is unknown, but it was agreed in 1962 that the US would participate in the subsequent evaluation of the Kestrel in the UK, this to be carried out by pilots from the three armed services of the United States. The US Army, who were looking to replace their Grumman Mohawk observation aircraft, were particularly interested, identifying the P.1127 as one of their preferred replacement aircraft and, following interest from Northrop, Hawker agreed in 1963 a collaborative agreement with them for the aircraft if the US Army should decide to purchase P.1127. However, internal services politicking resulted in the US Army being denied the ability to operate any aircraft other than helicopters, the agreement with Northrop coming to nothing.

In the event, the Tripartite Evaluation exposed pilots from the US Army, USAF and US Navy to the potentialities of V/STOL, particularly when the Kestrels arrived in the US after the trial and were distributed around the various research establishments. This brought the aircraft to a wider audience and, despite official responses denying interest in P.1127 or Kestrel by the armed forces, it is clear that many were impressed by the aircraft and its ability to provide true close support. As seen in the previous chapter, the USAF retained an unofficial interest in the concept by arranging in 1968 for two pilots to travel to Dunsfold to evaluate the latest iteration of the aircraft although nothing concrete came of the interest.

As it happened, it was the one service that had not been present at the Tripartite Evaluation trial that showed serious interest in acquiring Harrier – the United States Marine Corps. This service is charged with the amphibious assault of enemy territory and, as such, has a specific requirement for a close support aircraft to operate in defence of its ground forces, and the closer the better. USMC pilots got to fly the AV-6A Kestrel aircraft on arrival in the US and were favourably impressed. In 1963 the USMC had stated a requirement for a V/STOL tactical attack aircraft and just such an aircraft had arrived on their shores. Further reports reached the USMC regarding the improved aircraft represented by Harrier to be fitted with an engine of 21,500lb thrust which would allow a worthwhile warload to be carried. Colonel Tom Miller, head of the Air Weapons Requirements Branch, felt that Harrier could be the aircraft that the Marines were looking for and quietly arranged for a small group to travel to the UK to have a closer look at the aircraft.

So it was that, in September 1968, Colonel Tom Miller, Lieutenant Colonel Clarence 'Bud' Baker and Brigadier General W.G. Johnson arrived at the SBAC Air Show at Farnborough in civilian clothes and made contact with surprised Hawker Siddeley personnel. The cloak and dagger was for the benefit of their home audience, the USMC not wanting at this stage to alert US government officials to any interest in the potential purchase of a foreign aircraft. Bill Bedford, who had been expecting the pilots, stepped in and arrangements were made which resulted in Baker and Miller being given access to aircraft at Dunsfold for evaluation. Typically, the English weather did not co-operate so, with flying restricted, Duncan Simpson showed the pilots around the Dunsfold site. It should be noted here that Dunsfold had always had something of a 'cabin in the woods' feel, with major flight-test work being undertaken in Nissen huts buried in the trees and surrounded by primroses and animal life. According to Simpson, the response from the pilots was 'Gee, if you've developed this airplane in these surroundings, we're buying it!'

The flying evaluation was placed in the hands of John Farley who had been given responsibility for the USMC pilots. Some twenty flights were undertaken between 24 September and 3 October 1968. Farley's approach to the conversion to Harrier would have been very structured with little ad-libbing tolerated. Farley insisted that taxying be undertaken as a completely separate exercise and conducted under strict control to allow the pilot to experience the enormous thrust available from the Pegasus engine in a safe environment. In Farley's words, 'I wanted to shock (them) with the acceleration down the runway.' Baker, perhaps bridling slightly at this approach, (he had already told Farley that 'He didn't need a Brit to tell him how to taxi'), allowed the powerful acceleration to get away from him and, having been briefed to shut the throttle at 50 knots, had achieved 120 knots before he had a chance to bring the aircraft back under control, although not before the Harrier had rolled to starboard. Farley:

> the nose wheel came off the ground, the left outrigger came off the ground and he scraped the right hand tailplane tip along the ground ... and then it flopped back down again as it lost speed.

A chastened pilot followed Farley to the letter after that! The rest of the evaluation was uneventful and Miller went home full of praise for this machine, and intent on acquiring it for the Marines.[2] To achieve this, the idiosyncratic procurement process which is uniquely American had first to be tackled. The US Armed Forces procurement budgets are such that funding for equipment has to be approved by Congress on an annual basis. Any acquisition of Harriers by the US Marines would therefore have to clear three major obstacles: firstly, with procurement likely to stretch over several Congressional budget reviews, the chances of getting all that the Marines wanted against competition for funding from the USAF and US Navy, would be an uphill task. The second hurdle would be persuading Congress to approve purchase of a military aircraft from a foreign power, an almost unheard-of situation, although they had bought the Canberra (built by Martin as the B-57). It was tantamount to the US accepting that they were unable to produce such hardware themselves and, even more painful, those uppity English had achieved what the US could not. Getting that past

Congress would occupy the USMC procurement team for the next year. The third task was acquiring an aircraft that the US Navy – to which the USMC was subservient – did not have and had little knowledge of.

To correct this last situation, in January 1969, around the same time that the USAF pilots were there, a small team of US Navy test pilots from Patuxent River Naval Air Test Centre was sent to Dunsfold to carry out a formal naval preliminary evaluation. The DB Harrier XV281 and one of the early production machines, XV741, were made available for handling and nav/attack trials and a further aircraft to the latest specification, XV739, was available at Boscombe Down, although in the event this was not flown.

As the procurement process went through its many stages, it became known that the USMC was looking to purchase Harrier aircraft on the basis of minimum change from the RAF aircraft. It had further been decreed by Mendel Rivers, chairman of the House Armed Services Committee, that his support for the acquisition was conditional upon the aircraft being built in America, probably by Douglas, who were the suppliers of the A-4 to the US

AV-8A serial 158703 on Dunsfold's flight line. The aircraft was part of the second batch ordered and first flew on 21 September 1972. Note the formation lighting on the front fuselage and fin. (BAE Systems, courtesy of Brooklands Museum)

157

Navy and USMC, and that the purchase would be limited to 114 aircraft, later reduced to 110. However, the cost of transferring the manufacture of the aircraft to the US would mean an increase in the cost of $238.5 million and delay procurement by a year. For this reason, it fairly soon became apparent that the entire order would have to be completed in the UK but prior to that, Hawker Siddeley signed a fifteen-year licence agreement with McDonnell-Douglas allowing them to have the rights to the sale and manufacture of Harrier in the US.

So it was that the USMC was able to obtain funding in the FY1970 budget for the first tranche of twelve Harriers and, at the FY1971 appropriations hearings, it was agreed that further Harriers could be acquired and that they would indeed be built in the UK.

Thus the American Harrier, designated Mk 50 by Hawker Siddeley and AV-8A by the USMC joined the RAF aircraft in the Production Hangar at Dunsfold, the first AV-8A serialled 158384 flying on 20 November 1970. The first twelve aircraft were delivered with the Pegasus Mk 102 engine but were later retroactively fitted with the Mk 103 as it became available.

Douglas C-133B Cargomaster freighter at Dunsfold to collect an AV-8A, probably January 1971. (BAE Systems, courtesy of Brooklands Museum)

All twelve aircraft were complete by February 1972, which just left the small matter of how to get them across the Atlantic to their new home. It was decided that the first twelve aircraft would be sent as air freight, initially, in the hold of a Douglas C-133B Cargomaster freighter, a large, for its day, four-engined strategic cargo aircraft that could ship the aircraft and its various stores directly across the Atlantic. Having completed its flight test schedule, the first aircraft was broken down into major components – wing, fuselage and tailplane – and secured within specially-manufactured cradles for the journey to the US. Following the official handover of the first aircraft at Dunsfold to USMC representatives on 6 January 1971, the first of these outsize shopping trips was planned for the 24th. The C-133B having successfully located Dunsfold, the aircraft was landed and taxied to the end of the runway for the loading to take place. All went well and the first AV-8A was soon winging its way to its new home.

Later sorties were carried out using a Lockheed C-141A Starlifter, a four-jet long-range transport more suited to this particular role though cross-wind landings could be challenging. As it happened, the last pick up proved to be just such a landing. Peter Amos watched with interest as the pilot

> frightened himself by trying to land in the high crosswind, which also frightened us to death as we were watching it from the office window and could see it heading for us if he didn't catch it in time!

However, all was well and by March 1972 all twelve aircraft had safely reached their destinations in the US. Subsequent deliveries were crated and transported by road to Mildenhall for onward despatch, thus robbing the Dunsfold staff of the sight of these outsized aircraft winging their way into the airfield.[3]

Following the export of the first twelve AV-8A aircraft to the US, a further order, for eighteen aircraft, was placed following funding secured in 1971 for FY1972 purchases. Those aircraft were constructed and flown from Dunsfold between April and December 1972. As each year's funding was approved, further batches were constructed and flown from Dunsfold; thirty aircraft during 1973, another thirty in 1974 and twelve between March 1975 and January 1976. Finally, in 1975, funding was approved for the purchase of eight T. 2 trainers, designated TAV-8A in the US and Mk 54 in the UK, for delivery in 1975/6, these passing through Dunsfold between

Lockheed C-141A Starlifter which superseded the C-133B for later deliveries of AV-8As from Dunsfold. (BAE Systems, courtesy of Brooklands Museum)

July 1975 and October 1976. In all 102 AV-8A and eight TAV-8A aircraft were acquired by the US Navy for the USMC, all constructed by Hawker Siddeley, an enormous boost both for the company and for the UK Treasury.

In summary, the Harrier was, for the USMC, an outstanding success and confirmed their decision to move to a V/STOL-enabled force. Most pilots could not speak too highly of the AV-8A although it could, on occasions bite the unwary. One unfortunate trainee at MCAS Cherry Point in North Carolina, in attempting to make a transition from a VTO, failed to get properly airborne and came down hard a short distance from the take-off point causing the main undercarriage leg to fail. The aircraft continued at speed, hitting a drainage ditch which bounced the aircraft back into the air inverted before, shedding aircraft parts, hitting the parking ramp in front of the hangar and continuing *into* the hangar, now aflame, crashing into an A-4 jet and exiting the hangar through the rear doors. Not content with the destruction so far, the aircraft then entered the base parking lot and destroyed at least thirteen private vehicles! Sadly, the pilot died but, incredibly, no one else was injured – most personnel being absent at lunch.[4]

During the early sales efforts of the Harrier to the US, every effort was made to ensure that the aircraft was presented in its best light and, to rebut claims from some US sources that the aircraft had little load-carrying ability, in early September 1970, a Harrier GR.1, XV742, retained by HSA for trials, was temporarily repainted in USMC colours and loaded with a full 8,000lb complement of bombs and cannon so that photographic evidence could be obtained for use at the following week's Farnborough Air Show. The ensuing low-level, high-speed runs up and down the Dunsfold runway were purely for the benefit of the photographic department who announced that they were more than happy with the flying. Unfortunately, when the results reached Farley he was less than amused: 'The all-important … photographs produced from this expensive exercise were two blurred and dark photographs on which it is not even possible to clearly identify the stores carried.' Having lambasted all concerned, he concluded, 'As Tony Hawkes says "another victory like that and we are lost".'[5]

As a postscript to the American adventure it is worth noting one advantageous aspect of the USMC order; it included a requirement for the aircraft to be capable of operating with US stores, including the Philco Sidewinder air-to-air heat-seeking missile. Trials were undertaken in the UK to clear the installation, and operation, of this missile system to the AV-8A.

Harrier GR.1 XV742 in AV-8A livery for publicity shots of heavy stores carriage (8,000lb), September 1970. (BAE Systems, courtesy of Brooklands Museum)

At the time there was no requirement to have a similar ability on the Harrier GR.1 since it was a ground-attack aircraft, not a fighter. However, subsequent events in the South Atlantic ten years later would change this policy and the earlier work on missile carriage allowed operation of AIM9-L Sidewinders by the RAF Harrier GR.3s to be cleared in a matter of days for use in the Falklands War.

As the US order was being manufactured by Hawker Siddeley, news of another order reached Kingston with a requirement identified by the Spanish Navy for the Harrier in 1973. This interest was a result of a demonstration by John Farley aboard the Spanish carrier *Dédalo* the year before and resulted in an order for six single-seat and two two-seat Harriers. Delivery of AV-8A standard Harriers, designated AV-8S Matador, began in 1976 from Dunsfold and were made via the US due to sanctions still being in place because of political sensitivities concerning the Franco regime.

During the intensive effort to sell Harrier to the US armed forces, it had become apparent that there was no substitute for actual experience of flying the aircraft. Those who did get to fly the Harrier inevitably became converts, a point not lost on the HSA board. Thus, in 1970, a decision was made to construct a dedicated two-seat Harrier for demonstration purposes at company expense. Agreement was reached with contractors that all

Spanish AV-8S Matador makes a wet take-off from Dunsfold, June 1980. (BAE Systems, courtesy of Brooklands Museum)

AV-8A, 158969, here serialled XY125 and painted in RAF colours, probably for public display purposes. (BAE Systems, courtesy of Brooklands Museum)

installed equipment would similarly be provided at the contractor's expense. The civil serial G-VTOL was allocated for the aircraft together with a military serial ZA250 for when the aircraft needed to perform military demonstrations with ordnance.

The decision to provide a dedicated demonstration aircraft was not without precedent. During the sales campaign for the Hunter, a composite T.7 had been built from redundant sections and, serialled G-APUX, had become well known on the display circuit. Early demonstrations by the Harrier had also been facilitated by a GR.1, serialled G-VSTO, which carried out a number of demonstrations, including a series of flights in Switzerland which featured Farley in a spirited ascent out of a low-lying airfield straight up the side of the adjacent mountain.

G-VTOL, designated a Mk 52, the only one produced, was equipped with additional navigation and communications equipment to allow it to operate successfully globally. Yet, despite this impressive suite of kit, the early years of the aircraft were marred with a series of incidents that saw it returning more than once to Kingston for rebuild. Rolled out in an eye-catching livery of red, white and blue, first flight of the aircraft was achieved on 16 September 1971 with Simpson formating on the company HS.125 for air-to-air photography.[6]

Harrier Mk 52 G-VTOL in early livery in ferry configuration including extended wing-tips and servicing pod on the centre fuselage station. (BAE Systems, courtesy of Brooklands Museum)

Ill-luck struck just a month later on the aircraft's twelfth flight. As part of the work up for an important sales tour encompassing the Far East and India to be undertaken with G-VTOL and Tony Hawkes as HSA pilot, on 6 October 1971 Hawkes was completing the last flight prior to preparing the aircraft for the tour. This flight was to terminate with an 'end-stop' check to gather information on take-off distance for use when the aircraft was demonstrated on the Indian aircraft carrier *Vikrant*. The test comprised a short take off from a marked area on Dunsfold's runway mimicking the length of deck available on the *Vikrant*. As the end of the 'deck' was reached, the nozzles were dropped to 55 degrees and the aircraft quickly became airborne. At this point the test was over; the pilot was to return the aircraft to the runway and subsequently to the hangar. This did not happen. What did happen was that the aircraft appeared to remain airborne rather longer than expected and therefore touched down farther along the runway and at greater speed than expected. Braking was applied but had little effect; nozzle braking was then attempted but the aircraft continued at speed off the end of the runway, across the grass overshoot and descended a steep slope into a scrubby copse where it came to rest. The flight test engineer in the rear cockpit was able to extricate himself from the aircraft but Hawkes was unable to open the canopy due to the damage received and resorted to firing the canopy explosive mdc system to escape, from which he received minor injuries. The damage to G-VTOL was extensive, including to the front fuselage, undercarriage, wings and stores, and forced the return of the aircraft to Kingston for repair.

Having repaired G-VTOL, in 1972 a further attempt to get the aircraft out to India to demonstrate from the carrier INS *Vikrant* was staged with Farley carrying out the demonstrations and familiarisation flights with Indian Navy personnel. Despite many potential setbacks, this part of the tour was considered a great success and, on departure from India, the plan was to demonstrate the aircraft at several Middle Eastern locations. It was during a display for Abu Dhabi that it all went wrong. With the Ruler located at his palace at Al Ain, it was decided to carry out the demonstration there; Tony Hawkes would be the designated pilot for the aircraft. On 16 July, G-VTOL, now in a suitably 'desert' paint scheme, was flown to Al Ain, a dusty airstrip in the desert for demonstration to the Ruler and local officials. During the subsequent demonstration, with a local RAF officer in the rear seat, the aircraft was hovered and then moved slowly backwards at descending altitude into a dust cloud blown up by the aircraft, causing Hawkes to lose his horizon and, in the subsequent landing attempt, make heavy contact with

A sad looking G-VTOL lies in the sand at El Ain after Tony Hawkes' unfortunate accident, 16 July 1972. (BAE Systems, courtesy of Brooklands Museum)

the ground at an attitude that caused extensive damage. As the cloud cleared, G-VTOL lay drunkenly on the sand, its starboard outrigger destroyed, starboard wing on the ground and the nose crumpled and, probably, any hopes of selling Harrier into the Middle East lost.[7]

As G-VTOL was ferried back to Dunsfold aboard a cargo aircraft, the subsequent enquiry could not escape the conclusion that the pilot was at fault, the second incident with this aircraft and pilot in less than a year, and the reluctant conclusion was to move him from Dunsfold, another position being found on the civil programme at Woodford. To avoid any suggestion that the Harrier had some fundamental flaw, a single-seat Harrier was quickly 'rented' from the MOD and John Farley picked up the demonstration requirements to complete the Middle Eastern commitments but the chance for sales had been lost, no Harriers ever being sold into the Arabian Peninsula.

Following further repair, G-VTOL was again back in the demonstration business, this time for the Swiss Air Force at Dunsfold. Following Farley's impressive performance with G-VSTO in Switzerland, hopes were high that Harrier could replace the Hunter in this Alpine country. On 5 April 1973 the aircraft was aloft at Dunsfold with Farley in command and a Swiss Air Force pilot, Colonel H. Stauffer, in the front cockpit; following a touch and go, at about 200 feet, the engine speed started to decay rapidly and the evaluation pilot reported that he had 'lost the throttle'. Farley immediately selected the manual fuel-control system and took control to bring the aircraft in to a safe landing. While the engine fuel-control system took the blame, Farley believed

> there was nothing wrong with the aircraft, he had closed the fuel cock. I used the MFCS because we were low and slow in the circuit and I knew I probably only had one chance at a relight.[8]

Perhaps unsurprisingly, less than a week later, the Swiss pilot was again in trouble, this time in a single-seat Harrier – no Farley on hand this time to sort things out. The aircraft, XV276, was the first of the DB Harriers and had been retained at Dunsfold for trials work. On 10 April 1973 at 14.32, the colonel took off for his first Harrier solo to fly a circuit of the aerodrome. Two minutes later, on entering the downwind leg and reducing power, he inadvertently brought the throttle too far back and moved it into the HP cock 'off' position, thereby switching off the engine. Bringing the throttle forward again and relighting the engine would have recovered the situation but the pilot elected to eject, leaving the Harrier to find its own way down to earth in a flaming heap in fields on the Baynards Estate to the east of the aerodrome. While the pilot was unhurt, he believed that the blame lay squarely with the engine. The following week, at the Paris Air Show, the colonel was there, as was Farley, who knew there was nothing wrong with the engine, or the aircraft and took the HSA chairman's daughter up for a flight in G-VTOL to press home the point. An internal HSA memo made the cause of the crash clear: 'Pilot error. Pilot stop-cocked engine at low level.'[9]

Ironically, Farley knew better than most how easily one could make an incorrect selection: he had done just that himself a year or so earlier. On his return to Dunsfold in June 1972 after a series of fairly punishing displays at Lugarno and Grenchen in Switzerland, he espied the annual Kingston vs Dunsfold executives' cricket match in full swing below. Sensing a chance to impress the assembled worthies below with a small demo, Farley reached for the lever to bring the aircraft to hover by selecting full braking stop – on the throttle instead of the nozzle lever. As the engine wound down, he quickly relit it and pottered off into the circuit, no doubt wondering how it was that he had nearly lost the aircraft by a moment's ill attention.[10] After the loss of the DB aircraft, Hawker continued to woo the Swiss with Harrier but to no avail; catching everyone by surprise, the Swiss eventually decided to ignore all of the shiny new aircraft on offer and plumped for a further batch of refurbished Hunters, perhaps a consolation prize for Dunsfold.

Despite these various mishaps, G-VTOL went on to become a 'global' phenomenon and one of the most familiar aircraft to the general public and air show-goers. Eventually, retired in April 1989, the aircraft was donated to Brooklands Aviation Museum at Weybridge Surrey where it remains to this day.

G-VTOL was not the first of Hawker's, and Dunsfold's aircraft to find retirement in a museum. In August 1970 a notice from J.T. Lidbury, Hawker Siddeley's deputy chairman and managing director, appeared announcing the formation of a new National Aircraft collection at the former RAF Hendon in north London. It further announced that part of the museum would be formed as a memorial to Sir Sydney Camm and would contain exhibits ranging from the Cygnet, Camm's first solo design, to the Harrier. All well and good, but the only source for many of the exhibits would be Hawker Siddeley's collection of vintage aircraft at Dunsfold.

In an earlier chapter, it was seen how a diverse range of Hawker products had accumulated at Dunsfold, all at the time in flying condition.

So it was that the last Hurricane built, PZ865/G-AMAU, had migrated from Langley soon after Dunsfold opened for business with Hawker, to be followed by the Hart, G-ABMR, the Cygnet, G-EBMB, and the Tomtit, G-AFTA. Steps were taken to pass these valuable and, in the case of the Cygnet, unique airframes on to new homes. The reasons for this are not easy to discern, although cost of upkeep and concerns about their condition would have been foremost in the minds of the board. In 1965 the insurance premium for the Hurricane was £5,000 and for the Hart £1,000. To retain a Sea Fury in flying trim, as was the plan at the time, would cost £10,000 in insurance alone.[11] With regard to condition, the Cygnet had not been flown for some time, an assessment by the Chief Inspector in 1971 noting that, even in 1957, it 'caused considerable concern and apprehension'. So it was that, as early as 16 January 1968, J.T. Lidbury had announced to interested parties both within and outside Hawker Siddeley that a list of airframes would be made available for transfer to the nascent RAF Museum; the list comprised Dunsfold's Hurricane, Hart, Cygnet and Fury. Also included were Chester's Mosquito, Brough's Blackburn B2 and Hatfield's Cirrus Moth.[12]

Dunsfold's vintage aircraft prior to departure for pastures new. From left, Hurricane IIc PZ865, Hart G-ABMR and Cygnet G-EBMB. Note that the Harrier GR.1 has become bogged in the soft ground. (BAE Systems, courtesy of Brooklands Museum)

However, as word of these plans leaked out into the 'Heritage Community', various organisations cast their eyes over the potentialities of this feast and began pulling strings in an attempt to acquire one or more of the aircraft for themselves. Thus, on 2 December 1971, Air Commodore Wheeler for the Shuttleworth Collection, contacted Mr Bainbridge, HSA's PR head to enquire whether there was any chance of delaying decisions on final disposal of the aircraft so that 'one or two exchanges might be effected in components' that might be used on the Trust's rebuild of a Hawker Hind to flying condition. Previously, in 1967, an enquiry from the Trust had been made asking whether HSA planned to dispose of the Hurricane. The reply denying this spelled out that it was being lent to Hamish Mahaddie as part of the collection of flyable aircraft for the making of the film *The Battle of Britain* but that it would definitely be returning, but also notes that the Tomtit, passed to the Trust by July 1965, would return to Dunsfold for repainting in RAF colours.

Despite a rearguard action by Duncan Simpson to retain at least the Hurricane and Hart, firm instructions were issued on 17 November 1971 from on high to prepare for disposal of the Hurricane, Hart and Cygnet by June 1972. At the last moment, a deal was completed whereby the Hurricane would move to the RAF Memorial Flight at RAF Coltishall and they would supply a replacement Hurricane for the museum. On 10 April 1972, the Hart and Cygnet were prepared for transport and left Dunsfold for a new home at Hendon in the RAF Museum.[13]

As noted above, one of the aircraft to be offered to the RAF Museum was to be a 'Fury, in fact a Sea Fury. In summer 1962 the HSA board had agreed to the preservation in flying condition of a Sea Fury; this should not have presented any great challenge to the company which was awash with Sea Furies at the time, having purchased back from the Admiralty some 251 airframes for potential resale to third parties, but it appeared that it was not considered to be a priority for HSA management and it was left to Dunsfold staff to progress the idea. Fortuitously, in February 1963, Sea Fury FB. 11, serial TF956, had been identified at Lossiemouth as the earliest production machine and included in a batch of seven aircraft flown to Dunsfold and parked on the eastern dispersals along with those awaiting a future of some description.

TF956 had first flown at Hawker's Langley airfield on 5 September 1947, piloted by Frank Murphy, and was delivered to the Royal Navy on 8 October that year at RNAS Culdrose and placed into storage. Via various RNAS stations it joined No. 807 Squadron on HMS *Theseus* on 24 October 1950, flying 213 hours of operational sorties during the Korean War.

Following flak damage to the wing, the aircraft had returned to the UK in 1951 and, following repair, was returned to storage before issue to No. 738 Squadron. By 1954 TF956 was in storage and remained at various RN AHUs until January 1963 when it was sold to Hawker Siddeley Aviation and flown from Lossiemouth to Dunsfold by David Lockspeiser on 6 March 1963. There it was held pending a resale but, in the event, was moved to open storage on the eastern dispersals on 9 April 1964.

In May 1964 Duncan Simpson wrote an impassioned plea to the Chief Test Pilot asking for him to champion the preservation of the aircraft for return to flight as part of Hawker Siddeley's vintage flying collection, noting that 'shortly it will be too late; pieces are already being removed from the aircraft'. Eventually brought into the Production Hangar on 12 June 1964, an inspection of the airframe confirmed that it was in good condition. As the request for assistance and, more importantly, finance for the project ground its way up the corporate tree at HSA Group, so the aircraft sank further into the background although not before spending time at Kingston for 'overhaul'. In the end, it fell to the unofficial ministering of a couple of the production engineers to further the scheme, in particular Colin Balchin. As one of the electricians in the hangar, Colin took it upon himself to begin reconditioning some small electrical parts on the aircraft and, with no one showing any particular interest, the small parts led to rather larger parts and, slowly, the aircraft came back to life.[14] By December 1967 Simpson, busy calling in favours at RNAS Yeovilton in the hunt for remaining missing parts and further information on a suitable paint scheme, noted that 'Work is proceeding quietly at the back of the Production Hangar and the engine should go in shortly.' It was about this time that 'management' got involved, having belatedly become aware that an aircraft restoration project had been going on under their noses without their overt knowledge. Simpson, perhaps realising that the cat was well and truly out of the bag, commented ruefully that he hoped 'we can fend off the over-zealous accountants until we achieve [return to flight]'. By October 1968 Simpson replied to an enquiry from a serving pilot that, with the future of the entire vintage collection in doubt, the work on the Sea Fury 'has come to a grinding halt'. However, 'the aeroplane is 90%-95% toward flying' and he still hoped to get the Sea Fury back in the air.[15]

By 1970 hopes of flying the Sea Fury from Dunsfold had faded; in a response to Flight Lieutenant Russ Snadden, a keen supporter of the idea of returning a Sea Fury to the skies, Simpson, now chief test pilot, had to admit that 'the effort to make it fly again within Hawker walls has been defeated by our Harrier and Hunter programmes.' However, 'It now looks as if it will be returned to the Royal Navy at the Yeovilton Museum.' Yeovilton were naturally keen to acquire the airframe, given the work that had been expended on bringing it back to flyable status and because of its historic past, having seen action during the Korean War from HMS *Theseus*.

By 16 March 1971 the deal was done, TF956 being allocated to the Fleet Air Arm Museum Yeovilton, the aircraft leaving Dunsfold on 7 April by road. Following an 'unofficial' first flight on 16 January 1972, none other than Duncan Simpson carried out the first official flight from Yeovilton on the 19th, the aircraft carrying the B-serial G-9-395. In 1974 TF956 suffered major damage during a landing accident but was repaired and flying again for the next year's display season, including a visit to Dunsfold for Field Day. On 10 June 1989 TF956 was again in trouble and crashed into the Firth of Clyde during a display at Prestwick when the starboard undercarriage failed to lower. So much for the vintage aircraft, but what about the civil communications fleet?

In the 1950s the civil fleet had comprised two DH Rapide biplanes, G-AHGC, acquired by Hawker Aircraft in 1946, and G-ACPP, acquired in 1952, together with a Miles Whitney Straight, G-AEUJ, and an Avro Anson C.19, G-AHXK. By the mid-1960s the Avro C.19 had fallen by the wayside as had the Whitney Straight, leaving just two Rapides for all communications flights. The Rapides were, by the mid-60s, long in the tooth, having been built in 1944 and HSA really needed something more up-to-date and cost effective. The solution was the acquisition of a number of DH.104 Doves to be distributed around the group, including one for Dunsfold although Sir Harry Broadhurst's memo of 2 July 1965 on the subject was clear that it was to replace the Rapide at Dunsfold, not supplement it.

With the arrival of Dove Mk 8 G-ASMG in July, the two Rapides at Dunsfold, G-AHAG, acquired in 1963, and GAHGC, were considered surplus to requirements and appeared to be heading for oblivion. Indeed they were dismantled in October 1965 and added to the Social Club bonfire ready to be consumed on 5 November before being rescued by a timely offer from Scillonia Airways for use on the Isles of Scilly route and re-assembled and flown out in May 1966.[16] G-ASMG would go on to become one of Dunsfold's longest residents, still going strong in the early 1990s, before eventual retirement and replacement with a Jetstream 31, considered by many to be a retrograde step in terms of comfort and noise level, although undoubtedly rather quicker in the air. Also added to the fleet in the 1970s was a Piper Seminole PA-44 twin-engine aircraft, G-BGCO, to supplement the Dove. This aircraft remained until closure.

Chapter 10

Hawker Siddeley Enter the Trainer Market

The Folland Gnat was the first modern dedicated trainer design that the RAF had acquired, developed from the Gnat F.1 lightweight fighter and offered the service the opportunity to get its hands on a compact, lively aircraft that would certainly appeal to the potential fast jet students, and their tutors, at RAF Valley. That said, it also came with a number of less attractive attributes; the diminutive size of the airframe meant that those too large to squeeze into the cockpit had to receive their training on the T.7 Hunter; the instructor's view forward from the rear cockpit was very poor and the fuselage so densely crammed with the equipment required for its role that servicing was a nightmare. Added to these difficulties was the never completely settled matter of the longitudinal gearing to the tailplane that caused problems throughout its life, probably one concern that the student pilot could have done without. However, the aircraft did enter service, via the good offices of Hamble and Dunsfold, and was retained in use for the next sixteen years. There were those who found the decision to opt for the Gnat, rather than the Hunter to be inexplicable; but the promise of a cheap (£100,000) aircraft against the cost of a Hunter (£175,000) would have been a strong inducement.

However that may be, by the late 1960s it was clear that a Gnat replacement would be required before too long, as would be a replacement for the Hunter in the weapons training role and, likely, also the Hunting (BAC) Jet Provost. It so happened that, as these thoughts were coalescing in the minds of various design houses across the UK, the Kingston Design Office was feeling down on its luck. With the major work on design of the Harrier complete, no exciting new projects were being sketched on the drawing boards and thus the possibility of producing a dedicated trainer, as the Gnat had been, began to germinate. Quite what Camm's thoughts would have been on the subject can probably be guessed; Camm's team designed fighters, it was the only game to be in. No doubt a new fighter to take its place alongside the Hurricane, Tempest, Fury, Hunter and Harrier would

172

have been a fitting swansong for his long life in aviation, but he had died suddenly on the golf course in 1966 and was therefore not there to berate his staff as a *trainer*, for God's sake, began to be talked of in the Richmond Road project offices.

In the event, a replacement for Gnat started in 1964 with the issue of AST.362 by the RAF Operational Requirements Branch to industry to stimulate ideas for a future trainer. This called for a maximum speed ability around Mach 1.5 at altitude using two engines, adequate fuel reserves for typical training missions and operation from 6,000-foot runways. A benign stall was considered crucial although spinning ability was not felt to be so important. The lesson of adequate view from the rear cockpit had clearly been learned in the requirement in the AST for tandem seating with an 11-degree visual depression angle to be achieved over the front cockpit. The new aircraft would replace both Gnat and Hunter in the trainer role and enter service around 1974. Oh, and cheap – the new design must be cheap! The potential existed for collaboration with the French, who were looking for a replacement for the T-33 and Dassault Mystere IV which offered the chance of an increased market for the successful design.

HS Hawk T.1 XX154, the first Hawk to fly on 21st August 1974 from Dunsfold. The aircraft spent most of its life on development trials at Dunsfold and ministry establishments including DTEO Llanbedr. (BAE Systems, courtesy of Brooklands Museum)

From such uninspiring beginnings, Kingston Design sketched a trim little contribution under the title SGA.153 offering something like Mach 1.8 from either a twin- or single-engine turbofan arrangement from Rolls Royce, complete with two Aden cannon, weighing in at about 13,000lb. This offered the advantage of potential lightweight fighter sales to operators of the Gnat fighter, such as India, as well as into any future trainer market and was based on studies completed by HSA Hamble. From a further study of the AST came a slightly larger single-engine version titled HS.1173 that was as much light-strike as trainer and looked good on paper, offering a modest multi-role capability at the all-important low price. However, with the OR Branch insistent on two engines, Hawker Siddeley's designs were not acceptable and the question of collaboration with the French won the day with a Breguet design being jointly manufactured as the SEPECAT Jaguar.

However, it soon became obvious that the winning design would not fulfil the role required by the RAF at a price it could afford and thus Jaguar was re-allocated to other pastures while the need for a Gnat replacement continued, happily for Hawker Siddeley. At that time, one Gordon Hodson, a Folland ex-pat, was working from Kingston on Gnat in-service matters and, in an attempt to visualise just what a Gnat replacement for the RAF might consist of, in 1968 schemed a draft specification for just such an aircraft that eliminated all the bugs and niggles then current in the trainer community. This specification went the rounds of the design department at Kingston and, with the emphasis now being on finding a replacement in the basic trainer role for the BAC Jet Provost 5, brought forth initial sketches for a tandem-seat straight-winged aircraft of under 40-feet length powered by a 4,750lb engine known as Adour, which had been already developed for the Jaguar by a joint undertaking of Rolls Royce and Turbomeca. Crucially, the cost estimate per unit looked good at around £250,000, although this did not get you an engine to power the thing, and, with R&D costs included, could sell for around £370,000.

With preliminary designs looking more promising, likely markets were analysed for potential sales in both trainer and light-strike variants and the numbers proved sufficiently encouraging – sales of up to 1,000 were forecast – for work to continue on refining the design, now proceeding under the designation HS.1182. With a draft AST for a Jet Provost replacement available around early 1968, the design work looked to be on firmer footing, the aircraft now featuring modest sweep on wing and tail surfaces and a raised rear cockpit to offer the instructor some usable forward visibility.

Impressive line-up of Hawks on Dunsfold's flight line. Most are in training colours of red and white and destined for 4 FTS at Valley while the front Hawk, XX156, seen here in War Role guise was retained for various weapon-handing trials. Next to this is G-HAWK in a desert livery. (BAE Systems, courtesy of Brooklands Museum)

With the design looking distinctly unlike the AST requirement but offering improved performance and reliability, HSA issued its offering in a brochure as the 'HS.1182 Basic Trainer/Light Strike Aircraft', still with an Adour engine but with the intakes set high on the fuselage and elevators rather than all-moving tail.

A breakthrough of sorts was achieved in early 1970 with receipt of a new AST.397 and, later, a request for proposal (RFP) for an advanced trainer to replace the Jet Provost and, although not explicitly stated, a Gnat replacement also. HSA was pitched against BAC Warton with their P. 59 and P. 62 offering but, whereas BAC was suggesting a dual aircraft response to cover the basic and advanced training/light-strike requirement, Hawker Siddeley was seeking to cover the entire package of requirements with one airframe that could also answer the need to replace the Hunter T.7 and F.6 in the weapons training role. Through various design iterations the HSA aircraft slowly evolved into one that we would recognise today although still with the high-mounted intakes to reduce foreign object damage (FOD).

By 1971 it was clear that cost would likely decide whether it was HSA or BAC that won the trainer order and so HS.1182 was schemed with a Viper engine, the HS.1182V, and the design stripped to the bare bones to comply exactly with the ASR, this proposal being submitted despite rumblings of discontent at Kingston. Having got the Ministry's attention, a further detailed submission was made which also included two further proposals: the HS.1182AT, the ASR.397 submission but with an Adour in place of the Viper, and HS.1182AJ, the latest thinking on the project from the Kingston team and their preferred design. In October 1971 HS.1182AJ was declared the winning design with a requirement for 176 (175 plus one fatigue-test specimen) aircraft, but the battle was not yet over.

Almost all previous aircraft tenders had been based on a cost-plus agreement whereby the contractor's manufacturing costs were met by the government and a percentage added for the company's profit. For the first time the ASR.397 competition winner would be built under a fixed-price contract with built-in guarantees of performance and maintainability that could only be surmised when the aircraft was actually flying. In the event, the figures offered were fairly conservative and therefore allowed the company, as the aircraft progressed through the flight test development regime, to announce the design performance estimates being regularly exceeded, to the delight of the Kingston PR department and, more importantly, generating handsome payments to HSA as each milestone was completed successfully. This was just as well since the costings estimates supplied to MoD for the project had been tightly drawn and the contract profits for HSA would have been dismal without the maintainability and reliability clause payments, which triggered for payment in 1978.

The team chosen to complete the design was headed by Gordon Hudson, another ex-Folland designer, with Gordon Hodson as his deputy. During this period the Folland ejection seat was replaced at Ministry insistence with a Martin Baker unit and the Adour engine was equipped with a GTS (gas turbine starter) for relight in the air following flame-outs, due to the slow spool-up time of the Adour. The order would not include any prototype aircraft; all airframes would be built on production tooling from the start. Ability to accommodate four underwing pylons was also built into the design to improve its attraction to foreign air arms, although the RAF specification only called for two, together with capability to mount an Aden 30mm cannon on the centreline. As the design matured, the intakes were still mounted high but further wind-tunnel testing suggested that a low position would improve longitudinal stability at higher Mach numbers and the intakes were thus lowered to a position above the wing leading edge, incidentally giving a more pleasing profile. Unlike the Hunter and Gnat, which allowed the engine to be withdrawn rearwards for replacement, once the rear fuselage had been removed, the engine in the HS.1182 would be installed and removed from below, allowing control runs etc. to remain undisturbed. As the design was frozen in late summer 1972 into that recognisable today, the RAF bestowed the name Hawk on their new aircraft, this being formally announced in August 1973.[1]

With the requirement for good visibility from both cockpits implicit in the design, a novel arrangement was constructed at Dunsfold consisting of a cockpit mock-up mounted on a flat-bed truck which was driven up and down the runway to allow test pilot assessments of sighting calculations to be experienced in actuality rather than just in the designers' minds-eye.

Through late 1973 and the first months of 1974, the first Hawk, XX154, slowly came to life at Kingston until, on 31 July – the one-piece wing had arrived the day before – the aircraft arrived at Dunsfold for re-assembly in the Experimental Hangar. On 7 August 1974 the aircraft was positioned in one of the Hunter engine-pens and the engine successfully run. With its 'official' roll-out on 12 July, initial ground taxi tests commenced on the 20th and, with time running short to get the aircraft into the air and fit for an appearance at that year's Farnborough display, some flight-test work was delayed to allow a first flight late on Sunday evening 21 August. Duncan Simpson took the aircraft off the Dunsfold runway at 7.11pm for a flight of some fifty-three minutes. While all seemed set fair for the all-important Farnborough debut, those earlier taxi runs had highlighted a flaw with the steering; the Hawk could not turn corners easily on the ground. With no time to find a solution, the Hawker team resorted to towing the Hawk onto the runway for the start of its display and towing it off again once it had been completed. Few appeared to notice this strange behaviour, although it would no doubt have not gone unnoticed by the Alpha Jet team – the Hawk's main rival in the trainer market.[2]

With Farnborough out of the way, XX154 returned to Dunsfold Experimental Hangar and into a lay-up to allow for installation of the flight-test instrumentation package and addressing of the nose-wheel castoring. On completion, the first Hawk returned to investigation of the initial handling and performance aspects of the design. There was no time to lose as the production contract was tightly drawn and required deliveries to flying schools to begin in 1976. As it was, the second aircraft did not fly until May 1975, followed by the next four the same year. Those first

BAe Hawk T.1 XX264 following its return to Dunsfold for upgrading to T.1A standard in the War Role programme. All Red Arrows Aerobatic Team aircraft were so modified. (BAE Systems, courtesy of Brooklands Museum)

six aircraft were all fully instrumented to allow data acquisition to assist the flight development programme and were allocated to Boscombe Down as well as Dunsfold. Also based at Dunsfold for the trials was Hunter T.7 XL612, taken on charge from RAE Bedford to act as a chase aircraft for the early flights. With Harrier flight development also being carried out at Dunsfold, early in the programme Duncan Simpson appointed Andy Jones as Hawk project pilot and John Farley for the Harrier test programme, positions that both pilots were happy with. Andy Jones had joined HSA in 1970. As a former QFI on the Vampire T.11, he was well placed to bring this new trainer to peak condition. He was assisted on Hawk development by Jim Hawkins who had arrived in July 1973 and, later, by Chris Roberts, joining the team in 1979. Simpson was to retire from the role of chief test pilot in 1977, moving to a product support role at Dunsfold before becoming deputy director of SBAC, the CTP role being awarded to Farley with Jones as his deputy. Hawkins would now become lead Hawk pilot, mainly concentrating on the export Hawk, with Roberts as his No. 2.

Hawk Mk 50 G-HAWK carrying its military serial ZA101 while involved in weapon-carriage trials, June 1980. (BAE Systems, courtesy of Brooklands Museum)

With any new aircraft, there are many test points to be completed in the air, one of the higher risk activities being to put the aircraft into an intentional spin and work out the recovery technique so that service pilots will know what to do if they inadvertently enter a spin, for Hawk spinning, unlike the Gnat, would be part of the curriculum. The testing was to be carried out over Dunsfold and it was decided that the control responses and flight instruments would be monitored via a ground station so that the pilot would have safety monitoring assistance from another pilot during any difficult phases of the spinning. Thus, in July 1974, equipment was made available from Boscombe Down and installed in the first Hawk and in a ground station located adjacent to the ROC post on the south side of the airfield. In the event, the Hawk proved remarkably difficult to spin but, when it did, recovery was straightforward.[3]

With CA Release in April 1976, deliveries of Hawks to squadron service at the flying schools could begin although not before several niggling concerns with the aircraft had been addressed successfully. To improve the stall characteristics, the wing was altered to include wing fences and breaker strips, to give a benign stall with plenty of warning. At the same time, the addition of a row of vortex generators was added to address random pitch changes in the higher Mach range. Also changed was the flap arrangement following the discovery by Simpson that it was possible to stall the tailplane due to downwash from the powerful flaps. The flap slat was cut back on its outboard edge to prevent further incidents. No major changes to the aircraft had been found necessary, a quite remarkable situation and testimony to the skill with which the design had been formulated, especially since there had been no prototypes, the design moving straight into production working.

With the Hawk available for training use, it had been decided that the aircraft would first replace the Gnat and Hunter in the advanced flying and weapon-training roles and, later, the Jet Provost in the basic training role. Deliveries to squadrons commenced on 4 November 1976 with two aircraft to No. 4 FTS at RAF Valley; some twenty-five Hawks were on strength within a year. Those aircraft were painted in the then current training scheme of red, white and grey. Deliveries then began to No. 1 TWU at RAF Brawdy, the aircraft painted in the standard camouflage scheme. Included in the 175 aircraft for the RAF were twelve aircraft for the Red Arrows display team. These had minor modifications to allow for use of dyes and diesel fuel to produce coloured smoke as part of the display and changes to the fuel-control system to allow faster spool-up times for the Adour engine.

Some ingenuity was required to allow the broadly standard Hawks to produce coloured smoke, the testing being conducted at Dunsfold over a period of months. The eventual scheme consisted of a centreline gun-pod, modified by removal of the cannon and division of the pod into three compartments, to contain the diesel oil, red and blue dye. Smoke selection was via standard cockpit switches, the normal function of which was isolated and instead linked to the smoke-generation system. The oil, when ejected into the engine exhaust at the rear of the aircraft, produced white smoke with red or blue dye being added to produce the appropriate colour. Because of the cooler efflux from the Adour turbofan engine, in comparison to the Orpheus in the Gnat, the initial tests of the system resulted in unburnt oil and dye being sprayed across the aerodrome to the irritation of all concerned but, eventually, a suitable arrangement was found and testing proceeded relatively smoothly. It was easy to identify which of the engineering staff were engaged in the tests of the system since their overalls, and often skin, were dyed red or blue. Word has it that this fancy colour scheme extended to John Yoxall, the works manager's, cat!

Mark Gerrard, the flight test engineer on the smoke project remembered those days:

> The first Red Arrows Hawk was XX227. As it came down
> the production line at Dunsfold it looked like all the others,
> in yellow primer, except that it had the rudder painted red.

Also, in the cockpit were the switches for smoke on/smoke off and colour selection, as required for the demonstration team. Flight Testing started in the summer of 1980, and once the PFTS was complete, the next thing to look at was the smoke system. It became immediately apparent that something was not working as it should. At anything less than about 90% power the colours disappeared and the aircraft could only produce white smoke. Analysis of the film shot of the test runs clearly showed that the coloured dye was dropping out of the smoke plume, and the conclusion reached was that the temperature of the engine exhaust stream was too low to vaporise the dye.

The boffins in the fuel system department at Kingston concluded that what was required was a re-design of the pipe outlet to aid the vaporisation of the diesel/dye mix. Several designs were produced, but it was decided that it was going to be too expensive and time consuming to clear each of these designs for flight and accomplish flight tests. Accordingly it was decided that the various designs would be tested on the ground, with only the most promising design making it to flight test.

A ground test rig was designed, featuring a pressurised vessel for the dyed diesel and a structure to position the delivery pipe appropriately such that the aircraft could be lined up with the engine exhaust ready for ground running. There then followed a series of engine running ground tests at various power settings using the different pipe designs.

This was all in the days before environmental concerns were so paramount, which was probably just as well because the trials produced clouds of smelly, coloured smoke which drifted across the airfield in the direction of the wind. Windy days were avoided, of course, because of the potential effect on the test results, but light winds were acceptable. It was summertime, so time spent out on the airfield was always pleasant. The ground trials were not without their moments, as might have been expected, given the nature of the activity. On one occasion, the Flight Test Engineer was met with gales of laughter on his return to the office; there had been a pinhole leak in the pressure vessel, unnoticed by the test crew, which resulted in a fine blue mist emanating from the test rig. The aforementioned engineer was covered in blue spots.

Although consideration was given to wind direction when positioning the aircraft and the test rig, things were not guaranteed. On several occasions the cloud of smoke would be drifting safely away when a change in wind direction caused potential mayhem. The Rolls Royce rep was not amused to find his car covered with coloured spots that did not correspond to the colour of the car, and, of course, they had to be cleaned off quickly or they would become a permanent feature of the car's paint scheme. One day the same unfortunate Flight Test Engineer was hauled over the coals for allowing the smoke to drift across the office; it didn't smell very nice.

In the end, having tested various delivery nozzle designs of increasing complexity, it was decided that getting coloured smoke at low engine power settings was not going to be achieved and the project was halted. The Red Arrows aircraft stuck with the original straight pipe design, and to this day I believe it is true that coloured smoke can only be produced at high engine power settings.[4]

Eventually, it was concluded that, to get sufficient smoke production, the diesel needed to be injected into the hot core of the exhaust, maintained by flying at high RPM and by using airbrake extension in low-speed flight.

Following completion of flight testing at Dunsfold, the aircraft were flown to Bitteswell for application of the distinctive Red Arrows paint scheme and delivered from there. Those Hawks fell into the serial range XX291 to XX308. Also completed at Bitteswell were forty further aircraft withdrawn from the Dunsfold production line at finals stage and roaded to Bitteswell for final assembly and delivery; those Hawks were in the serial range XX291 to XX353, the flight testing being carried out at Bitteswell by Dunsfold pilots flown up for the day.

An additional aircraft joined the RAF Hawks on the production line at Dunsfold. The one and only Mk. 50 was the eighth aircraft on the line and was an entirely company-funded aircraft. Following the success of G-VTOL in touring the world to display the virtues of V/STOL to the masses, it was decided that a Hawk demonstrator would pay dividends in future export sales. An additional and very important reason for a company aircraft was to carry out additional trials for the export market, in particular, carriage and release tests for the additional pylons and for stores that were not in the UK inventory. The aircraft, registered G-HAWK, first flew on 17 May

Hawk 200 ZG200, the first single seat Hawk undergoes engine run in the detuner in May 1986. Note the hefty Instrumentation pack behind the pilot's seat. (BAE Systems courtesy of Brooklands Museum)

1976 from Dunsfold and became probably the most widely travelled Hawk in the world, visiting almost every continent in the pursuit of sales in what was a very tough market. G-HAWK was also added to the military register as ZA101. Civil-registered aircraft not being permitted to carry external stores, the company demonstrator flew with either registration although not both for the same flight. On retirement, this aircraft joined its stable mate G-VTOL at Brooklands Museum in January 2019.

As well as introducing the first British aircraft designed to the SI (metric) system and also one of the first to dispense with the prototype stage, Hawk was the first aircraft for Dunsfold which was actually substantially built at the airfield rather than only re-assembled and test flown. It may be instructive to examine this process in a little more detail.

The major components were manufactured at various of the company's sites – the wing, tailplane and fin at Brough, cockpit canopy at Hamble and fuselage sections at Kingston. All these major components would then find their way to Dunsfold on the back of various transports before materialising in Bay 2 of the Production Hangar which at that time was the Hawk 'erection floor'. The centre and rear fuselage would arrive already mated but the front fuselage would be delivered separately and would be installed in jigs that enabled them to be swung about their longitudinal axis through any angle to facilitate ease of access. Thus installed, the hydraulic systems, equipment shelves and electrical services would be installed – all the electrical looms and panels were manufactured in the electrical pen at Dunsfold – before the completed front moved across the bay to be mated to the centre and rear section and the fin fitted. Once complete, electrical and systems installation would continue and the cockpit canopy was fitted and cockpit pressure tested. Once all this work was complete, the fuselage would be relocated in Bay 1 – 'Finals' – for mating with the wing and tailplane as hydraulic systems, fuel-flow and electrical functioning were carried out. Once the aircraft was signed off as complete, it would leave the finals bay and trundle round to Bay 3 which at that time was the 'Flight Shed'. From there, the flight shed crew would take over and manage the initial engine runs and compass swing before preparing the aircraft for its first

Hawk Mk.50 G-HAWK in its 100-series configuration overflies Dunsfold. (BAE Systems, courtesy of Brooklands Museum)

flight. Engine running was conducted in one of the old Hunter detuner pens at the west end of the airfield, the Hawk jet-pipe being at about the same height as the Hunter's. Once securely held down, the aircraft would be run up by a Rolls Royce engineer and taken through its test points as often as required to clear the installation. Compass swing was undertaken on one of two compass beds, having the cardinal points and magnetic north marked out on the concrete base. Once ready for first flight, the aircraft would be taxied to the runway and engine checks completed before commencing the take-off roll before lifting off for the first flight. The aircraft would normally stay in the flight shed until the aircraft had completed its flight testing and 'finished flight' certificates signed; it would then relocate to the adjacent paint shop for its final coat of paint – flight testing was carried out with the aircraft in its primer finish – before a final test flight and delivery to the customer.

A few of the RAF Hawks were modified to carry and deploy an aerial target for gun-firing practice; Flight Test Engineer Mark Gerrard takes up the story.

> The banner target-towing trial was a lot of fun for me, because I was involved in almost every aspect of it. Not only did I run the aircraft & the trial, brief and debrief the pilot, analyse the results and produce the report, I also flew in the aircraft as Flight Test Observer.
>
> The RAF's gunnery target was a six feet by 30 feet banner towed behind a suitable aircraft on about 800 feet of nylon line. Its purpose was to be shot at by those being initiated in the gentle art of air-to-air gunnery, success or otherwise being determined by the number of holes in the thing at the end of a mission versus the number of rounds fired.
>
> The use of a wing mounted container for the banner would enhance performance and efficiency by carrying the target to the range area in a low drag configuration rather than dragging it off the ground and having the banner on tow all the way. To avoid an enormous amount of asymmetric drag, the towing point was on the rear fuselage, and in cruise mode with the banner stowed in its container the towing line reached from the release unit to the target in its pod under the port wing. The intent was that once the target towing aircraft reached the appropriate spot, the target would be deployed from its

container. There was, of course, no way of getting the banner back into its pod, so it would be towed back to base and released over the airfield.

A flight trials programme was devised, using XX278, to demonstrate banner deployment and release, and establish aircraft handling and performance with the banner on tow. Testing took place between September 1979 and March 1980. The first attempt at streaming the target, over the English Channel, resulted in failure of the weak link in the towline and the banner falling in the sea. A second attempt at a lower speed also ended with the banner in the sea. Heinz Frick, who was in the habit of drawing cartoons depicting various Dunsfold happenings, produced the 'We Keep Dropping Them' medal, featuring a comely young lady in the process of losing her underwear, with two bars for 'Hawk Banner 1' and 'Hawk Banner 2'. I suppose very politically incorrect by today's standards, but those were the days, my friend!

The boffins had a bit of a head scratch and decided that the cause of the problem was probably the presence of a Kevlar section of towline at the aircraft end, intended to protect the nylon cable from the engine exhaust heat. The Kevlar did not have the shock-absorbing properties of the nylon line, and the resulting shock loading was considered to be the cause of the weak link failures. Sure enough, deletion of the Kevlar led to a successful deployment. On this successful deployment flight, I flew as Flight Test Observer, with the late Jim Hawkins as pilot. After the successful stream, the object of the flight was to gain performance data with the banner on tow, in straight and level flight and in turns. As Flight Test Observer, I was busy writing down numbers from the cockpit gauges (no flight test instrumentation on XX278) during a left-hand turn when I felt a slight but distinct thump through the airframe. 'Jim, it just fell off!' I said, over the intercom. 'Are you sure?' came the immediate response. 'Absolutely,' I replied, 'I just felt it go.' 'OK,' said Jim, 'we'll have to follow it down to see where it goes.' There wasn't much doubt about where it was going; into the Channel, but Jim put XX278 into a tight descending left-hand spiral. 'Tell me when you can see it,' he said. By leaning backwards as far as I could and looking over my left shoulder I could just about see it 'In sight,' I said, 'Tighten the turn a bit', followed a few seconds later by 'It's in the water.' At that point, having established that the banner was on its way to the bottom of the sea and no apparent danger to anyone, we set course for home. Jim let me fly the aircraft back to Dunsfold, that being one of the highlights of my time as a Flight Test Engineer.

Post flight investigation showed that the towline had failed because it melted in the exhaust heat, vindicating the use of the Kevlar, but the Kevlar was unsatisfactory for the reason previously described. After a couple of unsuccessful attempts to make air-launching work using differing designs of towline, the RAF decided to abandon air launching and tow the banner off the ground.[5]

By 1979, with the RAF Hawk T. 1 aircraft working their way down the erection floor, other aircraft were apparent on the line. These were the first export Hawks, for Kenya or, as British Aerospace was – according to contract stipulation – forced to refer to them, 'an unnamed African country'. Those Hawks were identified as Mk 52 and were constructed to the '50 series' standard, having an uprated Adour Mk 851 engine delivering 5,340lb thrust and the addition of five-pylon capability for light strike/ ground attack. The order for twelve aircraft, serialled 1001 to 1012, proved trouble free and was delivered in batches between April 1980 and February 1981. Following them onto the Dunsfold line came the next export order, this time for Indonesia, a total of twenty Mk 53 Hawks serialled 5301 to 5320, these being delivered between September 1980 and March 1984. While these Mk 50 orders were welcome, British Aerospace had been studiously working behind the scenes to find a significant launch customer with which to demonstrate that Hawk had well and truly arrived on the international scene.

The market within which such a search was to be conducted was a truly competitive one, with Hawk being tendered against such aircraft as the Franco-German Alpha-Jet, the Italian MB.326 (later the MB.339) and the Swedish Saab 105B. As early as 1975 a concerted effort, including taking on loan XX156 to demonstrate in country, had been made to sell the aircraft to Egypt, then in need of an aircraft to replace their ageing MiG 15s and 17s in the training and ground-attack role and which could be assembled locally and later produced in country. Numbers in the order of 200 trainer/light

This RR Adour engine fell out of the aircraft as it was being installed following failure of the lifting strop. A pensive John Yoxall, Works Manager, is understandably unhappy. (BAE Systems, courtesy of Brooklands Museum)

attack were talked of with a further order for 100 fighter aircraft as an added carrot. Negotiations moved slowly but steadily and, in July 1977, a team from the Egyptian Air Force arrived at Dunsfold to evaluate the Hawk in both training and ground-attack roles, followed by a further visit to Egypt by G-HAWK in 1978. However, it was all in vain; the Egyptian Government signed an order for Alpha-Jet in October 1980 with small orders for the aircraft being followed by another small order for the Mirage 2000. With hindsight, the potential for large sales into Egypt had been undermined by the country entering into a non-aggression pact with Israel at the Camp David talks in 1978.

As the Egyptians had been the focus of HSA's attentions in the heat of the Middle East, a similar battle was being fought in the Arctic chill of northern Europe. As early as 1972, the company had been approached by its agent in Finland to alert it to a requirement in that country for an aircraft such as Hawk. By 1973 HSA, in the person of John Crampton, was briefing members of the Finnish Air Force on the finer points of the aircraft. As the competition developed, the company once again found itself in competition with Alpha-Jet, MB.339, CASA C.101, Saab 105 and the Czech L.39 Albatross, the Finns being meticulous in their assessment of each aircraft. Following the evaluation of the Hawk in 1975, at that time still under development, it would be another eighteen months before the contract was awarded to HSA, by then British Aerospace, for fifty aircraft, (designated Mk 51, the low mark number reflecting the long gestation period of the order) although it came with strings. The first batch of aircraft would be assembled at Dunsfold and delivered in early 1981 but later Hawks would be assembled in Finland from UK-produced kits and from locally-produced components and test flown from there. Added to this arrangement was the requirement for British Aerospace to arrange a 100 per cent off-set market whereby the cost of the order would be offset by orders for Finnish goods in a global market. Thanks to the tireless work of Colin Chandler and Ambrose Barber, this was achieved and indeed exceeded although much effort was expended in making it possible. As the first aircraft were assembled, Finnish engineers joined the Dunsfold engineering team; luckily conversations were conducted in English which many of them spoke, since no-one at Dunsfold had even a sprinkling of Finnish!

The Finnish aircraft were the last of the 50-Series; future orders would feature the '60-Series' Hawk with uprated engine – the Adour 861, of 5,700lb thrust, improved wing dressing featuring the 'three mini-fence' arrangement and upgraded wheels and tyres for 'hot and high operations' – the first order being for the newly independent Rhodesia, now to be known as Zimbabwe. This order was for eight Mk 60 aircraft, serialled 600 to 607, and the first four were delivered in July 1982 following due ceremony at Dunsfold. Pomp and ceremony notwithstanding, ten days after arrival in Zimbabwe, the aircraft were attacked by unknown insurgents who placed explosive devices down the engine intakes to cause considerable damage. The attack at the Thornhill base of the Air Force of Zimbabwe destroyed seven Hawker Hunters, a Cessna and one of the new Hawks, which was never replaced. Another Hunter and the other three Hawks were damaged although one Hawk was repaired locally and the other two returned, initially to Dunsfold, for repair. In the aftermath of the attack, elements within the government sought to lay the blame with white air force personnel and a number were arrested and tortured during what became an international *cause célèbre*. Ultimately all the detained servicemen obtained their release and left the country for new lives elsewhere. As the second batch of aircraft was nearing completion and preparation for the ferry flight to Zimbabwe,

G-HAWK fitted with ferry tanks. The maximum pitch angle attainable without dragging the tanks along the ground on take-off is being determined in the Experimental Hangar. (BAE Systems, courtesy of Brooklands Museum)

concerns about further attack were raised when a certain former Rhodesian Air Force pilot appeared and showed rather more interest than was prudent, including a phone call to Dunsfold. In the event, Dunsfold security was stepped up and the aircraft were eventually delivered safely.[6]

The next series of orders were for various Arabian countries and comprised modest numbers; the first of these was again subject to secrecy, being designated only 'Project 4B' and totalled eight Mk 61 Hawks serialled 501 to 508 destined for Dubai and delivered in 1983, plus an additional attrition replacement, coded 509, delivered in 1988. These were followed by sixteen Mk 63s for Abu Dhabi, serialled 1001 to 1016 and delivered through 1984 and 1985. Next came twelve Hawk Mk 64s for Kuwait serialled 140 to 151, delivered in 1985 and 1986 and, lastly, thirty Mk 65 aircraft for Saudi Arabia serialled 2110 to 2121 and 3751 to 3768 and delivered between October 1987 and October 1988. The last of the 60-series to be built at Dunsfold was to fulfil an order from Switzerland for twenty Mk 66 aircraft although only the first Hawk, H-1251, ZG974, was assembled and flown at Dunsfold in October 1989, the remainder being exported as kits for local assembly in Switzerland.

Unlike the RAF Hawks, the export aircraft carried a braking parachute for use in conditions where braking might be a problem. Testing of the system at Dunsfold had revealed that deployment of the chute caused the aircraft to yaw on landing and, therefore, the flight test engineer was stationed in the undershoot at the end of the runway to film the aircraft as it landed.

Mark Gerrard pulled the short straw:

> After a few [landings], Andy Jones, (Hawk Project Pilot), decided that it wasn't very safe having chaps in the undershoot area whilst aircraft were landing, so I changed the technique to set the camera to constant run as the aircraft was on short final and then run for the edge of the runway. There was some amusement in the pilot's office from watching a couple of Flight Test Engineers (I had an assistant sometimes) bravely running away … . It was clear that for some reason the parachute was off to one side, and this could have been the cause of the yaw.[7]

Since the braking chute would be used on the Finnish Hawks in wet and freezing conditions, it was decided that testing should be conducted to ensure chute behaviour in those conditions would be as normal. Mark Gerrard described the ensuing test.

> The possibility of the parachute becoming wet and freezing in its bay was considered to be a real risk, and it was decided that a suitable test should be performed.
>
> The plan was to give the brake parachute a good soaking, then install the wet package in the aircraft, take off and climb to 30,000 feet. The aircraft would then cruise around for a good long time to get the parachute pack cold and potentially freeze it. The aircraft would then return to Dunsfold and land as quickly as possible to ensure that if the parachute had become frozen it would still be so on landing. That would give us our best chance of determining whether cold soak and potential icing inhibited correct deployment of the parachute. This was duly done, with Jim Hawkins as the pilot and [Gerrard] as the [ground-based this time] Flight Test Engineer. Soaking and loading the parachute, take off, climb, cruise and descent all went without a hitch. On landing, Jim selected the parachute to stream, and there was no deployment. So it looked very much like the parachute did not care to be frozen, but of course we had to check back at the flight line. After a rapid

shutdown the brake parachute bay was duly opened, revealing the absence of the parachute. Jim became rather heated about this and accused us all, especially the Flight Test Engineer, of incompetence. Clearly we had failed to install the parachute; there could be no other explanation. This was not the case, however. The ground crew had installed the parachute in the bay and closed the door, observed by the FTE.

That left only one possibility; that the parachute door had somehow come open in flight and the parachute had fallen out. The brake parachute mechanism was specifically designed such that the parachute was secured to the airframe only on deployment, so if there were to be an inadvertent opening of the door the parachute would fall away. The mystery was that if the door had opened in flight, then how did it come to be closed on landing?

It was thought by some that a peculiarity of the airflow round the tail cone could have been responsible, and to investigate this potential phenomenon a special test was set up. The subject aircraft was to take off with the brake parachute door open, and climb away and accelerate as normal. A chase aircraft with a photographer would film the flight. Sure enough, as the test aircraft accelerated with the door open, the door was seen to close and, of course, the event was recorded on film. The parachute door remained closed throughout the remainder of the flight and landing. I cannot remember at what speed the door closed, and I cannot remember whether we ever repeated the wet parachute pack tests, but I suspect we did and the result was satisfactory. I suspect, although I don't know for sure, that those who thought there were some peculiarities about the airflow round the back of the aeroplane were vindicated.[8]

As the construction of the last RAF Hawk T. 1s ran its course at Dunsfold in 1982 with XX353 delivered on 9 February 1982, so plans developed to upgrade the aircraft from the Tactical Weapons Unit at Brawdy, and later Chivenor, to T. 1A standard. This requirement arose out of a request to British Aerospace from the Ministry of Defence on 4 April 1978 to offer a scheme to provide a maximum of ninety Hawk aircraft with a 'War Role' operational capability following initial discussions between the company and the Ministry for a 'Close Support' role for the Hawk in 1975. Central to the requirement was the ability to carry and release AIM-9G, later AIM-9L, Sidewinder air-to-air missiles and BL-755 cluster bombs on the inboard pylons with a Stage-2 proposal to carry drop tanks on the inboard pylons and Sidewinders or cluster bombs on the outboard pylons. Also included were upgrades to navigational and radio systems and new external lighting.[9]

In the event, only Stage-1 works were authorised, the close support role changes being omitted, the modifications to cover air-to-air requirements only. With a T. 1 completed on XX339 by 1982, the first aircraft, XX219, returned to Dunsfold in February 1983 and was followed by a further eighty-seven aircraft including ten Red Arrow Hawks. The modification works proved to be straightforward, allowing a quick turnaround of approximately six weeks for each aircraft, the last Hawk being XX256 which had arrived in February 1986 sporting the new 'Air Defence' grey paint scheme.

As the last war-role Hawk flew out, work quickly turned to the arrival at Dunsfold of the fuselage for the latest iteration of the Hawk family – the Hawk 200. The aircraft would stand normal practice on its head; instead of manufacturing a two-seat trainer from a single-seat fighter, British Aerospace would reverse the practice and produce a single-seat fighter from a trainer.

The idea of a single-seat version of the Hawk to provide a 'cheap' lightweight fighter/ground attack aircraft for nations with a modest defence budget had been around for some years and several attempts were made to bring the idea to fruition. Initial design studies for a single-seat version had been made in the mid-1970s, mainly revolving around the possible front fuselage changes required to produce a successful design. These were not proceeded with and the idea was mothballed. Then, in the late 1970s, further design work was carried out with the more powerful Adour 861 as the engine of choice but, again, with no funding available, the idea was dropped. Finally, in 1982, another design study was instigated to provide for an aircraft with increased firepower including integral twin cannon and provision for radar, 60-series engine and MIL-STD 1553 databus and, from this, private funding was made available in late-1983 for the construction of a single aircraft designated Hawk 200.

Work began at Kingston on the finalised design and manufacture, the bare fuselage arriving at Dunsfold in early 1986. A three-shift system of working was instituted on this aircraft only, to have it flightworthy for its inaugural appearance at that year's Farnborough display. The Hawk 200 was the first Kingston-designed aircraft to be fitted with a digital databus system to link the various avionics kits together; the first two aircraft also featured

Finnish Hawk Mk.51 HW319 in the turn-over rig, used to rotate the fuselage to remove foreign object debris prior to moving to final assembly, June 1982. (Author's collection)

built-in cannon armament, not seen at Dunsfold since the days of the Hunter, although these were deleted on production aircraft. First flight of the new aircraft, serialled ZG200, on 19 May 1986 was an incredible effort by all concerned at Kingston and Dunsfold, Chief Test Pilot Mike Snelling taking to the air for the one-hour-eighteen-minute flight. Work continued to bring the aircraft up to a peak of performance ready for the Farnborough Air Show under Project Pilot Jim Hawkins but, prior to Farnborough, it was planned to unveil the aircraft to the world at a special press day in early July. To this end Hawkins continued to polish his display, using the old eastern runway as his display axis. The light weight of the Hawk, certain avionics and weapons fits being absent from the first aircraft, and the uprated engine gave the aircraft a sprightly performance, utilised to the full in Hawkins' display manoeuvres, in particular, the ability to carry out high sustained G manoeuvring at low level.

On 2 July 1986, the day prior to the unveiling of the aircraft, Hawkins was again in the air to finalise his display, but this time using a new display axis. This was because a Finnish delegation was visiting and was keen to witness the performance of the Hawk from the senior mess on the north side of the airfield. At around 11.20am, following a series of tight rolling manoeuvres, the Hawk, in pulling through a loop, failed to complete the pull-out before hitting the ground to the south, just outside the aerodrome, destroying the aircraft and killing Hawkins instantly. While the subsequent inquest found a likely cause of death as due to 'g-loc' or G-induced loss of consciousness, the instrumentation traces suggested that the aircraft was in fact under control up to the point of impact. Whatever the cause of the crash, British Aerospace and Dunsfold had lost a respected and well-liked pilot, the first for the Kingston/Dunsfold sites since 'Wimpey' Wade's death in 1951. With the enquiry into the accident finding no fault with the aircraft, the BAe board decided to fund a further Hawk 200, which took to the air for the first time from Dunsfold on 24 April 1987, serialled ZH200.[10]

In tandem with work to develop the 200-series Hawk, work was also undertaken to produce the 100-series of aircraft. Development of this concept was centred at Dunsfold on G-HAWK and comprised a remodelled nose section grafted onto and over the original nose. An important milestone was the proving of the new long-nosed version aerodynamically and for spin clearance. G-HAWK first flew in the 100-series configuration on 1 October 1987, although as an aerodynamic prototype rather than with the full avionics kit. The finalised 100-series aircraft – the programme was completed at Warton – featured retention of two seats and upgrades to avionics and sensors to produce a capability to fit FLIR and laser sensors, RWR equipment, uprated Adour 871, MIL-STD 1553B databus and revised cockpit layout to provide MFDs and HOTAS controls.

Perhaps the greatest achievement for the Hawk and, at the time, for British Aerospace, was the successful sale of a Hawk derivative to the US Navy. This incredible result, in the face of intense competition both from Europe and from indigenous US companies, was all the more remarkable when one remembers that the US armed forces very seldom bought foreign aircraft; yet not only did they buy the Hawk, but the Harrier as well. This was an achievement for Kingston and Dunsfold that was of global significance, yet was missed or ignored by the UK press. It is not intended to dwell at length on the programme that resulted in the T-45 Goshawk since little of the work was carried out there. However, Dunsfold was central to efforts to complete the sale in several ways.

The programme for a trainer aircraft and associated systems for the US Navy to replace the Douglas A-4 Skyhawk in the training regime was called VTX-TS and, as is the way of things in the United States, was conducted over a period of years during which various company submissions were analysed and aircraft intensively studied. To accommodate access to the

Hawk, Dunsfold pilots were instrumental in ferrying the Hawk demonstrator G-HAWK to the US for demonstrations and familiarisation for the US Navy. Jim Hawkins and Chris Roberts flew across the Atlantic in May 1981 in G-HAWK to allow a closer acquaintance with the basic Hawk for decision makers and those with influence in the procurement process. Further flights to the US were made by Hawkins and Taylor Scott and by Roberts and Paul Hopkins on the third visit in 1986, along with Heinz Frick who joined the team later in the US.

At Dunsfold in 1983, as part of the work to support the BAe submission, work was carried out on take-off and landing procedures to fly the flight paths required for recovery to carrier decks as the US Navy Hawk would need to be carrier compatible and to this end a dummy carrier deck was marked out at the west end of Dunsfold's runway, equipped with a mirror landing sight which allowed a landing trajectory to be acquired by the pilot and the aircraft's glideslope to be monitored by a deck officer. Chris Roberts was heavily involved in the VTX-TS T-45 programme and recalls

> the no-flare landing using the mirror landing aid installed at Dunsfold. This was all about the difference between the way an Air Force pilot lands and the way a Navy pilot lands, and the implications on aircraft strength with regard to the vertical velocity on touch down. Simply put, if you could fly the Hawk slowly enough on the approach, it was strong enough to just drive it in without flare – but could you do this thousands of times without breaking it and how hard would too hard have to be?

To this end, G-HAWK was flown onto the runway using the mirror sight as would a pilot on carrier approach. Roberts again:

> The trial was to use the accurate glidepath at typical T-45 speeds and land without flare, as per a deck arrival. Proving that Hawk could fly the mirror approach without improved handling characteristics (that were considered necessary by some doubters) was important as was the data about the rate of descent on landing.

The outcome of this and other flight trials flown by Dunsfold's pilots was the successful sale of Hawk, named in the US T-45 Goshawk, to the US Navy, some 221 aircraft being manufactured jointly by BAe and MDC.

HAWKER SIDDELEY ENTER THE TRAINER MARKET

In the summer of 1988, both G-HAWK and ZH200 left the UK to participate in a global sales campaign in the Far East which encompassed displays in Australia as part of the country's bi-centennial celebrations. The tour was considered a great success with minimal problems with aircraft maintenance. However, on their return to the UK in October 1988, the aircraft were flown, not to Dunsfold, but to the company's airfield at Warton in Lancashire where a decision had been made to remove Hawk production from Dunsfold. Henceforth, all Hawk work would be based at Warton, the claim being made that Dunsfold could not cope with both Hawk and Harrier work. That Dunsfold had coped very well with combined Harrier and Hawk production for the past ten years was quietly forgotten, the decision being seen at Dunsfold as a purely political one intended to keep Warton in work at the expense of the southern sites. It was perhaps this decision which convinced staff at Kingston and Dunsfold that the political tectonics of the company were on the move. Henceforth, Dunsfold would have to rely on future Harrier orders for its survival.

Chapter 11

Harrier goes to War

A central tenet of the philosophy being generated at Kingston to 'explain' the reason for P.1127 in the 1960s was flexibility of operation; principally, this point was aimed at NATO air forces, but what was good for land-based aircraft surely also applied to the ship-borne variety? In the event, the specification for a naval P.1154 variant issued by the Admiralty was an endorsement of this truism, although internal politics meant that the demise of the large carrier that was implicit in acceptance of VSTOL at sea assured that the aircraft had a fierce struggle to be accepted. To many in the Royal Navy at the time, the aircraft carrier was seen as the embodiment of the UK's naval power and P.1154 threatened this. It also threatened plans for a new fleet of 'super-carriers', exemplified by CVA-01, that the Admiralty was battling to get laid down. Eventually, even plans for just a single new carrier were abandoned by the same Labour government that had earlier cancelled P.1154 and TSR.2, the assumption being that the RAF would provide cover for the Royal Navy globally, wherever required. With such ridiculous claims ringing in its ears, the Admiralty had to plan for a future that did not include a fixed-wing element although a purchase of F-4 Phantoms was allowed as a stop-gap and operated from HMS *Ark Royal* into the 1970s.

Of the existing carriers, *Victorious* was decommissioned in 1968, *Ark Royal* would be decommissioned in 1979, *Eagle* would be mothballed as a spares source for *Ark Royal* and *Hermes* was downgraded to a commando carrier to join HM Ships *Bulwark* and *Albion* in that role.

Notwithstanding the unlikelihood of the Fleet Air Arm continuing to field fixed-wing aircraft at sea, trials continued through the 1960s and early 1970s using Harriers to explore the opportunities for shipboard deployment. As early as 1963, in pursuit of the P.1154 project, XP831 had carried out a series of trials aboard *Ark Royal* at the hands of Bedford and Merewether, neither of whom had ever flown from a carrier previously. This was followed by trials aboard the commando carrier HMS *Bulwark* in 1966 with P.1127 XP984 by Bedford and RAE personnel and, in 1969,

198

with a Harrier GR.1, XV758. In August that year, a trial aboard the cruiser HMS *Blake* with Harrier GR.1 XV742, flying from the aft helicopter platform, presented no difficulties for the pilot. Later, in March 1970, further trials were completed aboard HMS *Eagle* as part of a plan to deploy RAF Harriers aboard the carriers as a component of future amphibious forces. Clearly, use of Harriers at sea would not present any insuperable problems, rather – as in the case of the US Marine Corps – the aircraft was shown to be eminently suited to a shipboard environment from where it could project a formidable presence at the battlefront.

Come what may, with the planned retirement of *Ark Royal* in the early 1970s and loss of her Phantoms and Buccaneers to the RAF, the Admiralty started planning replacements in the form of 'Through Deck Cruisers' to mount a squadron of anti-submarine helicopters. Displacing some 20,000 tons, the new 'cruisers' would have the ability to host RAF Harriers if required, but any mention of aircraft carriers was studiously avoided. The first of the new class, HMS *Invincible*, was launched in May 1977. Parallel to the fortunes of *Invincible*, two significant developments had occurred that would reap handsome rewards a few years later; firstly, the invention and development of the 'ski-ramp' or ski-jump as it was better known.

DB Harrier XV277 at Dunsfold with modified 'radar' nose and twin Martel anti-radiation/anti-ship missiles, May 1973. This radar and anti-ship package would form part of the Sea Harrier weapons system. (BAE Systems, courtesy of Brooklands Museum)

This device could be constructed at the forward end of a carrier's flight deck and, by imparting an upward trajectory to aircraft taking off, offer significant benefits in load-carrying ability. This would be particularly valuable when the aircraft in question had V/STOL capability – such as the Harrier. The second significant event was the agreement by the Treasury in 1971 that the Admiralty could pursue a version of the Harrier optimised for the maritime environment, although whether flown by RAF or Navy pilots, was not made clear. As one might expect in any missive from HM Treasury, the design was to be 'minimum change, minimum cost' and therefore could only encompass modest alterations.

The changes were required, firstly, to replace any components susceptible to saltwater corrosion and, secondly, to make the aircraft fit for service in its new designation – Fighter, Strike, Reconnaissance. To enhance its fighter role, the aircraft was restructured forward of the air intakes to accommodate a raised cockpit, improving rearward view and creating space for extra equipment and a re-contoured nose to take Blue Fox, a mono-pulse radar optimised for sea search with limited look-down ability, linked to a Ferranti navigation system tied to a Doppler radar. The design also embodied facilities to carry and fire AIM-9 Sidewinder air-to-air missiles and later, Sea Eagle – an advanced sea-skimming anti-ship missile. For the strike role, HSA would for the first time be designing an aircraft for carriage of nuclear weapons. The Sea Harrier would be capable of delivering the WE177 nuclear depth charge for use against enemy fleets, Sea Eagle or a range of standard bombs. The reconnaissance role was covered by carriage of a Vinten F95 camera on the starboard forward fuselage. The opportunity was also taken to completely revise the aircraft electrical system; the wiring used on the earlier Harriers – PTFE in 'lay-flat' sleeving – while adequate in the 1960s, was outdated and was replaced with cable looms of new, hardened material run in segregated bundles through the airframe.

The ski-jump was the subject of a thesis by one Lieutenant Commander Douglas Taylor in 1972 at Southampton University. Further study and funding from HSA led in 1976 to a study contract from MoD to HSA to build a ramp for practical testing. Rather than build this at Dunsfold, John Farley felt it would be more cost effective to build it at RAE Bedford to enable that establishment's scientists to be more closely involved.[1] Another of Dunsfold's DB Harriers, XV281, was used and completed the first trial launches in August 1977 with the ramp set at six degrees although later, angles of up to 20 degrees were tested. With the contract for Sea Harriers now a firm commitment, work began to retrofit a seven-degree ski-jump to HMS *Invincible*. Later, the next ship in the

Invincible-class – HMS *Illustrious* – would also gain a seven-degree ramp while *Ark Royal*, the last of the class would gain a 12-degree ramp as would HMS *Hermes*, converted back from a commando carrier.

With contract go-ahead received by HSA in May 1975 for twenty-four Sea Harrier FRS.1 aircraft – another ten aircraft were added in 1978 – the first three of which would act as development aircraft, production quickly got under way at Kingston with additional labour drafted in from Dunsfold. First flight was achieved at Dunsfold by XZ450 on 20 August 1978 by John Farley, this aircraft being used at the following week's Farnborough Air Show to demonstrate use of the ski-jump, specially constructed for the show. As part of the contract, two Hunter T.8 aircraft were modified at HSA Brough to T.8M standard with the Sea Harrier radar system to enable them to be used for systems development and, later, as weapons trainers with a third aircraft later modified to assist in the work. XL602 would spend a great deal of its new life at Dunsfold being used for a variety of trials and as a chase aircraft.

The first Sea Harrier FRS.1 was officially handed over to the Royal Navy on 18 June 1979. After the ceremony the aircraft, XZ451, was towed out of the flight shed onto the perimeter track from where, to the surprise of some and the panic of others, mainly journalists who had strayed too close, Mike Snelling took the Harrier off in a short take off to provide a spirited display for the assembled throng.

Sea Harrier FRS.1 XZ450, the first Sea Harrier to fly, in 1978, shown here on Dunsfold's flight line carrying Sea Eagle anti-shipping missile and sidewinder AIM-9G infra-red homing missiles. (BAE Image Systems, courtesy of Brooklands Museum)

As the number of available Sea Harriers increased, so they were made available to Boscombe Down and to the Sea Harrier Intensive Flying Trials Unit, otherwise known as 700A Squadron, under Lieutenant Commander 'Sharkey' Ward at RNAS Yeovilton. Ward, later CO of No. 801 Squadron, was considered by many to be 'Mr Sea-Harrier' since he had been involved with the procurement plan as an MoD desk officer prior to being given command of the first squadron of aircraft and, therefore, had an intimate knowledge of just what the Navy had acquired. As the FAA got to grips with its new aircraft, it quickly came to realise just what a capable aircraft the Sea Harrier was. Once 700A Squadron had completed its work, the pilots and aircraft were redistributed to form Nos. 800 and 801 Squadrons and No. 899 HQ and Training Squadron.

Also used for pilot training was Dunsfold's G-VTOL, which participated at Boscombe Down. Chris Roberts, recently arrived at Dunsfold from the RAF, was instrumental in this work, his excellent training including that of another future Dunsfold test pilot, Lieutenant Commander Rod Frederiksen.[2]

Type Operational Trials aboard *Hermes* during 1979-80 involved a variety of Sea Harriers, both those released to squadron use and those retained by Dunsfold for the various trials required to clear new systems. Present also

Hunter T.8M XL602 modified to allow training and development of Sea Harrier FRS.1 avionics package. Dunsfold, June 1990. (Author's collection)

was G-VTOL, allowing shipboard ski-jump training and familiarisation to be completed with the comfort of a safety pilot aboard the aircraft.

As the last few Sea Harrier deliveries were awaited from Dunsfold to Yeovilton in early 1982, one of those completely unexpected events occurred that would forever change the way that the world viewed the Harrier. In early April 1982 the dictatorship governing Argentina at that time sought to deflect internal unrest caused by government mismanagement of the economy by invading the British Protectorate of the Falkland Islands, some 300 miles off the coast of the mainland. With just a couple of days' notice of Argentina's intentions, the British government under Margaret Thatcher was caught on the hop and could do little to prevent the illegal seizure. However, with British territory under the control of a foreign power, the government did not wait long to order the islands liberated and a task force from the Royal Navy to sail with all speed to accomplish this.

Argentina, confident that it had read the signs of British disinterest correctly, was sure that the fait accompli would be accepted and massive demonstrations of support for the dictatorship erupted all over Argentina. It was clear to the UK government that air power would be key to regaining a foothold on the Falklands prior to any liberation force landing and, with that foremost in their minds, a taskforce slipped out of Portsmouth with HMS *Invincible*, and HMS *Hermes* as the flagship. Sea Harriers were flown onto the carriers at Portsmouth shortly before sailing and others joined both carriers as they slowly steamed south, followed in May by Harrier GR.3 aircraft from the RAF.

Meanwhile at Kingston and Dunsfold events moved quickly. Recognising that the main threat to the taskforce would be from the air, at Kingston work was started quickly on the design and construction of twin sidewinder pylon attachments to allow for up to four of the missiles to be carried in combat. At Dunsfold work was speeded up on the last two Sea Harriers still under construction, while Dunsfold's trials aircraft were prepared for despatch to Yeovilton to assist in pilot training. Also detached to Yeovilton was Lieutenant Commander Taylor Scott, one of the most recent test pilot arrivals at Dunsfold and still a Royal Navy reservist.

The Sea Harrier test fleet at Dunsfold was quickly despatched to the Royal Navy, XZ450 to HMS *Hermes* and XZ438, XZ439 to Yeovilton, later to be joined by XZ440. On arrival at Yeovilton, XZ438 was quickly utilised to test carriage of 330-gallon 'ferry' fuel tanks, which were considered important in any future efforts to reinforce the carrier squadrons. Concerns regarding the safety of the tanks appeared confirmed when XZ438 crashed

Sea Harrier FRS.1 XZ497 with Sea Eagle and twin Sidewinder launcher, developed in haste during the Falklands War. Note the post-Falklands toned-down colour scheme. (BAE Systems, courtesy of Brooklands Museum)

at Yeovilton on 17 May while taking off from the practice ski-jump due to a fuel imbalance. Mark Gerrard, the flight test engineer responsible for the aircraft described the events.

> The MoD had a requirement to clear ski jumping with the 330-gallon ferry drop tanks as part of support to the Falkland Islands campaign. The trial was run by A&AEE Boscombe Down … with support from BAe. That support comprised two FTE, John Edwards and myself, and one pilot (Mike Snelling). We had pretty much got to the end of the trial, with one flight left to do. The last flight was to be a take-off with full tanks, for performance and heavy weight handling characteristics, followed by a series of launches with mis-set trims for completeness of the flying qualities work, for which the tanks would be empty. The plan was that after take-off the aircraft would head out over the sea and dump fuel to empty the drop tanks in order to reduce to a sensible landing weight and get set up for the mis-trimmed portion of the test. Take off and climb out were completed without incident, and the pilot

proceeded to dump fuel as briefed. The ferry drop tanks were not gauged, so the only way to tell if they were empty was to dump fuel until the internal fuel gauge started to show a reduction, thus indicating that the drop tanks were empty. This was accomplished, and return to Yeovilton and landing were completed without incident.

Then it all went wrong. On the next ski jump launch, when the aircraft left the end of the ramp it began a roll to the right. As the bank angle increased the pilot ejected and the aircraft hit the ground in about a 90-degree bank with a small fire, a big bang and a large cloud of black smoke. The pilot [Lieutenant Commander David Poole] made, I think, one and a half swings on his parachute before reaching the ground. That was the end of XZ438.

The subsequent enquiry established that the cause of the accident was asymmetric loading of the aircraft, in excess of the ability of the flight-control system to keep the wings level, resulting from the starboard drop tank being almost completely full of fuel. There had been a fuel transfer failure of the starboard side, and thus when the pilot observed the internal fuel gauge reading decrease, only the port drop tank had emptied. It was interesting that the asymmetry hadn't been noticed by the pilot on landing, and there was no telemetry in those days for FTE monitoring. The board also found, if I remember correctly, that whilst accomplishing a trial of this nature with non-gauged drop tanks would normally be considered too risky, the urgency of getting the work done, because of the Falklands crisis, made the approach justifiable.

As a footnote, 330-gallon drop tanks were not cleared for ski jump take offs because the overall flying qualities in that configuration were considered to be unsatisfactory.[3]

XZ450 would also be lost, indeed was the first casualty of the Falklands War, when it was shot down over Goose Green by ground fire and the pilot Lieutenant Nick Taylor was killed. The aircraft had been the Sea Eagle trials aircraft and was therefore fully fitted for firing of the missile. Since the aircraft crashed on land, this information was then clearly in the hands of the Argentinian forces and it has been suggested, although never proved, that the assumption was made that all Sea Harriers had this capability and the Argentinian aircraft carrier, *Veinticinco de Mayo*, was moved well away from the taskforce.

It is not the intention here to recapitulate the story of the Falklands War which has been well told elsewhere but its importance to British Aerospace, the Royal Navy and to the Harrier itself cannot be understated.

By the time of the surrender of the Argentine forces, some twenty-eight Sea Harriers had taken part in the action together with fourteen RAF Harrier GR.3s. Losses of Sea Harriers amounted to six aircraft, of which two were to ground fire and four to accidents; none were attributable to air-to-air combat. Also lost were three Harrier GR.3s, all to ground fire. Against these losses should be balanced the loss of around 120 Argentine aircraft of which twenty-three were shot down by Sea Harriers. The success of the Sea Harrier as a fighter, while surprising to some in the military aviation world, did not surprise 'Sharkey' Ward. In the three years since the Royal Navy had taken delivery of the aircraft, a number of trials had been flown against the best fighters available. In the majority of engagements, the Harrier had come out on top, even against the F-15 (loss ratio 7:1) and F-5s of the USAF aggressor squadrons; against the F-4 Phantom, the RAF loss rate

Sea Harrier Mk 51 for India under construction in the Production Hangar, June 1982. (Author's collection)

was an embarrassing 25:1! The Harrier's incredible manoeuvrability and small size, coupled with the low exhaust signature, made it a very difficult target in any combat. When added to the professional training provided to RN and RAF pilots, the combination was a tough one to beat. The last word may safely be left to Admiral Sir Henry Leach, First Sea Lord: 'Without Sea Harrier there could have been no Task Force.'

As the unpleasantness in the South Atlantic receded, testing of the Sea Harrier at Dunsfold continued at a slower pace. One of the many requirements generated by the Navy Department, MoD was for a demonstration to determine the maximum weight at which the aircraft could maintain a hover. Calculations were made by flight test which suggested that with a 3,000lb load a steady hover should be feasible. Development Sea Harrier XZ497 was duly loaded with 1,000lb fuel each side and a 1,000lb inert bomb on the centreline pylon and, on 10 September 1982, Heinz Frick was given the task of demonstrating the hover. Having got airborne, Frick brought the aircraft round into the hover, established a nice steady position and checked off the engine temperatures – all was good – demonstration over. Because the Sea Harrier was too heavy to actually land from the hover, Frick started to move forward to transition the aircraft into normal flight for a conventional landing but, as he did so, the Harrier started to sink alarmingly and, as the ground came closer, he had to do something drastic or hit terra-firma. He took the only logical action and released the 1,000lb bomb which hit the ground beside the runway, allowing him to climb away for a successful and uneventful landing. On his return to the office

> I was called in to see the boss who had a stern look on his face. 'Nice job,' he said, 'pity you didn't drop the bloody bomb on the Production Manager's office.' Said manager ruled with a stern hand, was not too popular but ensured a most successful and safe Sea Harrier production run. Yet another contributor to the success of Dunsfold and the war in the south Atlantic.

For British Aerospace, and particularly Dunsfold, the most immediate effect of the Falklands War was the ordering of additional aircraft to replace the attrition encountered as part of the conflict. Between 1985 and 1988 some twenty-three new Sea Harriers were built at Dunsfold, together with four additional Harrier GR.3s and four T.4s for the RAF. As part of the new Sea Harrier order, immediate lessons learnt as a result of the Falklands conflict were embodied. The Phase 1 updates included the installation of AN/ALE

40 chaff and flare dispensers aft of the airbrake, addition of MADGE – Microwave Aircraft Digital Guidance Equipment – provision for Sea Eagle and twin Sidewinder carriage and introduction of twin electrical generators.

The additional Sea Harriers were not delivered to Yeovilton, being diverted instead to RAF St Athan in South Wales which had taken on the role of Services Modification Centre where the aircraft could have role equipment installed prior to despatch when required. In February 1988 a call was received from St Athan regarding electrical problems on ZE693, including non-functioning fuel flow, water injection and OAT displays. While St Athan were happy to question the workmanship at Dunsfold, it was equally clear that the circuits must have been functioning during ground and flight testing. Investigation confirmed serious problems with the electrical systems centred around a number of open circuits and suspicion fell on rodent activity within the cable ducts while the aircraft was in storage in a fairly remote hangar on the base. It was left to base personnel to rectify the faults so the full story of just what caused the problems was never revealed.

Just prior to the entry of the Sea Harrier into operational service, the second batch of Harrier GR.3s, ordered in 1978 were being finalised at Dunsfold. December 1981 saw the pilots busy clearing the PFTS for those aircraft in an effort to complete as many as possible before the end of the

Indian Sea Harrier Mk 51s IN616 to IN619 awaiting delivery, Dunsfold, April 1991. (Author's collection)

208

year – to please the accountants. There were twenty-four aircraft in the batch for delivery, although it was nearly only twenty-three. Heinz Frick takes up the story.

I did the first flight in Harrier XZ994 on 18th December and reported numerous snags. The jet was then worked on around Christmas and eventually pushed back on the line in the afternoon of New Year's Eve … . Eventually when the acceleration times (of the engine) were within fractions of a second correct, the jet was deemed ready to go. So in the afternoon of 31st December I got airborne, knowing that the only airfield open on New Year's Eve was Dunsfold … .

The take-off and climb proceeded normally towards the west. As I passed 35,000 feet there [was] a series of loud explosions from the engine, engine RPM decayed and jet pipe temperature shot up at an alarming rate. I immediately shut the engine down and commenced gliding at 250 knots. Gliding like a brick sxxt house must have been invented for the Harrier or maybe the F-104 and altitude was lost rapidly.

After a brief word with Air Traffic I commenced a relight, a procedure I knew well from my engine test days and, as luck would have it, the engine responded. I gently turned east and slowly increased engine RPM in an attempt to gain more height. Approaching 30,000 feet another series of bangs came from the engine and I knew the jet was not going to fly much longer. I throttled the engine to idle and began a descent towards the only runway I knew that would take a gliding Harrier – Boscombe Down. There was no need to call them since I knew they were shut, the radar controller wished me luck and I proceeded with my glide approach. I settled in the glide and joined the downwind leg at 10,000 feet, slowly increased speed to 250 knots to maintain adequate elevator control. I reduced speed to 80 knots just prior to touch down with the stick fully back and the aircraft proceeded to bounce on its main wheels like a wild bronco. I could of course only apply wheel brakes … and managed to use all 3,000 yards of runway.

Pleased to be on the ground I surveyed the scene, made the ejection seat safe ... and then slid down the wing. It was quickly getting dark and I waited a few minutes for some help. None came of course and I slowly started to walk towards habitation almost a mile away to phone base. I reached the main gate which was shut, but there was a light in the police post. The conversation went something like this:

Pilot: Anybody home?

Policeman: What the fxxx are you doing here? Sarge … there is a bloke dressed as a pilot on the wrong side of the fence!

Sarge: Tell him to get back over the fence; the fancy dress do in the mess doesn't start till 8pm.

Pilot: No, you don't understand, I have just landed and I need to get to a phone.

Policeman: You could not have done, the bloody airfield is shut.

Pilot: No, I have had a bit of a problem with a Harrier; it's on the airfield.

Policeman: We all have bloody problems with Harriers, noisy fxxxing things.

Pilot: Could I have a word with the Sergeant?

Policeman: Sarge, he wants a word with you … thinks he just landed a silent Harrier.

The sergeant now drags himself away from the telly greatly annoyed and peers through the fence.

Sarge: Hello Mr Frick, what are you doing here?

Policeman: Was he the one that went supersonic and broke the Arm Div windows? (Armament Division – a previous stunt in a Lightning).

We all burst out laughing, I much relieved, the Sergeant intrigued to find a Harrier somewhere in the dark and the policeman happy that he had kept Boscombe Down safe.

Meanwhile, back to Sea Harrier.

Delivery of the new batch of RN Sea Harriers and RAF GR.3s and T.4s was broadly complete by 1988, while a rather more significant Phase II update had been coming to fruition since 1983 during negotiations between BAe and the MoD. This was again as a result of the fortunes of the Sea Harrier during the Falklands conflict, during which it had become apparent that the Blue Fox radar had poor resolution when scanning in look-down mode and over land and, having acquired a target, the only effective missile available was the short-range AIM-9 Sidewinder.

The Sea Harrier Mid-Life Update (MLU) would produce a far more capable aircraft embodying a new pulse doppler multi-mode radar called Blue Vixen with enhanced look-down shoot-down and track while scan capability. This frequency-agile radar system was extremely jam-resistant and could interface with the Hughes AIM-120 AMRAAM BVR (beyond visual range) missile. Also included was a MIL-STD 1553B databus controlling the aircraft electronic systems. Externally, the aircraft would have an additional 13.75-inch plug inserted in the fuselage aft of the wing to enlarge the avionics bay, a revised leading edge to the wing and a re-profiled nose to accommodate the new radar scanner. The result of these changes would be the Sea Harrier FRS.2, one of the most advanced aircraft systems of its time.

Work on the new aircraft began with the withdrawal of ZA195, only delivered in 1984, from life as a replacement for XZ450 on Sea Eagle trials and its delivery to Kingston – airframes were structurally modified at Brough before their return south – as the first development batch aircraft (DB1). This was followed by XZ439 as DB2. ZA195 returned to Dunsfold in June 1988 and work began on the aircraft to rebuild it. The aircraft was ready for engine run by mid-September and flew in its new guise on 19 September 1988, a forty-minute check courtesy of Heinz Frick, while XZ439 first flew as an FRS.2 in March 1989. At this time, neither aircraft had its radar system fitted since this was still under development at Dunsfold and at Ferranti in Edinburgh. The upgrades to the Sea Harrier represented a step change in the capability of the aircraft and the extensive integration of the various new systems could have presented serious delays in obtaining CA release. To obviate this, an HS.125-600B executive jet was obtained and given the military serial ZF130, to be fitted out as a flying test-bed for the radar, weapons and avionics fit that Sea Harrier FRS.2 would carry. This arrived at Dunsfold in August 1988 and was hangared in the new Flight Shed.

The HS.125 would become a unique aircraft: capable of being flown as a 125 from the left-hand seat or as a Sea Harrier FRS.2 from the right; at the rear were positions for two flight observers. Installed in the aircraft over the next six months were the full Harrier avionics fit, comprehensive instrumentation system, Sidewinder acquisition round on the starboard wing

Sea Harrier FRS.2 ZA195, the first development aircraft for the Mid-Life Update to Sea Harrier, June 1989. (Author's collection)

and an AMRAAM missile simulation system, together with an upgraded electrical-generation system to power the various sub-systems; all this kit was housed in equipment crates which replaced most of the seats in the main cabin, making for a crowded aircraft. ZF130 flew for the first time in December 1988 but spent much of its first few months being used on the ground at Dunsfold integrating the avionics and instrumentation packages with the basic aircraft systems before intensive testing could begin.

The complete flightworthy radar package was fitted for the first time in July 1989, followed by a gamut of tests to prove the system was working correctly, leading to the first transmissions on 30 August 1989 and the first radar flight in September 1989. Over the next twelve months ZF130 continued with radar development, both in the air and on the ground. Such was the importance of maintaining secrecy about the system's capabilities that transmissions had to be shut down when overflights of Russian satellites were due, timings courtesy of MoD. As each development software stage was reached and cleared, so the mods were applied to the radar system in the DB aircraft. The HS.125 radar trials continued on an almost daily basis through to 1991, with ZF130 located in a remote area of the airfield using the traffic inbound to Gatwick Airport as convenient targets. The entire trial area was surrounded by fences and warning signs which, one day, almost proved its undoing.

212

While ground running, the aircraft was powered by two large mobile diesel ground-power units supplying A.C and D.C electrical power, parked under the tailplane of the aircraft. Also located there was another diesel generator powering an air-conditioning unit used to cool the aircraft on the ground. (The mass of equipment in the aircraft fuselage generated very high temperatures on the ground; the author once measured over 40 degrees Celsius during one summer test). Surrounding the aircraft when carrying out radar testing were two chain-link fences, one delineating the 'lethal' zone and the outer the 'danger' zone from radar transmissions. Warning notices and briefings made clear to all that entry into either of the zones during transmissions was strictly forbidden due to the danger to life. All well and good until one day one of the diesel generators had a very bad day; the cooling-fan bearing seized, driving the fan through the radiator and causing the generator to lose its coolant and immediately overheat. Within minutes, the unit was smoking and threatening to burst into flames just feet from the aircraft and its fuel tanks. Unfortunately, with the unit parked to the rear of the aircraft, the aircraft crew were ignorant of what was happening and, because of the limited visibility from the aircraft, also oblivious to the entire airfield's crash crews and their tenders parked just outside the radar warning zone desperate to enter and deal with the emergency. With the aircraft radios off to prevent extraneous interference with the testing, no warning of impending doom could reach the crew.

HS-125 ZF130, heavily modified to allow airborne testing and development of the Sea Harrier FRS.2's complex radar and weapons systems, June 1992. (Author's collection)

However, luck smiled on the righteous and inside the aircraft it was decided to call it a day; the systems were shut down and the door opened for some much-needed fresh air. The unexpected sight of a grand display of flashing blue lights, emergency crash tenders and sundry men in uniform was greeted with some surprise, as was the large smoke cloud at the rear of the aircraft. Rather surprisingly, the generator was still happily producing power even as its innards melted. It was quickly shut down with little harm done.

Following this a rethink of safety procedures resulted in future testing being carried out with the aircraft in contact with ATC. Also introduced once airborne radar testing commenced was a check on the aircraft as it taxied in post-flight using a Narda, a 'Geiger-counter'-type sensor to confirm that the radar had been switched off before irradiating the ground crew. Unfortunately, it was considered that one of the ground crew could be sacrificed and it was the author who got the job of standing in front of the aircraft as it taxied in – Narda, and little else, in hand.

The extended trials aboard ZF130 were further extended by the need to carry out the normal servicing required on this type of civil aircraft, including the complete stripping down of the aircraft to enable x-ray inspection of the structure. That the first of these became due shortly after the six months spent building out the fuselage suggested a drop-off somewhere but the checks had to be completed and the cabin rebuilt again. Eventually, the trials had progressed to a point where the radar and avionics package could be trialled by Boscombe Down and the Royal Navy and so, on 20 May 1991, the aircraft was flown down to Wiltshire, with Rod Frederiksen as trials pilot, for acceptance flights to begin. It was unfortunate that the radar system decided at this point to play up and, after three abortive flights, a meeting was called to decide the future, if any, of the trial. With a further troublesome test flight, the aircraft returned to Dunsfold in an effort to rectify the problem and to carry out further aircraft servicing, not returning to Boscombe until 17 June. Thereafter, the trials were rather more successful, the aircraft eventually returning to Dunsfold on 10 July.

Meanwhile, back with the DB aircraft, by 1990 XZ439 had had its radar package fitted while ZA195 continued handling trials with the full complement of AMRAAMs – two on under-fuselage pylons in lieu of the gun pods and two on the outboard wing pylons. The next stage was for the aircraft to undertake sea trials and, to this end, it may be useful to follow the aircraft through the various stages required to achieve this.

Before trials of the Harriers aboard one of the RN aircraft carriers could begin it was first necessary to ensure that the changes made to the aircraft would not react adversely to the various radar and radio emissions which it would encounter; carrier operations can be a very busy RF environment at times. To assess this, XZ439 was flown to Boscombe Down and spent the next week in the Radio-Frequency Environment Generator (REG) being bombarded with all of the various radio and radar emissions that it would encounter from ship's sensors. Such were the high powers of the various radio systems present that the entire building housing the REG operators was encased in a steel mesh Faraday cage to deflect any harmful waves, the Dunsfold crew keeping their heads down away from the equipment. Having passed this test, the aircraft weapon circuits were also checked to ensure that no external radio sources would fire or release weapons. With the testing complete, XZ439 also spent time at RNAS Yeovilton on ski-jump trials.

All was ready for the ship trial proper, the ground crew and flight test engineers from Dunsfold and Boscombe Down boarding *Ark Royal* at Portsmouth on 6 November 1990 prior to sailing for the Western Approaches and receiving the two DB Harriers en route, flown by Rod Frederiksen and Graham Tomlinson. Both pilots were recent arrivals at Dunsfold. 'Fred' Frederiksen, a Falklands veteran, had moved to Boscombe Down to take part in the clearance trials of the Phase-1 updates including a live firing of Sea Eagle in July 1984 from XZ440 against HMS *Devonshire*. In 1985 he returned to Yeovilton as CO of 800 Squadron. At the end of his time he was moved to a non-flying role and left the service shortly after to join BAe at Dunsfold in 1988 to participate in the FRS.2 trials. Graham Tomlinson had arrived at Dunsfold in January 1986 from the RAF. Prior to his arrival he had flown Harriers with 3 Squadron in Germany and, following a course with the ETPS, joined A Squadron at Boscombe Down, flying Tornados and Sea Harriers. In 1982, Tomlinson had received a three-year posting to the US to fly the AV-8B.

Over the following two weeks, multiple flights were made by both aircraft, including night flying, to assess aircraft suitability aboard ship and also to test weapons carriage and release. Despite poor weather, the trial was a success, the two aircraft flying off for Dunsfold on 15 November. Later trials would include demonstrations of LRU (line replaceable units) changes and, in early 1993, XZ439 transferring to Eglin in Florida for live AMRAAM firing trials, not returning to Dunsfold until late summer 1994. Interestingly, the aircraft was delivered to the US as deck cargo aboard the new *Atlantic Conveyor*, having flown into Liverpool Docks prior to a vertical landing on the quayside; all in a day's work for a Harrier.

Contract agreement for the upgrade works to be applied to service aircraft was received in December 1988 for conversion of around thirty Sea Harrier FRS.1s to FRS.2 standard.

As the Sea Harrier FRS.2 test points were steadily completed, so the production schedule for updating the production aircraft began with aircraft being withdrawn from active service and returned to Dunsfold to be stripped of their systems and roaded to Brough for the structural modifications to be implemented. The first of these aircraft was XZ497 which thus became P1 for the purposes of the update work and was flown into Dunsfold in June 1991, returning to Dunsfold early the following year and passing through to flight stage prior to despatch to Boscombe for yet more testing. Behind this aircraft came ZE695 (P2), delivered to the Royal Navy in a ceremony at Dunsfold in April 1993, and thereafter a further thirty aircraft, making thirty-four Sea Harriers upgraded to FRS.2 standard, including the two DB aircraft.

To further enhance the capabilities of the upgraded carrier air groups and back fill where attrition of airframes had occurred, a further contract

Harrier FRS.2 ZA195 during carrier qualification trials aboard *Ark Royal*, November 1990. The aircraft is carrying the full complement of four AIM120 AMRAAM missiles. (Author's collection)

was awarded to BAe for eighteen new-build Sea Harriers which would henceforth carry the designation FA.2, reflecting the loss of the nuclear strike role; FRS.2 was not wired for the WE177c weapon. This contract was activated in 1994 with deliveries beginning from Dunsfold in October 1995. ZH796 (NB01) was the first aircraft of the new batch handed over to the Royal Navy in a ceremony at Dunsfold on 20 October 1995, followed by the rest of the eighteen aircraft through to 1999. Eventually, all suitable FRS.1 airframes were upgraded, the RN standardising on the FA.2 designation which, with the new-build airframes, allowed the Royal Navy to field something like fifty aircraft split over the two front-line and the single HQ and training squadron.

With its capability fully modernised, the Royal Navy would be called on to participate in a number of localised wars and other areas of unrest, including UN peacekeeping roles in the Balkan conflicts policing the 'No Fly Zone' from carriers based in the Adriatic. These deployments, beginning in 1993 under the code name Operation DENY FLIGHT used Sea Harriers to carry out CAP, CAS and reconnaissance in support of UN assets and 'safe areas' although they were not permitted at this time to use their weapons, one Sea Harrier FRS.1 being shot down by a surface-to-air missile (SAM). Flights continued under Operation DETERMINED FORCE in 1995, by which time Harriers were allowed to use the full weapons suite available to them. Further troubles in the former Yugoslavian territories resulted in Sea Harrier deployment in March 1999 as part of NATO's Operation ALLIED FORCE to contain fighting in Kosovo, flying from HMS *Invincible* in concert with other NATO countries.

Perhaps surprisingly, despite the overwhelming superiority of Sea Harrier in the Falklands conflict and much subsequent interest in the aircraft and the V/STOL concept, no export orders were forthcoming. Indeed the first export order had been placed prior to the conflict by India following extensive sales campaigns by Kingston and some excellent display flying by John Farley in G-VTOL from their carrier, the INS *Vikrant*, in the early 1970s. The Indian requirement was to find a suitable replacement for its ageing Sea Hawks, with Sea Harrier up against the American A-4 Skyhawk and the French Étendard. The HSA team at the time felt that they had convinced the Indian Naval officers involved in the trial of the superiority of the aircraft and were confident of a sale although it would be another five years before anything concrete was heard on the subject. Eventually, by 1979, an order had been confirmed for six Sea Harrier FRS.1s and two T.4 trainers, to be designated FRS.51 and T.60 respectively. As an Indian

Navy team arrived at Dunsfold in September 1980 to train on Harrier and its systems, work began on construction of the aircraft with the first Sea Harrier IN602 handed over to the Indian Navy in a colourful ceremony at the aerodrome on 27 January 1983 with the aircraft garlanded in suitable flowery style. The Indian representative was keen to 'anoint' the aircraft with the traditional coconut milk and had to be urgently prevented from using the aircraft's nose as a suitable place to crack said nut!

The Indian Sea Harrier was broadly similar to the RN FRS.1 although it carried GOX instead of LOX and used the French Matra Magic AAM rather than the American Sidewinder, the latter being embargoed for India. The trainers were also broadly standard T.4N aircraft although the water-injection system was modified to allow selection of 'half water' to assist with the higher ambient conditions in India. The Indian project team included pilots and ground crew as one would expect, but also representatives from Indian industry, involved in overseeing the construction and testing of 'their' aircraft. The presence of these engineers could at times prove frustrating due to their insistence that everything was done correctly – quite rightly so – and matters reached a head with the completion of the last T.60, which the Indian engineers would not accept, there always being some further unhappiness that prevented them signing it off. The feeling grew that there were political reasons for this and the aircraft remained in the hangar at Dunsfold for months after completion, gathering dust. Eventually it was accepted long after the rest of the order had departed. Much of the concern regarding this last Harrier was the fact that it was 'bent'. It had been removed from the Kingston jig earlier than normal and suffered with subsequent manufacturing tolerances. Some creative arrangements had to be agreed with the Indian government for them to eventually accept the aircraft.[4]

Dunsfold's workload after the Falklands War was sustained at a high rate with Hawk export and Harrier GR.5 new-builds as well as the attrition batches of Sea Harrier and GR.3 Harriers to test and deliver. All this work had to be cleared by the test pilot team which, by this time, comprised a mix of ex-RAF and Royal Navy pilots. The Royal Navy was represented by Lieutenant Commander Taylor Scott, Lieutenant Commander Rod Frederiksen and Lieutenant Steve Thomas. Frederiksen had latterly been CO of 800 Squadron while Thomas was from the rival 801 Squadron; both had served with distinction during the Falklands War with Thomas credited with the destruction of three Argentine aircraft, for which he received the DSC, and Frederiksen with one enemy aircraft. Scott had remained in the UK to undertake training and assist the work-up of 809 Squadron at Yeovilton. Former RAF pilots included Heinz Frick, latterly an engine test pilot at Rolls Royce's Bristol facility, Jim Hawkins, who had come to Dunsfold via A&AEE Boscombe Down, Andy Jones, whose credentials included an exchange posting to the USAF flying F-106 Delta Darts, and Chris Roberts, ex-Red Arrows pilot, QFI and QWI. Also on the team was Mike Snelling, another Boscombe Down graduate, and Graham Tomlinson who arrived following a posting to the US to work on Harrier II testing. Paul Hopkins was also fortunate to obtain a posting in the US, undertaking a course at the US Navy Test Pilots School at Patuxent River, Maryland.

Together, this team of pilots carried out all of the, at times rigorous, test flying required by the company and, in two cases, lost their lives doing so.

Chapter 12

New Harriers for Old

On 23 April 1985, at Dunsfold, British Aerospace held what was effectively a mini-Farnborough Air Show; a display of static and flying aircraft and weapon systems from their extensive stable of products was presented to potential customers from around the world. In the commentary box was the redoubtable Raymond Baxter but the undoubted star of the show was the first RAF GR.5 Harrier ZD318 which was rolled out, still unpainted, to the acclaim of the world's aviation press. Just a week later, on the 30th, ZD318 would make its first flight there at the hands of Mike Snelling. The road to this second-generation aircraft had been a long and tortuous one which had started at Dunsfold twenty-five years before but, finally, Harrier was maturing into the workhorse of the battlefront that HSA had long believed was just around the corner.

Once Harrier was in service with the RAF and USMC, various design studies were instituted, both at Kingston and in the US, aimed at increasing the potential of the aircraft, principally by increasing the range and payload. At first this research revolved around a projected new engine – the Pegasus 15 – which would deliver something in the region of 24,500lb thrust although, because it would incorporate a 2.75-inch increase in fan diameter, would not be capable of retrofit to existing airframes. This project, designated AV-16, was pursued by HSA in partnership with McDonnell Douglas (MDC) in the US but eventually failed due to the severe global economic constraints resulting from the oil embargo of 1973.[1]

With the demise of the AV-16, more modest design changes were explored with which to enhance the performance of Harrier; these revolved principally around a new larger wing which could be retrofitted to existing aircraft. In the UK, despite HSA exploring ideas for a developed Harrier under project codes P.1184 and P.1185, the economic situation ruled out any worthwhile funding for a new aircraft and studies suggested that performance increases from just a new enlarged wing were probably not cost-effective. Meanwhile in the US, rather more intense research was proceeding at MDC

220

to come up with a Harrier that would have double the range or double the payload of existing AV-8As. The proposal was built around a new larger wing of supercritical profile manufactured from carbon-fibre composites. Also central to the new design were changes to the intake size and profile and further use of carbon-fibre composite in the front fuselage assembly. The new wing offered far greater internal fuel carriage and, with the other carbon-fibre assemblies, significant weight saving. Added to these changes, ideas first promoted at Kingston – use of 'LIDS' – lift improvement devices to increase available lift in the hover and 'LERX' – leading edge root extensions – to improve turning performance, would also be incorporated, together with 'DECS', a digital fuel control system.[2]

The US proposal, termed AV-8B, while slower than the AV-8A or Harrier, achieved the goal of doubling the range/payload of the aircraft from broadly the same engine. This remarkable performance was coupled with improvements to avionics, increased weapon deployment, self-protection equipment, improved visibility from a larger, raised cockpit and reduced pilot workload from an ergonomically-designed cockpit layout. As HSA's

Lift Improvement Devices (LIDs) being trialled on a Harrier GR.3 as part of the 'Big Wing Harrier' proposal for the GR.5. (BAE Systems, courtesy of Brooklands Museum)

partner in the US, MDC would be the lead manufacturer, should a market be found for the aircraft in the US armed forces, but a significant proportion would accrue to UK manufacturing resources, i.e. to HSA.

With a recommendation to proceed forthcoming in 1976 from the US Defense Systems Acquisition Review Council, MDC manufactured two prototypes, the first of which flew in November 1978, the two aircraft quickly moving into the flight-test regime to examine the design in more detail. The news was almost all good, a point not missed by observers in the UK. By 1980 the USMC made clear its intention to acquire the new aircraft in significant quantities – around 340 units though in the end only 286 were acquired – and to use it to replace not only its AV-8A but also the Douglas A-4 Skyhawk to become a completely V/STOL force. This was good news for British Aerospace since 40 per cent of manufacture, although not final assembly, would be carried out in the UK.

While it appeared that the USMC would get the Harrier replacement that it wanted, in the UK things were dragging on with no decision as to which way to go. A new Air Staff Requirement, ASR409, made clear that a Harrier replacement was sought and it was against this backdrop that HSA's research into a new 'big wing' had been undertaken. This proposal, identified as Harrier GR.5, was initially favoured by the RAF and competed against the US proposal, although it could not match the increase in load-carrying/sortie duration that AV-8B offered. With the cost effectiveness of the two proposals under scrutiny, the RAF's original stance that the AV-8B would be unlikely to suit their own use softened and the service began to look to the US aircraft as the potential replacement for the Harrier in the UK, albeit thoroughly anglicised to suit the different requirements of the northern European regime. With the possibility that AV-8B would not proceed unless the UK was onboard, the choice for MoD and the British government was clear; BAe could be responsible for 100 per cent of a small RAF order or be part of a much larger manufacturing operation by being part of the AV-8B programme. Rolls Royce were also keenly lobbying for AV-8B to go ahead with their engine installed, regardless of whether UK bought the product or not.

With the advent of the 1980s, decisions on the future of Harrier in the UK were in the hands of the Conservative government and on 25 June 1981 a Memorandum of Understanding (MoU) confirmed an order for sixty Harrier GR.5 aircraft, now using the original UK Harrier designation for the RAF version of AV-8B, for the RAF, plus two development aircraft. As usual the aircraft would represent a 'minimum change' from the baseline AV-8B

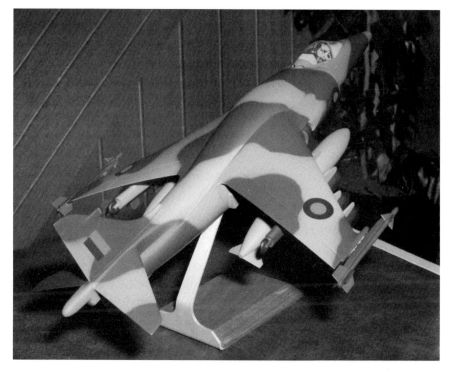

British Aerospace proposal for follow-on Harrier, colloquially the 'Big Wing Harrier', officially the Harrier GR.5. (BAE Systems, courtesy of Brooklands Museum)

manufactured for the USMC, most of the changes being in the avionics suite. However other changes were significant – the Stencel ejection seat would be replaced by a Martin-Baker unit, additional wing pylons for AAM would be fitted in front of the outrigger assemblies to free up other pylons for weapon/fuel carriage and nose profile would differ to accommodate UK sensors such as MIRLS. Also incorporated was local strengthening to the wing leading edges, intake lips, wraparound windscreen and nose cone to replace the bird-proofing required for Europe that had been removed from the design in the US. The USMC cannon of choice was the GAU-12/U Equalizer which used one of the under-fuselage pods for ammunition and the other for the cannon. The MOD preferred to use a twin-cannon armament as per the GR.3 and decided on the 25mm Aden which was lighter than the 30mm variety, a decision which they would come to regret later in the aircraft's service use.

Internally, the inertial navigation computer supplied by Litton would be replaced by a Ferranti unit and the Litton AN/ALR-67 ECM equipment was replaced by Marconi's ARI23333 Zeus EW system linked to MAWS (missile approach warning system) in the tail. In terms of weapon delivery, the LRMTS laser-designation system used on the GR.3 was not carried across to the new design; instead the US-derived ARBS (Angle Rate Bombing System) was retained, involving a tracking and target-lock facility generated by a TV sensor-head in the extreme nose which, in the low contrast environments of northern Europe, was less successful than on the AV-8B.

With the additional UK-sourced equipment, the build share between MDC and BAe approached a 50/50 split, though this was not sufficient for critics who decried the situation whereby the UK had become a mere sub-contractor to the US in terms of V/STOL technology. Those voices notwithstanding, Kingston got on with the job of producing the aircraft assemblies that fell to BAe as part of the bipartite agreement and mating them with the front fuselage sections when they arrived from MDC in St Louis. Following ZD318 down the line to Dunsfold came the second DB aircraft ZD319, flying for the first time on 31 July 1985 and, later, ZD320 which, although notionally the first production aircraft, would spend almost its entire life on development work. The next aircraft, ZD321, also joined the development work.

Official roll-out of the first Harrier GR.5 ZD318 at Dunsfold on 23 April 1985. (Author's collection)

The RAF received their first aircraft, ZD323, in May 1987 for familiarisation use and it was not until 1 July that deliveries started officially with the handover of ZD324 at a ceremony in the new Dunsfold Flight Shed. However, far from signalling the start of volume delivery to the RAF, this promising beginning was marred by an unexplained disaster which would effectively stop the process in its tracks. Taylor Scott had taken aircraft ZD325 up late in the day to carry out an oxygen flow test sortie on 22 October 1987 and was reported overdue at Dunsfold in the early evening. Meanwhile ATC had been unable to make contact with ZD325 as it crossed out over the sea and the aircraft was intercepted and filmed by an American C-5 aircraft as it headed west over the sea, south-west of Ireland. The film shot by the crew of the C-5 revealed that the cockpit was empty. Eventually the aircraft ran out of fuel and crashed into the ocean and was never recovered, but of the pilot there was initially no trace. Eventually Scott's body was found in Wiltshire and showed that the ejection sequence had not been activated. The drogue parachute had been fired through the canopy, releasing the pilot from the seat and dragging him out of the aircraft to his death. With this shocking death remaining a mystery, the entire GR.5 fleet was grounded. Since BAe were in the early stages of deliveries,

First flight of Harrier GR.5 ZD318 at Dunsfold on 30 April 1985 in the hands on Mike Snelling. (BAE Systems, courtesy of Brooklands Museum)

this meant that, as aircraft were completed at Dunsfold, they had their engines inhibited and were moved into temporary storage wherever space could be found. Later, temporary hangars were leased to get the aircraft under cover, these being erected on the disused runway adjacent to the new air traffic control tower.[3]

At the subsequent inquest, in the absence of definitive evidence, testimony was presented suggesting that the cockpit wander lamp could have fallen under the seat and caused the seat operating rods to become distorted, thus initiating the ejection sequence. It was a long shot that failed to convince many in the business but local protection to the sear rods under the seat was introduced in any event and the grounding lifted nine months later.[4]

With deliveries once more underway from Dunsfold, the first operational aircraft were delivered to No. 1 squadron at Wittering in May 1988 and, once this process was complete, the squadrons in Germany were the next to receive the new aircraft. As the Harrier GR.5s arrived, so the GR.3 aircraft became surplus and were brought back to the UK for storage at MUs so that, by 1990, the older aircraft had disappeared from the RAF's inventory. Some of the airframes had very low hours, those being mainly the post-Falklands War attrition replacement aircraft which had been under construction at Dunsfold in parallel with the first GR.5s, serialled ZD667 to ZD670, making 118 Harrier GR.3s produced plus twenty-eight T.2/T.4 trainers, the last of which, serialled ZD990 to ZD993, had also been constructed in 1986/7.

Following the forty-one Harrier GR.5s off the Dunsfold line came a further batch of nineteen aircraft designated GR.5A, these being an interim modification state between the GR.5 and the next full mark, the GR.7. The Harrier GR.7 would give the aircraft a full night-attack capability by installation of a GEC/Marconi FLIR (forward looking infra-red) unit above the nose of the aircraft and provision of night-vision goggles for the pilot. Also added at this time was a digital moving map display available via the head-down displays. These changes resulted in a modified aircraft nose profile with the FLIR mounted above the nose on the centreline and two 'horns' either side of the ARBS sensor housing the front Zeus sensors. ZD320 was the first aircraft so modified, a further thirty-three new-build GR.7 aircraft following and, later, the upgrading of all GR.5 and GR.5A Harriers. In total ninety-six Harrier GR.5/5A/7 aircraft were built, all at Dunsfold.

Having failed to secure funding either in the US or here for further uprating of the engine, the GR.5 and GR.7 aircraft had to make do with the Pegasus 11-21 (Mk 105) engine giving a maximum thrust of 21,750lb. However, some more modest work was carried out by Rolls Royce Bristol based on a design study engine called XG-15 which had run successfully at Bristol in 1984 and delivered 15 per cent more thrust (equal to another 3,000lb) than the existing Mk 105. From this, the Pegasus 11-61 was developed and a development engine installed in Harrier GR.5 ZD402 at Bristol. First flight was by Heinz Frick on 9 June 1989 and later by others including Chris Roberts; Andy Sephton, recruited from Farnborough, flew most of the sorties. Some fifty-seven flights were made, including new time-to-height records for V/STOL aircraft. While the engine was cleared for production for the USMC AV8B, as the Pegasus F402-RR-408 rated at 23,800lb thrust, funding was not available in the UK to cover the purchase of the engine for the Harrier so the GR.7 had to soldier on with the existing engine thrust as the aircraft weight inevitably increased over the years.[5] Not until the advent of the Harrier GR.9, after the closure of Dunsfold, would an improved engine, the Pegasus 107 at 23,800lb thrust, be fitted and then to only part of the Harrier force, only forty engines being acquired.

Publicity image following the handover of the first Harrier GR.5 ZD324 to the RAF at Dunsfold, 1 July 1987. (BAE Systems, courtesy of Brooklands Museum)

With the Harrier II so different from the Harrier I, it became more and more evident that the existing T.4 trainers could not provide a representative training regime for the pilots streamed onto the Harrier. Eventually a purchase of the trainer version of the AV-8B, the Harrier TAV-8B was agreed in 1990, thirteen aircraft designated Harrier T. 10 being contracted with BAe and MDC. These would be fitted with the equipment common to the GR.7 and be capable of use in wartime. Interestingly, this batch would be the first in the UK not to be built at Kingston/Dunsfold, the work being given to Warton on the basis that Dunsfold was 'too busy' with GR.7 and FA.2 work. The first aircraft, ZH653, also known as TX-01, first flew at Warton on 7 April 1994, piloted by Graham Tomlinson and Jim Ludford, arriving at Dunsfold later before moving on to Boscombe Down for service analysis. Once back at Dunsfold TX-01 spent much of its time on integration trials with the TIALD (thermal imaging and laser designation) pod developed for use in conjunction with Paveway LGB (laser-guided bombs).

One recurrent problem suffered by the Harrier GR.7 was the inability to fire the Aden 25mm cannon reliably, jams in the ammunition chutes being a regular occurrence. In a redesign of the gun in 1995 the opportunity was taken to incorporate link collection in the gun fairing as had been added to the Hunter four decades previously, and for the same reason, to prevent

Harrier GR.7 readied for weapon-handling sortie. The aircraft is seen here loaded with four SNEB rocket pods and AIM-9L Sidewinders on the outrigger pylons. Behind is one of the engine detuner pens. (BAE Systems, courtesy of Brooklands Museum)

damage to the aircraft or engine by ammunition links once ejected from the gun. Harrier ZD320 was chosen as the test aircraft and a full set of instrumentation fitted in autumn 1995 to collect data. This included pressure transducers fitted to the fuselage skin in front of the cannon muzzle on the port side and up to the air intake; also added were gun-gas-concentration sensors within the gunpod and within the fuselage engine bay. The addition of the link collectors made for a bulky pod but this was offset by improved LIDS effects in VTO.

Following flight trials with the new pods in April 1996 and ground firing in the Dunsfold butts in May, live-firing flights were carried out from Dunsfold at Lyme Bay. A problem was encountered with the gun during the firings where gun barrel internal skins were coming away, resulting in a debris field ahead of the aircraft causing structural damage as the aircraft flew through it. In September 1996 the aircraft was despatched to West Freugh for carriage and drop trials with Paveway 3 laser-guided bombs before returning in December for live gun-firing trials on the calibrated range. While further jams continued to pose problems, despite the rounds being Teflon coated in an effort to reduce the problem, the most serious difficulty was one that was unexpected. Analysis of the instrumentation traces showed a worrying build-up of gun gas in the forward fuselage and gun-pods to an extent that was considered to pose a risk. Remedy was sought in the cutting of multiple ventilation slots in the pod fairings, producing a most ungainly appearance but this did not cure the problem. Eventually, having produced the entire batch of pods and fairings, the project was quietly put to bed, the GR.7 never achieving a reliable gun option.

Also tested on ZD320 was the Canadian CRV-7 unguided rocket as an alternative to the SNEB Matra rocket of GR.3 vintage. The CRV-7 was carried in pylon-mounted pods holding nineteen rockets each. Live testing of these on ZD320 began in October 1995 and was successful, the weapon later joining the RAF armoury. Arming for live-firing trials such as these was latterly carried out in the former bulk fuel depot behind Canada House, the fuel paraphernalia having been cleared and earth banks raised for safety. Prior to this, live arming had been accomplished on the western ORP but this still resulted in some risk should weapons be fired inadvertently.

The last new weapon to be tested on the GR.7 at Dunsfold was the Brimstone anti-armour missile. This was a heavyweight fire-and-forget missile, three of which could be carried on each pylon. Unfortunately, work on testing the Brimstone system only got underway at Dunsfold after the closure announcement of June 1999, but initial jettison trials in the bomb

Harrier GR.5 ZD402 fitted with Pegasus 11-61 engine seen in the Production Hangar, June 1989. The aircraft was tested by Heinz Frick and Chris Roberts and would claim several 'time-to-height' records. The engine could produce 23,800lb thrust but was never ordered for the Harrier GR.7. (BAE Systems, courtesy of Brooklands Museum)

drop pit in August 1999 and carriage trials into November were achieved, ZD319 being the aircraft of choice for this trial. All went well until, on 23 November, the aircraft departed controlled flight and was temporarily grounded while investigations were carried out, not flying again until 12 January 2000.

While life at Dunsfold had certainly been busy for the Harrier II teams, it should not be thought that the Harrier I, known slightly pejoratively as 'tin-ships', was in any way a lost cause. Indeed, the Sea Harrier especially would come into its own in this same period. Going back now to the mid-1970s, HSA had continued in their tireless efforts to sell Harrier to an ungrateful world, but with strictly limited success. John Farley and the Kingston sales team were unstinting in presenting Harrier, usually G-VTOL, to any nation that showed any interest in the aircraft. One of these, perhaps surprisingly, was China and, in 1975, a delegation arrived in the UK with a brief to look over the aircraft. Having purchased a number of HS Trident airliners from Hatfield, it was to this factory that the delegation initially travelled and were later that day, 20 November, brought down to Dunsfold in one of the executive HS.125-600B twin jets, G-BCUX, piloted by the redoubtable Second World War night-fighter ace John 'Cat's Eyes' Cunningham for them to get up close to Harrier.

Following a tour of the hangars to see Harrier and Hawk, the delegation was entertained with a display of the HS.748 flown down from Woodford before boarding their transport for a short demonstration flight prior to return to Hatfield. As the aircraft lifted off heading east towards the main A281 road, a flock of birds rose in its path, and at 50 feet and 150 knots, multiple bird-strikes caused the engines to surge and flame out. With nowhere to go, Cunningham drew on his long and experienced career and, calling for undercarriage down and full flap, dropped the aircraft back onto the end of the runway. From there the aircraft careered onward, through the hedge at the end of the runway before hitting a ditch at the edge of the busy main road which tore the undercarriage off. Still at approximately 85 knots, the aircraft bounced across the road, coming to rest in the field beyond. Within seconds the crew had the seven passengers out as the aeroplane started to burn and bundled them away from the wreck. In a quite remarkable feat of control, Cunningham had got the aircraft down with almost no injuries to anyone aboard and, as the station fire crews arrived, all seemed to be under control.[6]

It was then that the fire crew found that there was wreckage under the aircraft that did not belong and realised they were looking at a Ford Cortina and its passengers which had been shunted by the aircraft as it crossed the road and carried with it into the field. In one of Dunsfold's most terrible ironies, the dead passengers included the wife and two children of one of their own pilots plus another three children on their way home from school. The subsequent inquest found no prior fault with either the aircraft or its handling by the crew after the bird strikes but did suggest that traffic lights be installed to control traffic on the A281 during active use of the runway, controlled by ATC. In the event, this suggestion was never implemented, although active bird-control procedures were evolved.

The following day, Harrier G-VTOL and Hawk XX156 were flown to Hatfield to provide a belated display of the capabilities of the two aircraft types, neither of which were subsequently purchased by China.

One day following the Falklands War, during a meeting between Colin Chandler and the Dunsfold pilots, Chandler explained that with few further orders for Sea Harrier pending it was likely that the production line would have to be closed unless the company could come up with ideas to prolong the life of Sea Harrier. The message was clear: 'the future of the Sea Harrier was very much in doubt unless we got our act together.' One of Dunsfold's pilots, Heinz Frick, decided to sit down and consider how the performance of the aircraft could be increased and the weight, and therefore cost, reduced. From this sprang the notion of stripping everything from the aircraft that was not needed for air combat, which chiefly meant the removal of the undercarriage! Slowly the idea took shape and one day 'suddenly the penny dropped – why not grab the thing out of the hover and put it straight inside the hangar'. From this evolved the idea of being able to refuel and re-arm the aircraft mechanically on smaller ships to increase the sortie rate and duration for aircraft at sea at reduced cost. The outcome of Frick's deliberations was presented initially to John Farley whose considered response was 'why haven't I thought of that?' The idea was then presented to John Fozard and the Future Projects Team at Kingston who believed it had sufficient merit to be worth further development. The concept, christened by Frick 'Sky Hook', evolved into a space-stabilised crane which would allow the undercarriage-less Harrier to lock onto its head while still in the air and be brought safely inboard for stowage in the ship's hangar.

Harrier T.10 ZH653 (TX01), seen here at Farnborough during detachment while Dunsfold's runway was resurfaced. The aircraft is heavily laden with drop tanks, AIM-9L Sidewinders and GBU-24 Paveway III laser-guided bombs. This aircraft was also used to test the Thermal Imaging and Laser Designator (TIALD) pod. (Author's collection)

By 1985 the concept was sufficiently mature to allow for flight testing at Dunsfold. Initially a hydraulic platform was borrowed from Guildford fire station, to the puzzlement of one of the firemen who wondered aloud 'what are you thinking – changing pilots in the hover?' However, the deal was done, the platform brought down to Dunsfold and Frick successfully attempted to formate on the top of the ladder with a Sea Harrier. With the idea looking entirely feasible, Fozard suggested a demonstration at the forthcoming British Aerospace Air Show scheduled for Dunsfold in April 1985 and for which a high-level crane was hired. A full mock-up of the space-stabilised capture-head and its sighting boards was mounted atop the crane and Frick, in Harrier G-VTOL, in front of the world's press successfully hovered within the small box of air within which a capture by the stabilised head would have been possible. With the item featuring on global news channels, BAe were becoming more confident that the concept had legs and continued with development. Regrettably, the Royal Navy was just not interested in the idea of modest ships with modest aircraft; what they wanted were big ships and big noisy aircraft and so the Sky Hook concept ultimately ran out of steam. One lasting memento of Sky Hook remained though; when G-VTOL was retired to Brooklands Aviation Museum a few years later, it still wore the Sky Hook logo penned by Frick, and retains it today.[7]

As deliveries of Sea Harrier FA.2 to the Royal Navy – both reworked from FRS. 1 and new build – began to reach the Navy in quantity, the need for a systems trainer began to make itself felt more urgently and, in the early 1990s, an order was placed for a number of Harrier trainers to be modified to carry out this role. Accordingly, as the first Harrier T.10s appeared and the workload of the RAF T.4 trainers reduced, those airframes with low hours were withdrawn and roaded to Dunsfold, together with some T.4Ns, to be converted into Royal Navy systems trainers designated Harrier T.8; T.6 was to have been a night-attack version of the T.4 which was not proceeded with. The T.8 would be a standard T.4 but with the addition of FA.2 avionics available in the front cockpit, except the radar system. The first fuselage, ZB605, arrived in Flight Test Operations hangar in October 1993 and proceeded with the refit and, by July 1994, had completed engine run; first flight was on 27 July. The aircraft wore a slightly incongruous appearance since the fuselage was grey but the wing, from another aircraft, was still in standard NATO camouflage. By September the aircraft was at West Freugh for armament trials before removal of the Instrumentation package and a spell at Boscombe Down in the REG. ZB605 was followed by a further six aircraft which would later take on the gloss black 'trainer' colours used by the RAF, giving it a somewhat more homogenous appearance.

In the late 1980s India, pleased with its initial batch of FRS.51 aircraft had placed a second order for aircraft in the serial range IN607 to IN623, these aircraft passing through production between 1988 and 1992. In all, India took delivery of twenty-three single-seat and two two-seat Sea Harriers.

Still with the Harrier I, by the mid-1990s Sea Harrier FA.2s, both new build and upgrade aircraft, were moving through the Production Hangar. In the FTO hangar upgrades to the development fleet aircraft were also being planned and implemented. In early 1997 ZA195 and XZ439, the FRS.2 development aircraft, were laid up and stripped to allow Phase 1 FIS updates to be applied to bring the aircraft up to full FA.2 standard. ZA195 was flying again by March of that year and completed by May 1997. At that point, the aircraft was laid up again and stripped, this time for Phase 2 upgrades, including installation of an IN/GPS system. The work included a complete continuity check of every electrical circuit on the aircraft lasting nearly six weeks, in an effort to generate a current modification status baseline due to the many different modifications carried out over its development life. The installation of IN/GPS came at a time when access to Global Positioning System technology was still a secret guarded closely by the US. Since access to the military GPS technology that allowed close positioning accuracy to be obtained was still secret, the aircraft was fitted with switching that allowed the pilot to destroy the codes in the control unit should it become necessary. That is hard to believe now with GPS access and equipment available to the world via phone apps.

The linked IN/GPS system not only gave pinpoint accuracy to the navigation and radar system but also allowed very accurate targeting during bombing, this being confirmed during trials with the system at West Freugh's bombing range during May and June 1998.

By the later 1990s the older pilots had all retired or moved to pastures new and a relatively new team had picked up the reins. Under Graham Tomlinson, Chief Test Pilot from 1994, were Bernie Scott and Mark Bowman, both ex-RAF, Jim Ludford, also ex-RAF and Commander Simon Hargreaves, ex-RN and Falklands veteran. Flying was restricted to Harrier, Hawk being but a memory until the last couple of years when Hawk again appeared in the production bays.

The purchase of redundant airframes for resale to other countries had a long tradition at Hawker and its subsidiary companies – the Tempest, Sea Fury and Hunter had all been utilised in this field. Yet, as the Harrier GR.5s were replaced in RAF service, re-purchase of the GR.3 aircraft becoming redundant does not appear to have been given any serious consideration.

Harrier T.8 ZB605, the first aircraft converted, outside Flight Test Operations in July 1994 with some of the staff responsible. (BAE Systems)

Perhaps this was due to the less than successful efforts of the HSA and BAe Sales team to persuade the world that what they really needed was a V/STOL aircraft for their air arms. More interest had been forthcoming from smaller navies; those in possession of wartime carriers were particularly interested since the cost of refurbishment to allow use of modern fast jets was often prohibitive. Harrier therefore offered a neat answer to this problem.

One of the countries caught in this situation was Brazil. As early as 1973, a sales team, accompanied by G-VTOL, John Farley and Don Riches, had attended the Sao Paulo International Aerospace Show, combining those flights with those to and from the Brazilian carrier *Minas Gerais*. This former Royal Navy carrier (HMS *Vengeance*) was not really suitable for modern fast jets; hence the interest in Harrier. Nothing came of this and the ship was withdrawn in 1987, apparently putting an end to any Brazilian interest in the Harrier. However, in July 1997, as a result either of further interest from the Brazilian Navy or a last push from BAe Sales, draft costs were collated to cover the recovery of redundant ex-USMC AV-8A aircraft from storage in the American desert base of Davis-Monthan at Pima, Arizona, and their subsequent shipment to Dunsfold for refurbishment and sale to Brazil. Ten single-seat and two trainer Harriers were budgeted for, at a price – with any spares packages – of between $500,000 and $1,000,000, with delivery to the buyer of the first aircraft by October 1998. Quite how far this plan went is unclear but appears to have been linked to another potential buyer for Harrier – this time in the private sector.[8]

The Swiss firm of Breitling had long been famous for its aviation chronographs and superior watches and over the years had used sponsorship of aviation and, in particular, aircraft display teams as advertising for its wares. In 1997 a further step in this promotional programme appears to have been considered, this time using the Harrier. Proposals were put together by BAe to supply five two-seat aircraft, of which two would be restored to flying condition for the actual display work with a third as back up and two further airframes for spares recovery. With no suitable aircraft available from UK sources, the preferred source would again be AV-8As from the desert storage facility of Davis-Monthan in the US. The aircraft would be required for the 1998 display season. Costs for the airframes were estimated at $550,000. Aircraft would be shipped to Dunsfold for strip and refurbishment, the costs including the provision by BAe of a suitable ground-crew team to service the aircraft through the display season with additional support based at Dunsfold, including pilot conversion. The indicative costs of this enterprise were reckoned at £3,775,000 at 1997 prices, a significant start-up outlay which, coupled with operating costs for the first season in the region of £729,000, may explain why the proposal was not followed up.[9]

Harrier GR.7 ZD319 undergoing jettison trials of Brimstone anti-armour missiles on the drop pit at Dunsfold, August 1999. (BAE Systems)

It would also have come up against CAA resistance to allowing a complex military aircraft to be operated in the private sector.

On 12 December 1994 a rather bedraggled XP984 arrived back at Dunsfold on a lorry. This aircraft had been the sixth prototype P.1127, carrying out much of the development work for the Kestrel. It had later been used for early ship-borne trials on HMS *Bulwark* before passing to RAE Bedford for use in various trials. In 1975 the aircraft had been damaged at Bedford, rendering it unflightworthy and had then passed to the Royal Navy Engineering College at Manadon. With closure of RNEC Manadon imminent, the airframe was offered for sale by Sotheby's in 1994; BAe had purchased it with a view to mounting as a gate guardian at Dunsfold. Viewed as a suitable training project for the apprentices, work slowly progressed on a cosmetic restoration before its eventual relocation to a suitable position inside the main gate. On the closure of Dunsfold, the aircraft was shipped to Brooklands Aviation Museum where it remains on display.

As a postscript to the continuing search for further work, an unusual exhibit appeared at the June 1995 Dunsfold Families Day – a mock-up of the Eurocopter Tiger Attack Helicopter. The aircraft was a collaborative project between Aerospatiale in France and MBB in West Germany, with the first prototype flown in April 1991. Unofficial discussions between France and the UK had continued for some time with the possibility of British participation, after it was revealed that the Army Air Corps was in the market for an attack helicopter. BAe became involved with the company potentially carrying out final assembly of any British order, the suggestion being that this work could come to Dunsfold. It must be said that the idea of switching from fast jet to helicopter production at Dunsfold was not exactly greeted with cries of joy and eventually the idea was dropped, Britain's Army Air Corps eventually going on to purchase the Boing AH-64D Apache Longbow with final assembly at Westland's facility at Yeovil in Somerset.

While on the subject of Dunsfold Families Day, or 'Field Day' as it was known internally, two fatalities served to dampen the enthusiasm normally involved in such displays. As described in Chapter 10, a civilian-registered Hunter had crashed with fatal consequences during rehearsals for the Families Day in summer 1998. Prior to this, in July 1989, Spitfire G-MKVC, belonging to Charles Church, had formed part of the flying display and was well received. In the early evening, the aircraft took off to return the short distance to its hangarage at Micheldever but, prior to being put away for the night, Church took the aircraft up for a last flight before nightfall. Following engine failure and an attempted emergency landing at Blackbushe, the aircraft went out of control and crashed at Hartley Wintney, killing Church.

Chapter 13

The End

On 24 June 1999 meetings of the entire workforce were informed that the decision to close Dunsfold had been confirmed by the main board of BAe with a termination date likely to be by the end of 2000. Most were shocked by the news, some merely saddened at what they saw as unnecessary muscle flexing by the northern dominated board. In truth, Dunsfold had been in an exposed position for some time; its major long-term programme on Hawk had been moved to Warton, Harrier was a programme running out of steam and, with the closure of the Kingston Design Office some time previously, any new design work was under the control of Warton, who were keen to promote their 'own' designs.

The seeds of closure had been sown many years prior, in the early 1970s. As part of the Labour Party's manifesto for the general election of February 1974, the party had committed itself to implementing widescale extensions to public ownership of major industries including the shipbuilding and aircraft industries. With its return to power weeks later, work had begun on turning this statement into reality and, in April 1975, a bill was placed before Parliament to allow the nationalisation of the two industries. In April 1977 the Aircraft and Shipbuilding Industries Act led to the creation of a new organisation named British Aerospace to which the assets of Hawker Siddeley Aviation, Hawker Siddeley Dynamics, British Aircraft Corporation and Scottish Aviation were allocated and Hawker Siddeley Aviation ceased to exist in any meaningful sense. The chairmanship of the new organisation fell to Labour Peer Lord Beswick, whose deputy, Alan Greenwood, had been chairman of BAC from 1976. Heading up the Aircraft Group would be Sir Frederick Page, formerly chief executive of English Electric and latterly chairman of the military aircraft division of BAC. Chief of the Dynamics Group would be George Jefferson, another former English Electric executive and later chairman of BAC Guided Weapons Division. Thus all three top posts within the new organisation had been handed to former BAC bosses; it was difficult not to conclude that Hawker Siddeley executives were being frozen out of the top roles in the new company.

As the new organisation began to bed in, no immediate changes were noticeable at Dunsfold although slowly over the following few years it became evident that budgets were being loosened and funding made available where previously the notoriously tight purse strings at Hawker Siddeley had been firmly tied. Public money was now available and soon began to be tapped for improvements to the aerodrome although the process was still in its infancy when the Labour government, mired in the infamous 'Winter of Discontent', was summarily dismissed at the ballot box and a Conservative administration returned to power under the leadership of Margaret Thatcher in spring 1979. As part of the new government's policy of returning nationalised industry to private ownership, the following year the British Aerospace Act 1980 saw BAe become a public limited company under the name British Aerospace plc in January 1981, shares in the new company being sold the following month with free shares made available for company staff.

As part of the process of nationalisation Admiral Sir Raymond Lygo had been recruited from the Royal Navy and took up the position of managing director of the Dynamics Division. After privatisation he became, in 1983, group managing director and quickly decided that there would need to be a 'massive rationalisation' of the company, principally by selling off the sites in the south of the country and moving the work to the north. In the mid-1980s, therefore, a development company, Arlington Securities,

Sea Hawk WV908 at Dunsfold in June 1995 prior to its refurbishment to flight. Behind can be seen P.1127 XP984, Sea Hawk WV911 (to be used for spares for the refurbishment of WV908) and, behind this, the sensor mast of the Eurocopter Tiger mock-up. (Author's collection)

was acquired and given the task of managing BAe's property portfolio and liquidating assets that the board decided could go.[1]

Restructuring in the group was nothing new but the post-privatisation world within BAe was viewed by many with a jaundiced eye. Bitteswell, the former Armstrong Whitworth aerodrome in Leicestershire, had long been used by the Hawker Siddeley Group as an overload production facility for other company products as well as producing the AW Argosy transport aircraft. As the Flight Test Centre for AWA, Bitteswell took major sub-assemblies from Baginton for assembly and flight test in a relationship similar to that between Kingston and Dunsfold. However, in 1965, following the cancellation by the Labour administration of the HS681 V/STOL tactical transport aircraft, the parent factory at Baginton was closed, leaving Bitteswell to soldier on alone. With off-load and repair contracts from other parts of the HSA group, Bitteswell remained in profitable use until, on 22 March 1982, closure of the site was announced with a cessation of operations in June that year, resulting in the loss of 1,000 jobs. Put up for sale in 1984 by BAe, the site eventually became an industrial centre and warehouse complex.

In 1986 attention turned to the southern sites, the so-called 'Kingsbridge' grouping of Weybridge/Kingston/Dunsfold. Initially, Kingston was identified as the first target, Weybridge being safe in the short term due to the fact that the group headquarters had been moved to Weybridge by Lord Beswick, the first chairman of BAe. However, with Kingston busy on Harrier and Weybridge only completing sub-assemblies for other sites, it was Weybridge that would feel the axe first.

In April 1986 a report entitled *Military Aircraft Division Rationalisation* unveiled 'Project W87', a plan to close the Weybridge site, widely regarded as the birthplace of aviation in Great Britain, by the end of 1987. It was possible that a small number of staff might remain on part of the site to support civil aviation technical requirements but the remainder would be cleared and sold for redevelopment given its 'having the highest potential sale value'. Military technical work would transfer to Warton, Brough and Kingston while 'It is planned that Dunsfold will continue *for the time being ... '*.[2]

Some 2,300 redundancies were anticipated out of a total staff count of just over 4,000 with up to 750 relocating to Kingston/Dunsfold. The closure announcement would be made in July/August 1987 with a complete closure anticipated by December that year and disposal of the site beginning around June 1988. The vast majority of the existing work packages would be transferred north to Warton, Preston, Salmesbury and Brough 'to protect the

Fairey Firefly WB271 visiting Dunsfold in June 1993. (Author's collection)

Fairey Firefly WB271 undergoing complete refurbishment in the FTO hangar, summer 2000. (Author's collection)

charging rates at those sites'. Care was to be taken to avoid the workforce recognising what was planned and, to this end, the 1986 apprentice intake would go ahead as planned to avoid giving 'too clear a warning signal'. Workforce reaction in terms of industrial action was carefully assessed and proved to be broadly accurate in its muted response to what many may have seen as inevitable so that, by 1988, the Weybridge Division was so in name only. A small but significant group of employees made the move from Weybridge to Dunsfold while rather more transferred to Kingston. In retrospect, it was the former who made the right choice.

With life settling down after this closure, a decision that many saw as misguided was made by the CSEU (Confederation of Shipbuilding and Engineering Unions) of which the Amalgamated Engineering Union was part, to campaign for a reduction in the working week from thirty-nine to thirty-five hours. With little incentive for industry leaders to acquiesce to such an increase in their labour costs, the path was clear for the unions to begin industrial action. A variety of manufacturing concerns nationwide were targeted for strike action, one of them being BAe's site at Kingston, Dunsfold not being required to join with the action at that stage.

The disruption to the Kingston site was severe and prolonged and degenerated into acrimonious exchanges at the gates as technical staff sought access through the picket line. In an ill-considered attempt to get some activity at the factory, Military Aircraft Division management dictated that workers from Dunsfold be moved to Kingston and, when those staff refused, they were suspended. Weekly payments from Dunsfold workers helped to keep them afloat but, with intransigence on both sides, little comfort could be found. In the long run the dispute was settled; the working week became thirty-seven-and-a-half hours with many workers simply completing their working week with an hour-and-a-half overtime to bring it back up to thirty-nine. The result was acclaimed a great victory by both sides but, inevitably, for the ordinary worker any victory was strictly Pyrrhic.[3]

Whether the plan to close Kingston arose directly from this action is difficult to say, but certainly its closure was part of the big sell-off plan and, in 1991, closure of the Kingston site was announced. With another 2,000 redundancies looming, the unions retained a specialist economic consultancy to consider ways to save the site. The 'Skypark Economic Development Area' was the response, offering space on the site for other industrial concerns coupled with a reserve of skilled labour available to relocating companies while BAe would retain a percentage of the site for a slimmed-down operation. Of course, those arguments, persuasive as they may have been, ignored the fact that the site was a valuable development asset to BAe, an important driver for its closure. With the last major aircraft assembly – AV-8B rear fuselage CUM205 – leaving the factory for Dunsfold on 20 February 1992, time was fast running out for the site.[4]

THE END

By the end of 1992 the presence of Hawkers at Kingston was no more. Design and engineering support staff were relocated to new offices on the RAE site at Farnborough; remaining production contract work was transferred to Dunsfold, comprising AV-8B rear fuselage assembly, Harrier GR.7 fuselage assembly and specialist disciplines. Some staff transferred to Dunsfold, mainly into the Black Hangar where the fuselage jigs were re-erected. Thus Dunsfold found itself in the position previously shared by Bitteswell, a not altogether comforting thought, in having lost its parent factory and being left to fend for itself in an increasingly politicised company environment with the northern sites becoming pre-eminent. Two years later the Hatfield site would suffer the same fate, the last aircraft flying out in 1994, and Hamble was hived off into a separate entity, leaving just Dunsfold remaining in the south from the previous empire of Hawker Siddeley Aviation.

By 1992 the Dunsfold site had been part of innumerable divisions within the industry. Formerly part of the Kingston/Brough division in the early days of BAe, it had then become part of MAD, the Military Aircraft Division, before changing to Military Aircraft and Aerostructures. Prior to this, as part of the Hawker Siddeley Group, it had been included in the Hawker Blackburn division.

The mid and late 1990s saw Dunsfold Harrier I Production completing the FA.2 Sea Harrier new-build (delivered 24 December 1998) and MLU (mid-life update) aircraft, while Harrier II was carrying out a series of upgrades and modifications to GR.7 RTW (return to work) and the remaining GR.5 Harriers. In Flight Test Operations, work revolved around trials of FA.2 radar software, IN/GPS integration, Harrier T.10 TIALD integration, GR.7 25mm cannon firing and other works. In the pipeline for Harrier I was design work for the integration of JTIDS (joint tactical information and display system) into the FA.2 and the trials HS.125, leading to flight trials in 2000/01 while Harrier II was working towards integration of Brimstone, an anti-armour missile, and Storm Shadow, a stealthy air-launched cruise missile, for GR.7. Around the corner was further work that would upgrade the databus and avionics systems in GR.7 to allow carriage of smart weapons and AMRAAM, together with an uprated engine to become the Harrier GR.9.

While all this sounded promising for Dunsfold, funding for much of the future work was not guaranteed and, even with it, the workload graphs showed a worrying reduction leading up to the end of the century. Unless additional work could, or would, be moved south from Warton,

Flight Test Operations staff pose with two of the development fleet aircraft: Sea Harrier FRS.2 XZ439 and Harrier GR.7 ZD320, January 2000. (BAE Systems)

Salmesbury and Brough, the situation could prove worrying. Against this background, however, a 'Five Year Development Plan' for the Dunsfold site was published in November 1998. This offered a rolling plan to upgrade the aerodrome's facilities through major infrastructure projects 'to support the short and medium-term business strategy for the Dunsfold site'.[5]

The report identified the key disciplines at Dunsfold as 'Design and Engineering; Systems Development; Integration and Test; Development Flight Testing and Analysis; Production Flight Testing; Aircraft Final Assembly; RTW Systems Upgrades; RTW Structural Upgrades; Major Structural Assembly; Electrical Manufacture and Customer Support'.

As part of the programme, several key work packages were identified. It was hoped to acquire a Return to Works programme for the refurbishment of Kuwaiti Hawk Mk 64 aircraft; these had been taken by Iraq during the crisis leading up to the First Gulf War and only returned to Kuwait after the cessation of hostilities. Because the aircraft could not be considered airworthy, they had been taxied along the main road from Iraq back into Kuwait using their Adour engines. If nothing else, a major rework of the engines would be required. Also planned for construction in 2000 were works to increase the length of useable runway to allow for safe take off and landing of Harrier GR.7 and T.10 during CASOM (Storm Shadow) trials when the aircraft would be heavily laden. Other work packages would be actively sought from the Services and other parts of the company to maintain workloads at reasonable levels. The number of technical staff in 1998 was 189, with 502 Production staff and 373 others, a total of 1,064.

Also budgeted for in the plan were new buildings comprising security gatehouse, personnel and training school, conference centre, administration, dynamic test facility and sports and social club, most of these entailing demolition of the existing facilities; these works were costed at some £2.45m. Also allowed for was a new production facility, costed at £1.5m to allow for additional Hawk and Harrier RTW packages to come to Dunsfold, planned for 2001 with the potential for a further new hangar in 2002 dependent on workload, possibly replacing the existing production facilities. Work was already in play to improve the Hawk Engine Running Pen with refurbishment of the brickwork and new detuner costed at £220,000.[6]

Other improvements were related to increased requirements for health and safety including the provision of sprinkler fire-control systems in the FTO hangar and the logistics centre, improvements to the main drainage system for the social club and Primemeads Cottage. On the airfield, improvements included the extension of the east end runway, already mentioned, upgrades to runway approach and taxiway lighting, upgrades to ATC facilities, repairs to perimeter track and aircraft parking area, repairs to

Production staff pose with the last Harrier T.10, ZH662, and the last Sea Harrier FA.2, ZH802. The cockpit carries a scrawled reference to 'The last of the Dunsfold many' and, below it, the ironic 'Investors in People'. (BAE Systems)

eastern and western ORPs, replacement of runway crash nets, replacement of DME and UHF ground movement base station equipment.

Already under construction in 1998 were major improvements to site security installations, the most obvious of which was the creation of two secure citadels on the north side of the airfield, one encompassing FTO and Tempest hangars and systems development building in the west and the other, the main Production and Black hangars in the east. A new external security fence and CCTV across the site was included. Additional security works were allowed for in the five-year plan, including further extension of CCTV coverage. Entry to the internal citadels was by means of access-controlled pedestrian gates and large electronically-operated main gates to allow for aircraft movement. Further work was planned to improve and upgrade the IT network across the site, with provision of fibre-optic trunk and upgrade to a new Windows-based infrastructure, the work to be funded centrally.

All in all, the report suggested continued financial support for Dunsfold into the twenty-first century. The reality would be rather different.

The first two Kuwaiti Hawks eventually reached Dunsfold in early 1998, courtesy of a Kuwaiti C-130 Hercules which flew in on 26 January, the work being carried out in Bay 2 of the Production Hangar, and were delivered back on 2 September 1999. Thereafter, eight further Hawks returned in pairs for rework, making ten in total, the last making the journey around Easter 2000. The last two of the original twelve were considered beyond economical repair.

Also returning to Dunsfold in 1999 were further Hawks, this time from Indonesia,the company purchasing five Mk 53 aircraft for possible resale: L5306, L5315, L5317, L5319 and L5320. In the end, events overtook this plan and the later aircraft were transferred from Bay 2 to FR Aviation at Bournemouth Airport for completion.

On the Harrier II front, work continued on RTW upgrades to GR.7 and T.10, these aircraft being joined by a couple of their predecessors in the shape of two T.4 RAF trainers. These had been purchased to fill a gap in the training requirement for the Indian Navy but, again, time constraints would not allow their completion at Dunsfold, the aircraft moving to Yeovilton with an engineering crew for completion and delivery. The aircraft came in as ZB600 and ZB602 and left as IN656 and IN655 respectively.[7]

Meanwhile, in the FTO hangar, some rather older airframes had appeared. One of these, the Sea Hawk FGA.6, WV908, which had been the subject of a two-year refurbishment for the Royal Navy Historic Flight, handed over in November 1997 – had returned with cracking of the jet-pipe

Harrier T.10 undergoing calibration of strain gauging in the rig in FTO hangar, 2000. (Author's collection)

heat shield and had been the subject of a fairly complex repair. This was joined by its Naval stablemate, Fairey Firefly Mk 5 WB271 which was the subject of a rebuild, including replacement of its electrical systems. The work necessitated a complete strip down to bare metal and manufacture of replacement electrical looms, the work stretching over many months and the aircraft eventually moving back to Yeovilton by road. The aircraft survived until 2003, being destroyed in a fatal crash at Duxford on 12 July. Also entering FTO in 2000 was the gate guard P.1127, XP984, for breakdown and transport to its new home at Brooklands Museum.

Over the fifty years that BAe and its predecessor companies had operated from Dunsfold Aerodrome, changes had slowly occurred to the landscape of the site that had made it less of a 'hole-in-the-woods' operation and more amenable for its users. However, most of those changes had only occurred post-1980. Until then, apart from the new Production Hangar and canteen, the site was still very much as it was when Hawkers had arrived back in 1951, including numerous Nissen huts, some functioning as repositories for complex and expensive computer equipment and instrument-repair facilities. After 1980 the face of Dunsfold began to change: slowly the old huts were demolished and replaced by new buildings or by Portacabins, a small township of which grew up to the west of the Experimental Hangar.

The senior mess and administration functions, up until then also tenants of Nissen huts, got smart timber-clad premises in which to work and dine.

The Black Hangar, for many years a stores location, was cleared in the post-Falklands period and a production line installed to cater for further batches of Sea Harrier FRS.1s and Harrier GR.3 and T.4 aircraft. Later, with the arrival of the rump of the former Kingston production capability, those lines were cleared and jigs for AV-8B fuselages installed. Out on the airfield itself, a new air traffic control tower emerged in 1979, adjacent to the disused western runway, to replace the facility at the top of the old watch-room on the northern perimeter, and topped with a radar dish, taking over from the previous one which until then had stood atop a lattice steelwork tower in front of the experimental building, erected in 1958. The crash barriers formerly installed at each end of the runway were joined by aircraft approach lighting and an ILS installation. In the summer of 1996 the runway was closed to traffic and a construction company tasked with a complete resurfacing of its 6,000 feet over several months. Some production flying was permitted from the northern taxiway but the development aircraft moved to Farnborough for the duration of the work and continued their flight-test activities from a secluded hangar.

Dunsfold from the east. Just visible in the lower left corner is the HS Trident, flown in for trials by RFD-GQ, September 1987. (Author's collection)

THE END

On 22 February 1985 a rather more far-reaching move saw the demise of the experimental department at Dunsfold, the first department to arrive at the aerodrome in 1951, and the amalgamation of its work and personnel into production and a new department termed DASG – the Development Aircraft Support Group. This department remained in the Experimental Hangar and was joined by the Flight Shed function previously housed in Bay 3 of the Production Hangar. As part of the upgrade to facilities, the former Experimental Hangar was radically reconstructed on the same footprint, but much modernised with the addition at the front of new office space, eventually housing Flight Test and Flight Test Instrumentation functions. Later the Black Hangar would also get a more modest makeover, eventually becoming olive green rather than black, although still retaining its unofficial name until closure. Also in the mid-1980s, on the hardstandings once used by Airwork, DH, an aviation servicing company obtained permission to construct a hangar for the refurbishment of HS.125 executive jets with access to the perimeter track and the aerodrome's facilities. The hangar would house some rather exotic aircraft during its life, including a Spitfire refurbishment and a Hawker Tempest restoration. At one stage a line of DH Sea Vixen fighters graced the forecourt although none reached airworthy status before their removal from the aerodrome.

Across on the south side of the airfield, other changes were in train. Dating from wartime use, the two fuel-pumping stations, one just inside the 'Compasses' gate and the other behind Canada House on the former Benbow Lane, had become derelict. Both were swept away, with the western one remodelled to become an arming area for live weapons fit. This was designed in such a way that personnel were housed in the centre of a large 'roundabout'. Once the aircraft was armed, the layout allowed it to taxi out to the runway without pointing its weapons at the support staff. Similarly, on return, staff were in no danger as the aircraft taxied back into the area with any unused ordnance. Surrounding the area was a high earthen bund to absorb blast or bullets should something go awry. While this sounds unlikely, an incident in the Experimental Hangar in years past pointed to the dangers involved. A pre-flight check on a Hunter had included function of the gun trigger which promptly expelled a 30mm cannon shell, still in the cannon breech, at great velocity across the hangar and straight through the wall and to freedom somewhere in the vicinity of the canteen. That no one was injured was luck rather than judgement.

Also on the south east side of the airfield, the hardstandings once home to Mitchells and later Sea Furies, became home to a rather more advanced aircraft, a Trident airliner. This had arrived in the mid-1980s for use by the safety equipment company RFD-GQ and ended up on its belly after many trials of pneumatic lifting bags and other kit. To the rear of this hardstanding was a blister hangar, erected in 1964 as a store for engines and seats. With its own boiler heating system, this hangar later became a store for USMC equipment, proudly proclaiming its allegiance on the door – 'US Government Property – Department of Defense'. At the front of this line of hardstandings was a facility to allow the safe jettisoning of stores and the filming of their release to ensure that jettison tests in flight would not endanger the aircraft. The area was spartan, with photographic reference lines marked out on the ground and a large pit let into the surface filled with sand and, later, mattresses to give the weapon a soft landing. Here were tested the jettison of AMRAAM from the Sea Harrier FRS 2 and, one of its last tasks, test drops of Brimstone anti-armour missiles, courtesy of the author in 1999. Looking now at the western extremes of the airfield, in the mid-1970s, a new flight line was laid out on the stub of the western disused runway and a flight-line hut erected to shelter staff working on the line. From there, almost all military flights took place although previously those flights had originated from the aircraft parking area in front of the armoury at the east end of the airfield where little or no shelter was available. Prior to the development of the new arming point behind Canada House, live weapons trials had started from the western ORP where, in earlier years, the first hovers of the P.1127 had taken place.

On the northern fringe of the 'factory' site and between the Experimental Hangar and the engine detuners, the previous Nissen huts housing flight test and the radio workshop had given way to a new avionics building. Adjacent to this was another new building – EETS - for the testing of avionic equipment and, next to this, some of the last remaining Portacabins from the shanty town of the 1970s. These cabins formed the basis of the 'Dynamic Test Facility', originally for development of the LRMTS equipment fitted to the Harrier GR.3. From there, a clear sighting range was available right across the airfield to targets on the south side. Later, the cabins became home for development of the Ferranti Blue Fox radar for Sea Harrier FRS.1s. Just to the north of the cabins, a couple of others remained which belatedly housed members of the Grantex team. This operation was shrouded in secrecy; their aircraft were hangared in the former DASG hangar, renamed as Flight Test Operations and serviced by staff from Mann Aviation. Discussion of their surveillance activities on behalf of government ministries was not encouraged. Between the FTO hangar and avionics building, the last hangar to be erected was the

The Royal Observer Corps bunker on the southern edge of the airfield. Designed to allow a small contingent to observe and report on nuclear explosions in the event of war, the bunker was fully proofed against nuclear fall-out. (Author's collection)

Tempest or 'strip' hangar, where aircraft returning for major modifications could be stripped out ready for removal to the Production Hangar.

Following the closure announcement on 24 June 1999, the Union presence at Dunsfold initiated a study to identify potential ways in which the aerodrome might remain in operation. Their report, *The Case for BAe Dunsfold*, sought to illustrate the economic viability of the site since this was one of the key planks of the BAe case for closure. It was careful to point out that, far from being an uneconomic location with high overheads, Dunsfold in fact had the lowest charging rate in MA&A, at £45.00 per hour against, for example, Warton/Salmesbury at £70.00 per hour.[8]

The report suggested a number of ways by which Dunsfold could remain commercially active into the twenty-first century. With the EFA project being mired in endless delays, it was noted that life extension of Harrier II through various RTW programmes would be required to provide continuing aircraft capability to the RAF to fill any shortfall and that Dunsfold was the natural location for this work to be carried out. Work to upgrade the Harrier II fleet from GR.7/7A to GR.9 standard was also likely to be required, again with Dunsfold being the lead site. Further reduction of the charging rate could be achieved by allowing use of unused parts of the aerodrome by third parties such as sub-contractors, and by allowing use of the airfield facilities by other aviation-related concerns. Relocation of the Farnborough office to Dunsfold was also suggested as a cost-cutting move for the company.

Unfortunately, like the Kingston campaign, all of this missed the point that the company saw Dunsfold as a development opportunity which would generate what they anticipated would be a large cash inflow into the company with the added benefit of Dunsfold's remaining work being shared among the northern sites to strengthen their own workbase. In the event, release of the document did not persuade the company to think again; it declined to continue negotiations and re-issued the Notice of Redundancy to the Dunsfold staff.

While most staff felt that they were being treated unfairly by the company, measures taken to mitigate the worst excesses of redundancy were put in place. Accommodation was provided to Guildford job centre to allow direct access to vacancies and advice from staff; outside employment agencies were given access to allow screening of staff for potential relocation to other areas of work. Re-skilling courses were made available, both through the unions and the company again, to assist in relocation to other areas of work and staff allowed to leave without affecting their redundancy package wherever possible.

By August 2000 activity was starting to slow; development aircraft were being flown out of Dunsfold for the last time to new homes at Boscombe Down, Yeovilton or Warton. The last flights of military aircraft under BAe administration occurred in September with Harrier FA.2 ZH802 departing to Yeovilton on the 14th, piloted by Simon Hargreaves, and Harrier T. 10 ZH662 flying out on the 21st to Boscombe Down, also in the hands of Hargreaves. This last was a Warton product, the irony of which needs no explanation. Some civil communications flights continued including the Piper Seminole hack G-BGCO to Warton on the 27th, and flight operations finally closed down on 29 September 2000, forty-nine years after BAe's predecessor company, Hawker Aircraft's, arrival back in 1951.[9]

In October 2000 most staff had departed, just a few stalwarts remaining to clear and tidy the site. By December the aerodrome was eerily quiet. Enquiries from potential new occupiers had slowed; the most promising, from FR Aviation, was to wither on the vine as pressure from local residents built to ensure that the local authority enforced what was regarded as a cast-iron guarantee that BAe should return the site to agriculture. In the event, despite legal action, this would never happen, the site instead being sold as one lot to a development company, but that is altogether another story.

THE END

Because of the compact nature of Dunsfold Aerodrome and the isolation engendered by the need to work behind the veil of the Official Secrets Act, Dunsfold had always a sense of close community, as something separate from what happened beyond the fences. Indeed it is the one consistent theme that has run through the many, many conversations undertaken by the author with ex-staff. Heinz Frick, former Chief Test Pilot, perhaps expressed it best:

> When I was in my teens determined to have a career as a fighter pilot I bought the book Neville Duke wrote about his flying career. After a heroic time in the war he made a tremendous, historic contribution to the advancement of fighter aircraft at Dunsfold. Little did I realise that, after hard work and a considerable amount of luck, I would also end up working at Dunsfold test flying world-beating jets. Test flying is a most satisfying part of the development of a modern fighter but cannot be achieved without the skill and dedication of engineers, designers and all supporting staff. I still remember my first flight in a Sea Harrier when the inertial system failed in fairly poor weather. The instruments told me I was heading west but Dunsfold Air Traffic Control saw me on radar heading south. It was their skill that got me back to the airfield for a safe vertical landing in front of a Chinese delegation.
>
> Dunsfold was the place where hundreds of parts from all over the country were assembled and tested. It was always a privilege to walk out to a jet and see the engineers who built it assembled to see the aircraft on its first flight. All versions of the Harrier are world-beating fighters. The Hawks, too, are world-beating trainers and ground-attack machines. The whole team at Dunsfold can be extremely proud of what we achieved for Hawker Siddeley, British Aerospace and the country. We delivered aircraft all over the world, often across deserts and oceans, invariably a little short of fuel. All these ferry flights to every continent were a complete success thanks to the teamwork back at home at Dunsfold. Sadly some of the test flying did not go according plan; that is the nature of getting the maximum performance from the jets. The good and happy morale of all that worked at Dunsfold allowed us to continue and overcome the darkest of days. What a privilege to have been part of a world beating team, and working in the Surrey countryside.

Notes

Chapter 1
1. National Archives, Kew (NA, Kew): Avia 65/80
2. NA, Kew: DEFE7/516
3. Ibid.: AVIA 65/80
4. Ibid.: AVIA55/25
5. Ibid.
6. Ibid.
7. Ibid.
8. Ibid.
9. Ibid.
10. Ibid.
11. Ibid.: DEFE7/516
12. Ibid.: CO537/2604
13. Ibid.: AIR16/1122, FCO7/834
14. Ibid.: AIR16/1127
15. Ibid.: AIR16/1122
16. Ibid.: AIR16/1127
17. Ibid.: AVIA 65/80
18. Ibid.: AIR16/1122
19. Ibid.
20. Ibid.: FC07/834
21. Ibid.
22. Ibid.: FCO7/834, AVIA 65/1941
23. Ibid.: FO371/185039
24. Ibid.: FCO7/834

Chapter 2
1. BAE Systems, courtesy of Brooklands Museum: HAL/SHK/002
2. Ibid., HAL/SHK/002
3. Ibid., HAL/SHK/011

4. NA, Kew: AVIA53-13
5. Neville Duke Log, Tangmere Aviation Museum: 2007.084.001.004.
6. Dow, Andrew, *Pegasus – The Heart of the Harrier*, p. 54, fn. 18.
7. Neville Duke Log, op. cit., 2007.084.001.004.
8. Duke, Neville, *Test Pilot*, p. 193.
9. BAE Systems, courtesy of Brooklands Museum. HAL/HIS/007
10. NA, Kew: AVIA 65/80
11. Ibid.
12. Ibid.
13. Neville Duke Log, op. cit., 2007.084.001.004.
14. Duke, *Test Pilot*, op. cit., p. 15.
15. Neville Duke Log, op. cit., 2007.084.001.004.

Chapter 3

1. *Flight*, 29 May 1953.
2. *Aeroplane*, 29 May 1953
3. BAE Systems, op. cit., HAL/HIS/082
4. Neville Duke Log, op. cit., 2007.084.001.004.
5. BAE Systems, op. cit., HAL/HUN/116
6. Neville Duke Log, op. cit., 2007.084.001.004.
7. All papers relating to the du Boulay action are held at NA, Kew, AVIA 65/536 and AIR 2-12325
8. Ibid.
9. NA, Kew: AVIA 65/536
10. Ibid.
11. BAE Systems, op. cit., HAL/MIS/092
12. Neville Duke Log, op. cit, 2007.084.001.004.

Chapter 4

1. BAE Systems, op. cit., HAL/PRJ/058
2. Ibid., HAL/PRJ/057
3. NA, Kew: AVIA 65/80
4. BAE Systems, op. cit., HAL/PRJ/001, 033, 034, 043, 051, 059
5. Martell-Mead, Paul, and Hygate, Barrie, *Hawker P.1103 & P.1121 – Camm's Last Fighter Projects*, 2015, p. 36.
6. NA, Kew: AVIA65/60
7. Ibid.
8. Ibid.
9. Ibid.
10. Ibid.

11. Ibid.
12. Ibid.
13. Ibid.
14. Ibid.
15. Ibid.,AVIA 65/1942 and AVIA 65/1941
16. Ibid., AVIA 65/1942 and AVIA65/1941, pt 2
17. *BAe Link* magazine, issue 3, July 1979
18. Pers comm, Peter Amos
19. NA, Kew: AVIA 65/1942
20. Ibid.
21. Ibid.: AVIA 65/1941
22. Ibid.: AVIA 65/1942 pt 2

Chapter 5
 1. *Hawker Association Newsletter*
 2. BAE Systems, courtesy of Brooklands Museum. HAL/HIS/164
 3. Interview Colin Balchin, 23 January 2017
 4. Pers comm, Peter Amos
 5. BAE Systems, op. cit., HAL/HUN/143
 6. Ibid.
 7. Ibid.
 8. Ibid.
 9. Ibid.
10. Ibid.
11. Ibid.
12. Super Hunter brochure, March 1971, via Peter Amos
13. Phipp, Mike, with Hayward, Eric, *Hunter One – the Jet Heritage Story*
14. Air Accidents Investigation Branch: AAIB Bulletin No: 10/99 Ref: EW/C98/6/1 Category 1.1. October 1999.

Chapter 6
 1. Via Philip Jarrett
 2. NA, Kew: AIR2/17677
 3. Ibid.
 4. *The Aeroplane*, 23 September 1949.
 5. John Judge Log, via Peter Amos
 6. McCloskey, Keith, *Airwork – A History*, p. 56
 7. NA, Kew: AVIA65/1941
 8. Via Peter Amos

9. Curtis, Duncan, *The Canadair Sabre in RAF Service*, p. 9.
10. BAE Systems, courtesy of Brooklands Museum. Dunsfold Tower Logs and via Peter Amos
11. Ibid., Dunsfold Tower Logs
12. *Air Britain Digest*, January 1960.
13. NA, Kew: AVIA65/636
14. Pers comm Reg Dennis
15. Bingham, Victor, *Folland Gnat*, p.21; James, Derek, *Spirit of Hamble – Folland Aircraft*, p. 17.
16. Via Peter Amos
17. Interview, Chris Roberts 5 January 2018
18. Pers comm, Peter Amos

Chapter 7
1. NATO Document M.C.48 – item no. 5: *Measures to Enable NATO Forces to Survive Soviet Atomic Attack.*
2. BAE Systems. op. cit., HAL/HIS/006
3. Ibid.
4. Ibid.
5. Ibid.
6. Ibid.
7. Ibid., HAL/HIS/127
8. Report of Loss of P.1127 second prototype, XP836, on 14 December 1961; Record of images of XP836 post-crash. BAE Systems, op. cit., HAL/P27/033
9. Dow, op. cit., p. 194
10. BAE Systems, op. cit. HAL/P27/130
11. Dow, op. cit., p. 210

Chapter 8
1. BAE Systems courtesy of Brooklands Museum: HAL/P27/138
2. Dow, Andrew, *Pegasus – The Heart of the Harrier*, p. 276
3. BAE Systems, courtesy of Brooklands Museum: HAL/PRJ/029
4. Interview John Parrott 16 February 2017
5. BAE Systems, courtesy of Brooklands Museum: HAL/PRJ/029
6. Dow, op. cit., p. 277
7. Ibid., p. 285
8. BAE Systems, courtesy of Brooklands Museum: HAL/HIS/004
9. BAE Systems, courtesy of Brooklands Museum: HAL/P27/130

10. BAE Systems, courtesy of Brooklands Museum: HAL/P27/129
11. BAE Systems, courtesy of Brooklands Museum: HAL/P27/137
12. Pers comm Peter Amos
13. *Flight International* 11 Jan 1968.
14. Proceeding of a Board of Enquiry into an Aircraft Accident convened on 28 January 1969.
15. BAE Systems, courtesy of Brooklands Museum HAS/HEX/021. Interview Dick Wise 11 May 2017.

Chapter 9

1. BAE Systems, courtesy of Brooklands Museum: HAL/P27/138, and Report by John P Reeder and Fred Drinkwater, NASA Langley 24 July 1962.
2. Interview John Farley 19 October 2016
3. Pers comm Peter Amos
4. BAE Systems, courtesy of Brooklands Museum HAS/HRG/097
5. BAE Systems, courtesy of Brooklands Museum: HAL/MIS/016
6. BAE Systems, courtesy of Brooklands Museum: HSA/HR2/013
7. BAE Systems, courtesy of Brooklands Museum: HSA/HR2/008
8. Interview John Farley 19 October 2016
9. BAE Systems, courtesy of Brooklands Museum: HSA/HRG/097
10. Interview John Farley 19 October 2016
11. BAE Systems, courtesy of Brooklands Museum: HAL/HIS/015
12. BAE Systems, courtesy of Brooklands Museum: HAL/HIS/014
13. BAE Systems, courtesy of Brooklands Museum: HAL/HIS/014
14. Interview Colin Balchin 23 January 2017
15. BAE Systems, courtesy of Brooklands Museum: HAL/SFY/001
16. Pers comm Peter Amos

Chapter 10

1. BAE Systems, courtesy of Brooklands Museum: HSA/HK1/001
2. BAE Systems, courtesy of Brooklands Museum: HAL/HIS/018
3. BAE Systems, courtesy of Brooklands Museum: HAS/HK1/058
4. Pers comm Mark Gerrard
5. Ibid.
6. Cole, Barbara, *Sabotage and Torture*.
7. Pers comm Mark Gerrard
8. Ibid.
9. BAE Systems, courtesy of Brooklands Museum: HSA/HK1/020, 022
10. BAE Systems, courtesy of Brooklands Museum: BAE/HKS/018

Chapter 11

1. John Farley, John, *A View from the Hover*, p. 102
2. Interview Chris Roberts, 5 January 2018
3. Pers comm Mark Gerrard
4. Interview Chris Roberts, 5 January 2018

Chapter 12

1. Dow, op. cit., p. 364
2. Ibid.
3. Inquest report via *Flight International*, 9 April 1988
4. Ibid.
5. Dow, op. cit., p. 450
6. Air Accidents Investigation Branch AAIB Report 1/77 issued by Department of Trade 8/2/1977. *Surrey Advertiser*, 21 November 1975
7. Interview Heinz Frick, 4 December 2018
8. BAE Systems, courtesy of Brooklands Museum: HAS/FTS/012
9. Ibid.

Chapter 13

1. Lygo, Adm. Sir Raymond, *Collision Course – Lygo Shoots Back*, p. 446
2. BAE Systems, courtesy of Brooklands Museum: BAE/MAN/005
3. BAE Systems, courtesy of Brooklands Museum: BAE/MAN/022
4. *The Comet*, 21 February 1992
5. BAE Systems, courtesy of Brooklands Museum: HAL/MIS/174
6. Ibid.
7. Pers Comm Bill Anderson
8. BAE Systems, courtesy of Brooklands Museum: HAL/MIS/174
9. BAE Systems, courtesy of Brooklands Museum: Dunsfold Tower Logs

Appendix 1

Instrumentation Systems for Airborne Data Acquisition

As will be clear from the foregoing story, much of Dunsfold's work involved the testing of aircraft to clear airframe and systems equipment for release to service. Over the period of this book, the methods by which information on aircraft and systems performance was gathered changed quite fundamentally. In the 1950s the standard method of gathering data was by means of what was known as an automatic observer panel (AOP). This relatively simple technique utilised a secondary instrument panel located in some convenient part of the aircraft, the instruments of which were filmed by cine camera and, once the film had been developed, the results could be read and subsequently analysed. The automatic observer could record typically up to ten different types of data, although in the Sea Hawk trials undertaken by Hawker Aircraft, up to twenty types were recorded.

By the 1960s the AOP was being overtaken by early electric sensors sending their readings to paper trace recorders and later, to wire recorders; in the 1970s, the advent of digital electronic systems allowed much larger amounts of data to be recorded. At Dunsfold, this process of recording and analysing instrumentation data was the province of the Flight Test Instrumentation Department. Rod Hunt, former Group Leader FTI, explains how it worked.

> The Flight Test Instrumentation (FTI) department at Dunsfold was responsible for the collection, recording, replaying and processing of all the sensor information from the instrumented test aircraft.
>
> During the 1980s through to 2000+ there was a total of ten test aircraft – Hawk single-seater (ZH200), four Harrier Ground Reconnaissance (GR) aircraft ZD318, ZD319, ZD320 and ZD321, each one going through various upgrades Mk 5, Mk 7, Mk 9. Also a two-seater T. 10 Trainer Harrier

(ZH653), and two Sea Harriers, ZA195 and XZ439, and a specially adapted HS.125 commercial aircraft (ZF130).

Each test aircraft was fitted with a bespoke instrumentation system IDAS (Integrated Data Acquisition System), designed in-house by the Instrumentation and Electronics (I&E) department at BAe Kingston and developed by FTI at Dunsfold. The instrumentation system collected 'low-level' sensor information, conditioned it, digitised this information and sent it along an Instrumentation Data-Bus to be recorded on an 'agile' magnetic tape recorder (each tape 1 inch wide, 6,800 feet long). The word 'agile' is used to describe the way data was recorded, dependent upon the amount of data sent to the recorder at any specific time, so slow data traffic – the recorder would go slower while for vast amounts of data it would speed up. This way data packing-density was maximised. The tape recorder was housed in the rear equipment bay from where it could be winched out for tape replacement or in for storage ready for trial.

Each Harrier aircraft (production and development) had various systems and 'black boxes' fitted around the aircraft. These 'boxes' communicated with each other via various databuses. The IDAS would 'listen-in' to these communication messages that were travelling up and down the buses, and record all the communications on the tape recorder. Instrumentation video recorders were fitted that could record what the pilot saw on the two head-down Multi-Purpose Colour Displays (MPCDs) as well as what he was seeing in the Head-Up Display (HUD). These video signals were mixed to record MPCD and HUD imagery as well as moving map (giving the aircraft's location). Wet film cameras could be fitted to the underwing or centreline pylons to film the way in which the various stores left the aircraft when released or fired.

Typical standard parameters recorded included acceleration – normal, lateral and longitudinal 'g'; airspeed; altitude; rates – roll, pitch and yaw (deg/sec); surface angle – aileron, flaps, rudder, tailplane, airbrake; nozzle angle; temperatures – outside air, various equipment bays; pressures – hydraulic etc.; avionics databus data; radar databus data. Alongside these 'standard' parameters, special instrumentation sensors would be commissioned, and recorded by IDAS, for specific ground or flight trials. An example could be that high frequency accelerations would need to be recorded to capture the vibration experienced on any of the 'stores' (e.g. weapons, fuel tanks etc.) that were carried on any of the pylons under the aircraft's wing or fuselage.

For each trial sortie, the instrumentation was programmed, via a Ground Support Unit, to record those parameters needed for that sortie. The tape recorder was loaded with a new tape and checks were made to ensure the IDAS was working as required. The instrumentation system was controlled by the pilot via a special IDAS display unit fitted in the cockpit. The pilot could monitor and interrogate the IDAS and could use it as a timing method for recording particular events during the sortie.

Once the aircraft had carried out its designated trial, the aircraft would land, the magnetic and video tapes would be unloaded, along with any wet-film recorders. The video tapes would usually be handed to Flight Test to be used in their pilot debrief following each sortie. Checks would be carried out to ensure the IDAS had performed correctly and the aircraft's instrumentation would be prepared for the next trial.

The large magnetic data tape would be taken to the Flight Test Instrumentation Data Reduction (FTDR) room where software was created, and loaded onto the Ground Station (to mimic the flight trial requirements) and the tape replayed. Calibration details were added during the replay to allow the data to be reduced and for analysis engineers to view the appropriate parameters in 'real units' (e.g. feet, degrees, degrees/second, knots etc. – instead of just 1s and 0s). Various forms of printouts, along with re-formatted data tapes could be provided to the specialist engineers to carry out the detailed analysis of how the aircraft and/or its systems performed during the sortie. All of this data would be readily available for future analysis usually only a couple of hours later.

Trials supported by FTI included various system and performance trials and integration, weapon pit drop, rough ground trials, onboard ship trials, weapon release and firing trials (both in UK and in USA) night vision goggle integration, Aden gun firing trials.

Appendix 2

Supermarine Attacker F.1, FB.2.
Breakdown of Movements at Dunsfold

Serial no	Flown Gatwick to Dunsfold for test	Delivery by Shorts to Abbotsinch	Notes
Attacker F.1			
WA207?	28/02/1955		Possibly WA507
WA474	26/03/1956	19/04/1956	
WA476	20/06/1955	27/06/1955	Force landed at Stretton en route. Scrapped 1958
WA479?	12/03/1956	20/03/1956	
WA484	20/01/1956	01/02/1956	
WA486	24/08/1955	31/08/1955	Scrapped 31/8/58
WA487	03/02/1956	07/02/1956	
WA488	15/02/1956	05/03/1956	
WA489	02/08/1955	17/08/1956	
WA491?	14/03/1956	21/03/1956	To Lasham
WA497	12/12/1955	20/01/1956	
WA508	23/11/1955	17/01/1956	Serial shown incorrectly as WA548
WA513	28/06/1955	04 or 08/07/1955	Scrapped 7/58
WA515	24/10/1955	01/11/1955	
WA516	18/01/1955	08/02/1955	Scrapped 7/58
WA518	03/03/1955	15/03/1955	
WA519	21/03/1955	04/05/1955	
WA521?	02/05/1955	16/05/1955	Serial shown incorrectly as WG521, Returned to Gatwick
WA523	02/03/1955	24/3/55	
WA523	03/08/1955	18/08/1955	Scrapped 31/8/58
WA525	23/05/1955	09/06/1955	Scrapped 7/58
WA527?	19/09/1955		

263

Serial no	Flown Gatwick to Dunsfold for test	Delivery by Shorts to Abbotsinch	Notes
WA527	14 or 24/10/1955	01/11/1955	
WA531	12/07/1955		
WA531			Returned to Gatwick 15/7/55
WA531	02/08/1955	17/08/1955	Scrapped 31/8/58
WA534	28/11/1955	05/12/1955	Possible confusion with WA834
WA585?	24/03/1955		Possibly WA485
WA506		21/02/1955	Delivery Dunsfold to Stretton (possibly WA506)
WA834	28/11/1955	05/12/1955	
Attacker FB.2			
WK319	08/03/1956	15/03/1956	Scrapped 31/8/58
WK321	26/09/1955	12/10/1955	
WK325	30/06/1955	04/07/1955	Delivery aborted due to aileron trouble
WK325		07/07/1955	
WK326	29/08/1955	05/09/1955	
WK327	23/02/1956	07/03/1956	Serial shown incorrectly as WA325
WK328	31/05/1955	09/06/1955	Serial shown incorrectly as WA328
WK338	18/05/1955	02/06/1955	Scrapped 31/8/58
Attacker FB.2			
WP275?	28/02/1955		See entry below
WP275	14/04/1955	02/06/1955	
WP279	26/10/1955	02/11/1955	Serial shown incorrectly as WA279.
WP291	23/03/1956	16/04/1956	
Attacker FB.2			
WT851	02/12/1955	Returned to Gatwick 6/12/55	
WZ278	11/2/55?	08/03/1955	

Courtesy of Peter Amos, 2019

Appendix 3

Canadair Sabre: Breakdown of Movements at Dunsfold

Date	Aircraft	Canadian Serial	RAF Serial	Pilot	Destination	Notes
04/11/1954	Sabre 4	19512	XB609		Benson	delivery by RAF
09/11/1954	Sabre 4	19538	XB635		Benson	delivery by RAF
01/12/1954	Sabre 4	19475	XB544		Lynham	delivery by RAF
15/12/1954	Sabre 2	19308				from West Raynham to N. Luffenham RCAF visitor
30/12/1954	Sabre 4	19715	XD714		Benson	delivery by RAF
17/01/1955	Sabre 4	19868	XB855		Benson	delivery by RAF
18/01/1955	Sabre 4		XB521		Dunsfold	From Manston, flown in by RAF
02/02/1955	Sabre 4	19828	XB941		Lynham	delivery by RAF
03/03/1955	Sabre 4	19628	XD754		Lynham	delivery by RAF
28/03/1955	Sabre 4	19663	XB551		Dunsfold	From Kemble, flown in by RAF
28/03/1955	Sabre 4	19888	XB997		Dunsfold	From Kemble, flown in by RAF
01/04/1955	Sabre 4	19706	XB868		Lynham	delivery by RAF
06/04/1955	Sabre 4	19561	XB675		Dunsfold	From Kemble, flown in by RAF
06/04/1955	Sabre 4	19524	XB621		Benson	delivery by RAF
14/04/1955	Sabre 4	19888	XB997		Kemble	delivery by RAF
19/04/1955	Sabre 4	19561	XB675		Benson	delivery by RAF

Date	Aircraft	Canadian Serial	RAF Serial	Pilot	Destination	Notes
25/04/1955	Sabre 4	19645	XB791		Benson	delivery by RAF
16/05/1955	Sabre 4	19565	XB679		Lynham	delivery by RAF
02/06/1955	Sabre 4	19490	XB583		Benson	delivery by RAF
02/06/1955	Sabre 4	19470	XB739		Benson	delivery by RAF
27/06/1955	Sabre 4	19602	XD728		Kemble	delivery by RAF
07/07/1955	Sabre 4	19589	XB703		Benson	delivery by RAF
11/07/1955	Sabre 4	19822	XB935		Dunsfold	From Tangmere, flown in by RAF
15/07/1955	Sabre 4	19555	XB669		Kemble	delivery by RAF
02/08/1955	Sabre 4		XB9424		Dunsfold	From Manston, flown in by RAF
10/08/1955	Sabre 4		XB843		Dunsfold	From Germany via Manston, flown in by RAF
10/08/1955	Sabre 4		XB842		Dunsfold	From Germany via Manston, flown in by RAF
26/08/1955	Sabre 4	19840	XB953		Dunsfold	From Germany via Manston, flown in by RAF, cleared customs Dunsfold
26/08/1955	Sabre 4	19864	XB851		Dunsfold	From Germany via Manston, flown in by RAF, cleared customs Dunsfold
26/08/1955	Sabre 4	19886	XB995		Dunsfold	From Germany via Manston, flown in by RAF, cleared customs Dunsfold
31/08/1955	Sabre 4	19794	XB917		Dunsfold	From Benson, flown in by RAF
07/09/1955	Sabre 4	19572	XB686		Dunsfold	From Benson, flown in by RAF
07/09/1955	Sabre 4	19845	XB958		Dunsfold	From Benson, flown in by RAF
07/09/1955	Sabre 4	19826	XB939		Dunsfold	From Benson, flown in by RAF
07/09/1955	Sabre 4	19857	XB650		Dunsfold	From Benson, flown in by RAF
12/09/1955	Sabre 4	19522	XB619		Dunsfold	From Benson, flown in by RAF

Date	Type	C/N	Serial	Location	Notes
19/09/1955	Sabre 4	19467	XB536	Dunsfold	From Benson, flown in by RAF
22/09/1955	Sabre 4	19620	XB746	Dunsfold	From Benson, flown in by RAF
22/09/1955	Sabre 4	19874	XB983	Dunsfold	From Benson, flown in by RAF
27/09/1955	Sabre 4	19511	XB608	Dunsfold	From Benson, flown in by RAF
03/10/1955	Sabre 4	19748	XB885	Dunsfold	From Benson, flown in by RAF
03/10/1955	Sabre 4	19792	XB915	Dunsfold	From Benson, flown in by RAF
04/10/1955	Sabre 4	13325		Dunsfold	From Prestwick, visitor USAF, returned same day
17/10/1955	Sabre 4	19733	XB870	Dunsfold	From Benson, flown in by RAF
20/10/1955	Sabre 4	19700	XB862	Dunsfold	From Benson, flown in by RAF
10/11/1955	Sabre 4	19688	XB834	Dunsfold	From Benson, flown in by RAF
10/11/1955	Sabre 4	19694	XB856	Dunsfold	From Benson, flown in by RAF
15/11/1955	Sabre 4	24476		Dunsfold	From Prestwick, visitor USAF, returned next day
12/01/1956	Sabre 4	19544	XB641	Marseille–Marignane	Delivered by USAF
27/01/1956	Sabre 4	19570	XB684	Marseille–Marignane	Delivered by USAF
27/01/1956	Sabre 4	19865	XB852	Dunsfold	From Benson, flown in by RAF
27/01/1956	Sabre 4	19528	XB625	Dunsfold	From Benson, flown in by RAF
10/02/1956	Sabre 4	19882	XB991	Chambley	Delivered by USAF
28/02/1956	Sabre 4	19633	XB759	Marseille–Marignane	Delivered by USAF
08/03/1956	Sabre 4	19859	XB771	Dunsfold	From Benson, flown in by RAF
16/03/1956	Sabre 4	19661	XB807	Marseille–Marignane	Delivered by USAF
16/04/1956	Sabre		XD?11731	Dunsfold	From Linton, flown in by RAF
16/04/1956	Sabre	17795		Dunsfold	From Linton, flown in by RAF
16/04/1956	Sabre	?		Dunsfold	From Linton, flown in by RAF
17/04/1956	Sabre 4	19772	XD770	Dunsfold	From Linton, flown in by RAF. Scrapped Lasham

Date	Aircraft	Canadian Serial	RAF Serial	Pilot	Destination	Notes
18/04/1956	Sabre 4	19464	XB533		Dunsfold	From Kemble, flown in by RAF
19/04/1956	Sabre 4	19817	XB930		Dunsfold	From Benson, flown in by RAF
19/04/1956	Sabre	13496			Dunsfold	From Prestwick, visitor USAF, returned next day
20/04/1956	Sabre 4	19542	XB639		Marseille–Marignane	Delivery by USAF
20/04/1956	Sabre	19848	XB961		Dunsfold	From Benson, flown in by RAF
25/04/1956	Sabre	19823	XB736		Dunsfold	From Linton, flown in by RAF
03/05/1956	Sabre	19839	XB952		Dunsfold	From Benson, flown in by RAF
03/05/1956	Sabre	19877	XB986		Dunsfold	From Benson, flown in by RAF
07/05/1956	Sabre	?			Dunsfold	From Linton, flown in by RAF
07/05/1956	Sabre	?			Dunsfold	From Linton, flown in by RAF
08/05/1956	Sabre 4	19864			Munich	Delivered by USAF
09/05/1956	Sabre	19533	XB630		Dunsfold	From Benson, flown in by RAF
09/05/1956	Sabre	19784	XB896		Dunsfold	From Benson, flown in by RAF
09/05/1956	Sabre	19890	XB999		Dunsfold	From Benson, flown in by RAF
10/05/1956	Sabre	19527	XB624		Dunsfold	From Benson, flown in by RAF
10/05/1956	Sabre	19540	XB637		Dunsfold	From Benson, flown in by RAF
10/05/1956	Sabre	19726	XD725		Dunsfold	From Linton, flown in by RAF
11/05/1956	Sabre 4	19696	XB858		Spangdahlem	Delivered by USAF
14/05/1956	Sabre	?			Dunsfold	From Benson, flown in by RAF
14/05/1956	Sabre				Dunsfold	From Benson, flown in by RAF
14/05/1956	Sabre				Dunsfold	From Benson, flown in by RAF
15/05/1956	Sabre	19707	XD706		Dunsfold	From Linton, flown in by RAF
16/05/1956	Sabre	?			Dunsfold	From Benson, flown in by RAF

Date	Type	Serial	Code	Location	Notes
16/05/1956	Sabre	?		Dunsfold	From Benson, flown in by RAF
16/05/1956	Sabre	?		Dunsfold	From Benson, flown in by RAF
17/05/1956	Sabre	19663	XB551	Prestwick	Delivered by USAF
18/05/1956	Sabre	19875	XB948	Dunsfold	From Benson, flown in by RAF
18/05/1956	Sabre	19869	XB978	Dunsfold	From Benson, flown in by RAF
22/05/1956	Sabre	19478	XB547	Lasham	Delivered by Airwork
22/05/1956	Sabre	19835	XB948	Lasham	Delivered by Airwork
22/05/1956	Sabre	?		Lasham	Delivered by Airwork
22/05/1956	Sabre	19485	XB578	Lasham	Delivered by Airwork
22/05/1956	Sabre	19540	XB637	Lasham	Delivered by Airwork
23/05/1956	Sabre	19707	XD706	Lasham	Delivered by Airwork
23/05/1956	Sabre	?		Lasham	Delivered by Airwork
23/05/1956	Sabre	19533	XB630	Lasham	Delivered by Airwork
23/05/1956	Sabre	19488	XB581	Lasham	Delivered by Airwork
23/05/1956	Sabre	?		Lasham	Delivered by Airwork
23/05/1956	Sabre	?		Lasham	Delivered by Airwork
24/05/1956	Sabre 4	19822	XB935	Chambley-Bussieres	Delivered by USAF
24/05/1956	Sabre	19720	XD719	Lasham	Delivered by Airwork
25/05/1956	Sabre 4	19489	XB582	Dunsfold	From Benson, flown in by RAF
31/05/1956	Sabre	19595	XB709	Marseille–Marignane	Delivered by USAF
31/05/1956	Sabre	19811	XB924	Marseille–Marignane	Delivered by USAF
06/06/1956	Sabre		X?790	Dunsfold	From Benson, flown in by RAF
12/06/1956	Sabre	19829	XB9424	Marseille–Marignane	Delivered by USAF
12/06/1956	Sabre	19695	XB857	Marseille–Marignane	Delivered by USAF
21/06/1956	Sabre 4	19832	XB945	Bitburg	Delivered by USAF
30/06/1956	Sabre	19838	XB951	Marseille–Marignane	Delivered by USAF

Date	Aircraft	Canadian Serial	RAF Serial	Pilot	Destination	Notes
06/07/1956	Sabre	19830	XB943		Pratica de Mare	Delivered by USAF
12/07/1956	Sabre	19804	XB917		Pratica de Mare	Delivered by USAF
10/08/1956	Sabre	19722	XD721		Chambley-Bussieres	Delivered by USAF
10/08/1956	Sabre	19616	XB742		Chambley-Bussieres	Delivered by USAF
21/08/1956	Sabre	19467	XB536		Chambley-Bussieres	Delivered by USAF
07/09/1956	Sabre	19841	XB954		Chambley-Bussieres	Delivered by USAF
07/09/1956	Sabre	19554	XB668		Chambley-Bussieres	Delivered by USAF
12/09/1956	Sabre	19766	XD764		Chambley-Bussieres	Delivered by USAF. Returned to Dunsfold
12/09/1956	Sabre	19749	XD731		Chambley-Bussieres	Delivered by USAF. Returned to Dunsfold
19/09/1956	Sabre	19404	XB532		Prestwick	Delivered by USAF
19/09/1956	Sabre	19766	XD764		Prestwick	Delivered by USAF
25/09/1956	Sabre	19803			Chambley-Bussieres	Delivered by USAF
25/09/1956	Sabre	19464	XB533		Chambley-Bussieres	Delivered by USAF
26/09/1956	Sabre	19620	XB746	FU-620	Dunsfold	From Linton, flown in by Airwork
05/10/1956	Sabre	19748	XB885		Chaumont-Semoutiers	Delivered by USAF
05/10/1956	Sabre	19620	XB746		Chaumont-Semoutiers	Delivered by USAF
15/10/1956	Sabre	19839	XB952		Toul-Rosières	Delivered by USAF
15/10/1956	Sabre	19792	XB915		Toul-Rosières	Delivered by USAF
27/10/1956	Sabre	19601	XB727		Dunsfold	From Lasham, flown in by Airwork
30/10/1956	Sabre	19874	XB983		Rome	Delivered by USAF
30/10/1956	Sabre	19835	XB948		Rome	Delivered by USAF
06/11/1956	Sabre	19511	XB608		Rome	Delivered by USAF

CANADAIR SABRE

Date	Type	C/N	Serial	Pilot	Location	Remarks
06/11/1956	Sabre	19601	XB727		Rome	Delivered by USAF
08/11/1956	Sabre	19817	XB930		Bitburg	Delivered by USAF
08/11/1956	Sabre	19724	XD723		Bitburg	Delivered by USAF
20/11/1956	Sabre	19810	XB923		Chambley-Bussieres	Delivered by USAF
20/11/1956	Sabre	19644	XB770		Chambley-Bussieres	Delivered by USAF
03/12/1956	Sabre	19877	XB986	Tyszko		
03/12/1956	Sabre	19720	XD719	Tyszko	From Lasham	
04/12/1956	Sabre	19784	XB896	Tyszko		
05/12/1956	Sabre	19784	XB896	Sparkes		
06/12/1956	Sabre	19877	XB986	Sparkes	Delivery to Manston	
06/12/1956	Sabre	19874	XB983	Tyszko		
11/12/1956	Sabre	19720	XD719	Tyszko		
12/12/1956	Sabre	19784	XB896	Lt Fisher	Fürstenfeldbruck	
13/12/1956	Sabre	19720	XD719	Tyszko		
13/12/1956	Sabre	19639	XB765	Tyszko		
18/12/1956	Sabre	19639	XB765	Sparkes		
27/12/1956	Sabre	19739	XB765	Tyszko		
29/12/1956	Sabre	19720	XD719	Tyszko		
29/12/1956	Sabre	19739	XB876	Tyszko		
02/01/1957	Sabre	19639	XB876	Tyszko		
02/01/1957	Sabre	19720	XD719	Tyszko		
02/01/1957	Sabre	19739	XB765	Tyszko		
03/01/1957	Sabre	19639	XB765	Tyszko		
03/01/1957	Sabre	19739	XB876	Sparkes		
03/01/1957	Sabre	19720	XD719	Tyszko		
03/01/1957	Sabre	19528	XB625	Tyszko		

271

Date	Aircraft	Canadian Serial	RAF Serial	Pilot	Destination	Notes
03/01/1957	Sabre	19639	XB765	Col Smith		
03/01/1957	Sabre	19720	XD719	Tyszko		
07/01/1957	Sabre	19730	XD729	Sparkes		
07/01/1957	Sabre	19572	XB686	Tyszko		
09/01/1957	Sabre	19572	XB686	Tyszko		
09/01/1957	Sabre	19528	XB625	Tyszko		
10/01/1957	Sabre	19739	XB876	Sparkes	Fürstenfeldbruck	
10/01/1957	Sabre	19639	XB765	Kuchman	Fürstenfeldbruck	
10/01/1957	Sabre	19720	XD719	Catlin	Fürstenfeldbruck	
12/01/1957	Sabre	19528	XB625	Tyszko		
16/01/1957	Sabre	19572	XB686	Sparkes		
16/01/1957	Sabre	19488	XB581	Rhodes	From Lasham	
17/01/1957	Sabre	19528	XB625	Sparkes		
17/01/1957	Sabre	19737	XB874	Rhodes		
18/01/1957	Sabre	19737	XB874	Sparkes		
18/01/1957	Sabre	19848	XB961	Rhodes		
18/01/1957	Sabre	19572	XB686	Smith		
18/01/1957	Sabre	19737	XB876	Sparkes		
21/01/1957	Sabre	19848	XB961	Tyszko	To Lasham	
22/01/1957	Sabre	19528	XB625	Tyszko	To Lasham	
04/02/1957	Sabre	19572	XB686	Sparkes	Châteauroux-Déols	
04/02/1957	Sabre	19737	XB876	Catlin	Châteauroux-Déols	
04/02/1957	Sabre	19488	XB581	Tyszko		
04/02/1957	Sabre	19754	XD736	Tyszko		

Date		Serial	Code	Pilot	Note	Remarks
06/02/1957	Sabre	19493	XB586	Tyszko		
06/02/1957	Sabre	19848	XB961	Tyszko	From Lasham	
06/02/1956	Sabre	19528	XB625		From Lasham	
11/02/1957	Sabre	19493	XB586	Tyszko		
12/02/1957	Sabre	19496	XB589	Tyszko		seen at Lasham 16/5/59
12/02/1957	Sabre	19493	XB586	Tyszko		
13/02/1957	Sabre	19754	XD736	Capt Fonk?		
13/02/1957	Sabre	19493	XB586	Tyszko		
13/02/1957	Sabre	19528	XB625	Capt Fonk?		
15/02/1957	Sabre	19488	XB581	Sparkes		
18/02/1957	Sabre	19754	XD736	Sparkes		
18/02/1957	Sabre	19493	XB586	Tyszko		
18/02/1957	Sabre	19848	XB961	Sparkes		
19/02/1957	Sabre	19528	XB625	Kochman	To Munich	
19/02/1957	Sabre	19754	XD736	Landford?	To Munich	
20/02/1957	Sabre	19488	XB581	Sparkes		
20/02/1957	Sabre	19848	XB961	Sparkes		
20/02/1957	Sabre	19493	XB586	Tyszko		
20/02/1957	Sabre	19628	XB754	Tyszko		
21/02/1957	Sabre	19845	XB958	Tyszko		
21/02/1957	Sabre	19488	XB581	Sparkes	To Bitburg	
22/02/1957	Sabre	19493	XB586	Catlin		
22/02/1957	Sabre	19845	XB958	Catlin		
25/02/1957	Sabre	19845	XB958	Sparkes		
25/02/1957	Sabre	19493	XB586	Sparkes		

Date	Aircraft	Canadian Serial	RAF Serial	Pilot	Destination	Notes
27/02/1957	Sabre	19848	XB961	Sparkes		
28/02/1957	Sabre	19845	XB958	Sparkes	DBLS	
28/02/1957	Sabre	19848	XB961	Catlin	DBLS	
01/03/1957	Sabre	19628	XB754	unknown		
04/03/1957	Sabre	19628	XB754	Tyszko		
04/03/1957	Sabre	19649	XB795	Tyszko		
07/03/1957	Sabre	19628	XB754	Tyszko		
07/03/1957	Sabre	19649	XB795	Sparkes		
08/03/1957	Sabre	19649	XB795	Sparkes	Marseille–Marignane	
12/03/1957	Sabre	19493	XB586	Tyszko	local	
12/03/1957	Sabre	19628	XB754	Tyszko	local	
13/03/1957	Sabre	19493	XB586	Sparkes	to Weathersfield	
13/03/1957	Sabre	19493	XB586	Sparkes	from Weathersfield	
13/03/1957	Sabre	19505	XB598	Tyszko	local	
14/03/1957	Sabre	19493	XB586	Sparkes	local	
14/03/1957	Sabre	19505	XB598	Sparkes	local	
15/03/1957	Sabre	19628	XB754	Tyszko	local	
18/03/1957	Sabre	19505	XB598	Kockman?	Marseille–Marignane	
18/03/1957	Sabre	19493	XB586	Lankford?	Marseille–Marignane	
20/03/1957	Sabre	19859	XB771	Tyszko	local	
20/03/1957	Sabre	19628	XB754	Sparkes	local	
21/03/1957	Sabre	19628	XB754	Sparkes	local	
22/03/1957	Sabre	19628	XB754	Sparkes	Châteauroux-Déols	
22/03/1957	Sabre	19618	XB744	Tyszko	local	

CANADAIR SABRE

25/03/1957	Sabre	19682	XB828	Tyszko	local
25/03/1957	Sabre	19859	XB771	Helmmore	local
25/03/1957	Sabre	19618	XB744	Tyszko	local
26/03/1957	Sabre	19682	XB828	Sparkes	local
26/03/1957	Sabre	19859	XB771	Sparkes	local
29/03/1957	Sabre	19859	XB771	Helmore	local
29/03/1957	Sabre	19618	XB744	Sparkes	local
29/03/1957	Sabre	19859	XB771	Catlin?	local
29/03/1957	Sabre	19618	XB744	Sparkes	Toul-Rosières
29/03/1957	Sabre	19682	XB828	Catlin?	Toul-Rosières
02/04/1957	Sabre	19859	XB771	Tyszko	local
04/04/1957	Sabre	19859	XB771	Catlin?	
04/04/1957	Sabre	19859	XB771	Catlin?	Fürstenfeldbruck
09/04/1957	Sabre	19733	XB870	Tyszko	local
11/04/1957	Sabre	19733	XB870	Sparkes	To Wethersfield
11/04/1957	Sabre	19733	XB870	Sparkes	From Wethersfield
12/04/1957	Sabre	19733	XB870	Sparkes	Rome
15/04/1957	Sabre	19524	XB621	Hunt	From Liverpool
15/04/1957	Sabre	19524	XB621	Sparkes	local
15/04/1957	Sabre	19648	XB794	Helmore	local
16/04/1957	Sabre	19648	XB794	Sparkes	local
16/04/1957	Sabre	19736	XB873	Hunt	From Liverpool
16/04/1957	Sabre	19860	XB772	Helmore	local
23/04/1957	Sabre	19860	XB772	Helmore	local
23/04/1957	Sabre	19648	XB794	Sparkes	local

Date	Aircraft	Canadian Serial	RAF Serial	Pilot	Destination	Notes
23/04/1957	Sabre	19736	XB873	Sparkes	local	
26/04/1957	Sabre	19860	XB772	Sparkes	local	
26/04/1957	Sabre	19648	XB794	Sparkes	local	
26/04/1957	Sabre	19524	XB621	Sparkes	local	
29/04/1957	Sabre	19648	XB794	Catlin	Ypenburg	
29/04/1957	Sabre	19524	XB621	Sparkes	Ypenburg	
29/04/1957	Sabre	19736	XB873	Helmore	local	
30/04/1957	Sabre	19851	XB975	Helmore	local	
30/04/1957	Sabre	19556	XB670	Hunt	From Speke Liverpool	
01/05/1957	Sabre	19736	XB873	Sparkes	local	
01/05/1957	Sabre	19556	XB670	Sparkes	local	
02/05/1957	Sabre	19688	XB834	Helmore	local	
03/05/1957	Sabre	19860	XB772	Sparkes	local	
03/05/1957	Sabre	19494	XB587	Hunt	From Liverpool	
03/05/1957	Sabre	19688	XB834	Tyszko	local	
03/05/1957	Sabre	19494	XB587	Catlin	local	
06/05/1957	Sabre	19494	XB587	Catlin	local	
06/05/1957	Sabre	19860	XB772	Catlin	Ypenburg	
06/05/1957	Sabre	19736	XB873	Thorough	Ypenburg	
08/05/1957	Sabre	19851	XB975	Rhodes	local	
08/05/1957	Sabre	19566	XB680	Rhodes	local	
10/05/1957	Sabre	19688	XB834	Catlin	local	
10/05/1957	Sabre	19566	XB680	Catlin	local	
13/05/1957	Sabre	19688	XB834	F/Lt Manuel?	Ypenburg	

276

CANADAIR SABRE

Date	Type	Serial	Serial2	Pilot	Notes
14/05/1957	Sabre	19566	XB680	F/Lt Manuel?	local
15/05/1957	Sabre	19851	XB975	Trauhman	local
15/05/1957	Sabre	19613	XB739	Helmore	local
16/05/1957	Sabre	1435		Capt Sullivan	local
16/05/1957	Sabre	19613	XB739	Capt Sullivan	Charles?
16/05/1957	Sabre	19851	XB975	Lt Manuel	Charles?
18/05/1957	Sabre	19566	XB680	Helmore	local
20/05/1957	Sabre	19593	XB707	Hunt	From Speke
20/05/1957	Sabre	19494	XB587	Helmore	local
21/05/1957	Sabre	19593	XB707	Sparkes	local
22/05/1957	Sabre	19556	XB670	Helmore	local
22/05/1957	Sabre	19494	XB587	Helmore	local
23/05/1957	Sabre	19556	XB670	Sparkes	local
23/05/1957	Sabre	19494	XB587	Sparkes	local
23/05/1957	Sabre	19475	XB544	Helmore	local
27/05/1957	Sabre	19556	XB670	Sparkes	Ypenburg
27/05/1957	Sabre	19589	XB703	Tyszko	local
28/05/1957	Sabre	19475	XB544	Helmore	local
28/05/1957	Sabre	19539	XB636	Tyszko	local
28/05/1957	Sabre	19593	XB707	Helmore	local
29/05/1957	Sabre	19475	XB544	Sparkes	local
29/05/1957	Sabre	19593	XB707	Sparkes	To Wethersfield
29/05/1957	Sabre	19593	XB707	Sparkes	From Wethersfield
29/05/1957	Sabre	19539	XB636	Helmore	local
29/05/1957	Sabre	19539	XB636	Sparkes	local
30/05/1957	Sabre	19756	XD754	Hunt	From Liverpool

Date	Aircraft	Canadian Serial	RAF Serial	Pilot	Destination	Notes
31/05/1957	Sabre	19539	XB636	Sparkes	local	
31/05/1957	Sabre	19756	XD754	Sparkes	local	
31/05/1957	Sabre	19539	XB636	Sparkes	Toul-Rosières	
31/05/1957	Sabre	19593	XB707	Catlin	Toul-Rosières	
03/06/1957	Sabre	19706	XB868	Hunt	From Liverpool	
05/06/1957	Sabre	19706	XB868	Sparkes	local	
05/06/1957	Sabre	19756	XD754	Manuel	To Chambrey France	
05/06/1957	Sabre	19475	XB544	Lt Lockley	To Chambery France	
05/06/1957	Sabre	19718	XD717	Helmore	local	
06/06/1957	Sabre	19718	XD717	Helmore	local	
07/06/1957	Sabre	19718	XD717	Helmore	local	
11/06/1957	Sabre	19718	XD717	Helmore	local	
12/06/1957	Sabre	19718	XD717	Helmore	local	
12/06/1957	Sabre	19718	XD717	Sparkes	local	
12/06/1957	Sabre	19706	XB868	Helmore	local	
13/06/1957	Sabre	19706	XB868	Sparkes	local	
14/06/1957	Sabre	19718	XD717	Sparkes	local	
14/06/1957	Sabre	19706	XB868	Sparkes	To Ypenburg	
17/06/1957	Sabre	19678	XB824	Helmore	local	
18/06/1957	Sabre	19646	XB792	Tyszko	From Liverpool	
18/06/1957	Sabre	19678	XB824	Sparkes	local	
19/06/1957	Sabre	19623	XB749	Hunt	From Liverpool	
19/06/1957	Sabre	19726	XD725	Helmore	local	
20/06/1957	Sabre	19646	XB792	Sparkes	local	

Date	Type	Number	Code	Pilot	Route
20/06/1957	Sabre	19628	XB754	Sparkes	local
20/06/1957	Sabre	19646	XB792	Sparkes	local
20/06/1957	Sabre	19623	XB749	Sparkes	local
20/06/1957	Sabre	19678	XB824	Sparkes	local
20/06/1957	Sabre	19726	XD725	Tyszko	local
21/06/1957	Sabre	19726	XD725	Sparkes	
21/06/1957	Sabre	19718	XD717	Helmore	
21/06/1957	Sabre	19646	XB792	Sparkes	To Ypenburg
21/06/1957	Sabre	19623	XB749	Lockley	To Ypenburg
21/06/1957	Sabre	19678	XB824	Manuel	To Ypenburg
24/06/1957	Sabre	19726	XD725	Sparkes	local
25/06/1957	Sabre	19718	XD717	Sparkes	local
25/06/1957	Sabre	19718	XD717	Sparkes	local
25/06/1957	Sabre	19718	XD717	Helmore	local
26/06/1957	Sabre	19718	XD717	Sparkes	local
26/06/1957	Sabre	19494	XB587	Helmore	local
26/06/1957	Sabre	19726	XD725	Sparkes	local
27/06/1957	Sabre	19527	XB624	Helmore	local
27/06/1957	Sabre	19762	XD760	Hunt	From Liverpool
27/06/1957	Sabre	19726	XD725	Sparkes	local
27/06/1957	Sabre	19494	XB587	Helmore	local
27/06/1957	Sabre	19762	XD760	Sparkes	local
28/06/1957	Sabre	19762	XD760	Sparkes	local
28/06/1957	Sabre	19494	XB587	Sparkes	local
28/06/1957	Sabre	19527	XB624	Sparkes	local
01/07/1957	Sabre	19857	XB650	Helmore	local

Date	Aircraft	Canadian Serial	RAF Serial	Pilot	Destination	Notes
02/07/1957	Sabre	19520	XB617	Hunt	From Liverpool	
02/07/1957	Sabre	19762	XD760	Catlin	Fürstenfeldbruck	
02/07/1957	Sabre	19494	XB587	Sparkes	Fürstenfeldbruck	
03/07/1957	Sabre	19726	XD725	Lockley	Fürstenfeldbruck	
03/07/1957	Sabre	19718	XD717	Manuel	Fürstenfeldbruck	
05/07/1957	Sabre	19527	XB624	Sparkes	local	
05/07/1957	Sabre	19520	XB617	Sparkes	local	
08/07/1957	Sabre	19520	XB617	Helmore	local	
09/07/1957	Sabre	19520	XB617	Tyszko	local	
09/07/1957	Sabre	19857	XB650	Sullivan	local	
09/07/1957	Sabre	19791	XB914	Helmore	local	
11/07/1957	Sabre	19520	XB617	Sullivan	local	
11/07/1957	Sabre	19857	XB650	Sullivan	local	
15/07/1957	Sabre	19791	XB914	Helmore	local	
15/07/1957	Sabre	19890	XB999	Helmore	local	
16/07/1957	Sabre	19791	XB914	Tyszko	local	
16/07/1957	Sabre	19520	XB617	Sullivan	To Ypenburg	
16/07/1957	Sabre	19527	XB624	Sparkes	To Ypenburg	
16/07/1957	Sabre	19585	XB699	Kampschoran?	To Ypenburg	
17/07/1957	Sabre	19791	XB914	Tyszko	local	
17/07/1957	Sabre	19890	XB999	Helmore	local	
18/07/1957	Sabre	19791	XB914	Sparkes	local	
18/07/1957	Sabre	19890	XB999	Sparkes	local	
06/08/1957	Sabre	19457	XB650	Rhodes	From Liverpool	

Date	Type	Number	Reg	Pilot	Route
06/08/1957	Sabre	19849	XB973	Hunt	From Liverpool
06/08/1957	Sabre	19759	XD757	Tyszko	From Liverpool
07/08/1957	Sabre	19791	XB914	Tyszko	local
10/08/1957	Sabre	19767	XD765	Hunt	From speke
10/08/1957	Sabre	19606	XB732	Helmore	From Speke
12/08/1957	Sabre	19826	XB939	Tyszko	local
13/08/1957	Sabre	19606	XB732	Tyszko	local
13/08/1957	Sabre	19791	XB914	Sparkes	local
13/08/1957	Sabre	19457	XB650	Sparkes	local
14/08/1957	Sabre	19791	XB914	Tyszko	local
14/08/1957	Sabre	19890	XB999	Tyszko	local
16/08/1957	Sabre	19826	XB939	Tyszko	local
19/08/1957	Sabre	19759	XD757	Sparkes	local
19/08/1957	Sabre	19890	XB999	Sparkes	local
19/08/1957	Sabre	19621	XB747	Tyszko	local
19/08/1957	Sabre	19451		Kampschoran?	To Ypenburg
19/08/1957	Sabre	19849	XB973	Sparkes	local
19/08/1957	Sabre	19621	XB747	Tyszko	local
20/08/1957	Sabre	19791	XB914	Tyszko	local
20/08/1957	Sabre	19621	XB747	Sparkes	local
20/08/1957	Sabre	19890	XB999	Kampschoran?	Ypenburg
21/08/1957	Sabre	19621	XB747	Sparkes	local
21/08/1957	Sabre	19676	XB822	Sparkes	local
21/08/1957	Sabre	19606	XB732	Sparkes	local
22/08/1957	Sabre	19826	XB939	Sparkes	local
22/08/1957	Sabre	19767	XD765	Sparkes	local

Date	Aircraft	Canadian Serial	RAF Serial	Pilot	Destination	Notes
22/08/1957	Sabre	19849	XB973	Solomon	Burtonwood	
22/08/1957	Sabre	19759	XD757	Kampschoran?	Burtonwood	
23/08/1957	Sabre	19826	XB939	Sparkes	local	
23/08/1957	Sabre	19606	XB732	Sparkes	To Ypenburg	
26/08/1957	Sabre	19621	XB747	Tyszko	local	
27/08/1957	Sabre	19767	XD765	Kampschoran?	To Ypenburg	
28/08/1957	Sabre	19621	XB747	Tyszko	local	
28/08/1957	Sabre	19791	XB914	Tyszko	local	
28/08/1957	Sabre	19621	XB747	Tyszko	local	
29/08/1957	Sabre	19826	XB939	Kampschoran?	To Ypenburg	
30/08/1957	Sabre	19485	XB578	Tyszko	local	
30/08/1957	Sabre	19791	XB914	Tyszko	local	
02/09/1957	Sabre	19489	XB582	Tyszko	local	
04/09/1957	Sabre	19621	XB747	Sparkes	local	
04/09/1957	Sabre	19485	XB578	Tyszko	local	
05/09/1957	Sabre	19674	XB820	Tyszko	From Liverpool	
05/09/1957	Sabre	19485	XB578	Sparkes	local	
05/09/1957	Sabre	19791	XB914	Sparkes	local	
05/09/1957	Sabre	19621	XB747	Sparkes	To Manston	
06/09/1957	Sabre	19840	XB953	Tyszko	local	
09/09/1957	Sabre	19485	XB578	Tyszko	local	
10/09/1957	Sabre	19674	XB820	Sullivan	local	
10/09/1957	Sabre	19840	XB953	Tyszko	local	
12/09/1957	Sabre	19840	XB953	Tyszko	local	

CANADAIR SABRE

12/09/1957	Sabre	19485	XB578	Kampschoran?	Châteauroux-Déols
12/09/1957	Sabre	19791	XB914	Olsen	Châteauroux-Déols
17/09/1957	Sabre	19825	XB938	Hunt	From Liverpool
17/09/1957	Sabre	19489	XB582	Tyszko	local
18/09/1957	Sabre	19674	XB820	Sullivan	local
20/09/1957	Sabre	19674	XB820	Sullivan	local
20/09/1957	Sabre	19700	XB862	Tyszko	local
25/09/1957	Sabre	19610	XB736	Tyszko	local
26/09/1957	Sabre	19825	XB938	Sullivan	local
26/09/1957	Sabre	19840	XB953	Sullivan	local
26/09/1957	Sabre	19795	XB918	Hunt	From Liverpool
26/09/1957	Sabre	19674	XB820	Kampschoran?	To Ypenburg
26/09/1957	Sabre	19840	XB953	Olsen	To Ypenburg
27/09/1957	Sabre	19702	XB864	Tyszko	local
27/09/1957	Sabre	19795	XB918	Sullivan	local
27/09/1957	Sabre	19489	XB582	Sullivan	local
27/09/1957	Sabre	19489	XB582	Sullivan	local
30/09/1957	Sabre	19610	XB736	Tyszko	local
30/09/1957	Sabre	19702	XB864	Tyszko	local
30/09/1957	Sabre	19610	XB736	Tyszko	local
01/10/1957	Sabre	19489	XB582	Sparkes	local
01/10/1957	Sabre	19702	XB864	Sparkes	local
02/10/1957	Sabre	19610	XB736	Sparkes	local
02/10/1957	Sabre	19702	XB864	Sparkes	local
02/10/1957	Sabre	19700	XB862	Sparkes	local
03/10/1957	Sabre	19759	XD757	Sparkes	local

Date	Aircraft	Canadian Serial	RAF Serial	Pilot	Destination	Notes
03/10/1957	Sabre	19700	XB862	Sullivan	local	
03/10/1957	Sabre	19610	XB736	Sparkes	To Manston	
03/10/1957	Sabre	19702	XB864	Sullivan	To Burtonwood	
04/10/1957	Sabre	19825	XB938	Tyszko	local	
09/10/1957	Sabre	19825	XB938	Hunt	local	
09/10/1957	Sabre	19489	XB582	Hunt	local	
11/10/1957	Sabre	19825	XB938	Hunt	local	
11/10/1957	Sabre	19738	XB875	Hunt	local	
12/10/1957	Sabre	19738	XB875	Hunt	local	
14/10/1957	Sabre	19700	XB862	Sparkes	local	
14/10/1957	Sabre	19825	XB938	Sparkes	local	
15/10/1957	Sabre	19738	XB875	Tyszko	local	
17/10/1957	Sabre	19738	XB875	Tyszko	local	
21/10/1957	Sabre	19738	XB875	Sparkes	local	
21/10/1957	Sabre	19883	XB992	Tyszko	local	
22/10/1957	Sabre	19700	XB862	Tyszko	local	
22/10/1957	Sabre	19738	XB875	Sparkes	local	
22/10/1957	Sabre	19795	XB918	Tyszko	local	
23/10/1957	Sabre	19795	XB918	Tyszko	local	
25/10/1957	Sabre	19738	XB875	Sparkes	local	
25/10/1957	Sabre	19489	XB582	Sparkes	local	
30/10/1957	Sabre	19795	XB918	Tyszko	local	
31/10/1957	Sabre	19883	XB992	Tyszko	local	
01/11/1957	Sabre	19489	XB582	Tyszko	local	

Date	Type	Serial	XB	Pilot	Note	Remarks
01/11/1957	Sabre	19785	XB897	Hunt	From Liverpool	
01/11/1957	Sabre	19700	XB862	Tyszko	local	
04/11/1957	Sabre	19489	XB582	Sparkes	local	
04/11/1957	Sabre	19700	XB862	Sparkes	local	
04/11/1957	Sabre	19825	XB938	Tyszko	local	
04/11/1957	Sabre	19785	XB897	Sparkes	local	
04/11/1957	Sabre	19738	XB875	Sparkes	local	
05/11/1957	Sabre	19700	XB862	Sullivan	To Burtonwood	
05/11/1957	Sabre	19738	XB875	Lt Clark	To Burtonwood	
06/11/1957	Sabre	19489	XB582	Sparkes	local	
06/11/1957	Sabre	19540	XB637	Tyszko	local	
06/11/1957	Sabre	19825	XB938	Sparkes	local	
08/11/1957	Sabre	19489	XB582	Sparkes	To Ypenburg	
08/11/1957	Sabre	19590	XB704	Tyszko	local	
08/11/1957	Sabre	19697	XB859	Hunt	local	
22/11/1957	Sabre	19785	XB897	Sparkes	local	
22/11/1957	Sabre	19795	XB918	Tyszko	local	
22/11/1957	Sabre	19825	XB938	Sparkes	local	
22/11/1957	Sabre	19522	XB619	Tyszko	local	
22/11/1957	Sabre	19697	XB859	Sparkes	local	
22/11/1957	Sabre	19540	XB637	Tyszko	Flame out	
23/11/1957	Sabre	19522	XB619	Tyszko	local	
25/11/1957	Sabre	19697	XB859	Sparkes	To Chambley?	
25/11/1957	Sabre	19825	XB938	Clark	To Chambley?	
26/11/1957	Sabre	19833	XB946	Tyszko	local	Typo? 19833 was Aviation Traders refurb. Seen Dunsfold 6/8/58

Date	Aircraft	Canadian Serial	RAF Serial	Pilot	Destination	Notes
29/11/1957	Sabre	19883	XB992	Tyszko	local	
29/11/1957	Sabre	19771	XD769	Tyszko	local	
29/11/1957	Sabre	19590	XB704	Sullivan	local	
29/11/1957	Sabre	19522	XB619	Tyszko	local	seen at Dunsfold 3/4/58
02/12/1957	Sabre	19785	XB897	Sullivan	local	
02/12/1957	Sabre	19785	XB897	Sullivan	To Etaue?	
09/12/1957	Sabre	19725	XD724	Hunt	From Speke	
09/12/1957	Sabre	19795	XB918	Sparkes	A.T.	
10/12/1957	Sabre	19771	XD769	Tyszko	local	seen at Lasham 16/5/59
16/12/1957	Sabre	19590	XB704	Tyszko	local	
16/12/1957	Sabre	19529	XB626	Tyszko	local	Seen at Dunsfold 3/4/58. At Lasham 5/59
19/12/1957	Sabre	19725	XD724	Sparkes	local	
19/12/1957	Sabre	19540	XB637	Tyszko	local	
19/12/1957	Sabre	19771	XD769	Tyszko	local	
19/12/1957	Sabre	19590	XB704	Tyszko	local	
19/12/1957	Sabre	19883	XB992	Sparkes	local	
24/12/1957	Sabre	19478	XB547	Tyszko	local	
30/12/1957	Sabre	19725	XD724	Sparkes	local	
30/12/1957	Sabre	19883	XB992	Sparkes	local	
01/01/1958	Sabre	19540	XB637	Tyszko	local	
02/01/1958	Sabre	19725	XD724	Sparkes	Furstenfeldbruck	
03/01/1958	Sabre	19734	XB871	Rhodes	From Liverpool	seen at Dunsfold 3/4/58. Stored Lasham
03/01/1958	Sabre	19764	XD762	Tyszko	From Liverpool	seen at Dunsfold 3/4/58. Stored Lasham

03/01/1958	Sabre	19472	XB541	Hunt	From Liverpool	seen at Dunsfold 3/4/58. Stored Lasham
03/01/1958	Sabre	19728	XD727	Onion	From Liverpool	seen at Dunsfold 3/4/58. Stored Lasham
03/01/1958	Sabre	19540	XB637	Tyszko		
07/01/1958	Sabre	19883	XB992	Tyszko		
07/01/1958	Sabre	19795	XB918	Sparkes		
07/01/1958	Sabre	19540	XB637	Tyszko		
07/01/1958	Sabre	19771	XD769	Sparkes		seen at Lasham 16/5/59
08/01/1958	Sabre	19795	XB918	Sparkes		
08/01/1958	Sabre	19478	XB547	Tyszko		seen at Lasham 16/5/59
08/01/1958	Sabre	19883	XB992	Sparkes		seen at Lasham 16/5/59
08/01/1958	Sabre	19540	XB637	Sparkes		seen at Dunsfold 6/8/58
13/01/1958	Sabre	19795	XB918	Clark	To Manston	XD774

Appendix 4

Sea Fury: Breakdown of Movements at Dunsfold

Mark	Serial	B-Reg	Arrived Dunsfold	Departed Dunsfold	Notes
FB.11	TF956	G-9-395	06/03/1963	07/04/1971	To RNAS Yeovilton
FB.11	VR930		03/04/1963	15/01/1965	To Museum RAF Colerne
FB.11	WE687		18/11/1960	15/02/1962	Scrapped at Dunsfold
FB.11	WE709		14/03/1963	23/11/1964	Scrapped at Dunsfold
FB.11	WE717			1963	Scrapped at Dunsfold
FB.11	WE790	G-9-46	30/12/1958	1966	Earmarked for Cuba, Lets Fire School Netherlands
FB.11	WE790	G-9-46	30/12/1958	1966	Earmarked for Cuba. Lets Fire School Netherlands
FB.11	WE792		17/02/1961	29/02/1964	To Lets Fire School Netherlands
FB.11	WE800	G-9-42	23/01/1959	1964	To Deleen Fire School Netherlands
FB.11	WE800	G-9-42	23/01/1959	1964	To Deelen Fire School Netherlands
FB.11	WG594	G-9-41	27/10/1960	13/04/1964	Earmarked for Cuba. Lets Fire School Netherlands
FB.11	WG594	G-9-41	27/10/1960	1962	B-reg NTU. Dunsfold by road. Lets Fire School

FB.11	WG596		09/04/1963	23/11/1964	Scrapped at Dunsfold
FB.11	WG599	G-9-66	28/02/1963	19/09/1963	To Germany D-CACY
FB.11	WG622	G-9-47	27/01/1959	23/03/1964	Earmarked for Cuba. Lets Fire School Netherlands
FB.11	WG622	G-9-47	27/01/1959	23/03/1964	To Lets Fire School Netherlands
FB.11	WG623		08/11/1960	07/03/1964	To Lets Fire School Netherlands
FB.11	WG626	G-9-37	02/01/1959	17/05/1964	Earmarked for Cuba. Lets Fire School Netherlands
FB.11	WG626	G-9-37	02/01/1959	23/03/1964	Earmarked for Cuba. Lets Fire School Netherlands
FB.11	WH593	G-9-38	02/01/1959	17/05/1964	Earmarked for Cuba. Lets Fire School Netherlands
FB.11	WH593	G-9-38	02/01/1959	1964	Earmarked for Cuba. Lets Fire School Netherlands
FB.11	WJ244		07/02/1963	13/07/1967	To Germany for spares
FB.11	WJ288		12/03/1963	01/09/1966	Towed to Biggin Hill
FB.11	WJ290		02/12/1960	10/02/1964	To Museum of Aircraft Deelen Netherlands
FB.11	WM484	G-9-48	27/10/1960	1964	Earmarked for Cuba. Lets Fire School Netherlands
FB.11	WM492		1961	1964	Lets Fire School Netherlands
FB.11	WM493	G-9-43	30/12/1958	01/06/1964	Earmarked for Cuba. Lets Fire School Netherlands
FB.11	WM493	G-9-43	30/12/1958	01/06/1964	To ETS Netherlands
FB.11	WM494	G-9-44	08/01/1959	1964	Earmarked for Cuba. Lets Fire School Netherlands
FB.11	WM494	G-9-44	08/01/1959	1964	To Lets Fire School Netherlands
FB.11	WN484	G-9-48	27/10/1960	1964	B-reg NTU. Dunsfold by road. Lets Fire School
FB.11	WZ632	G-9-45	21/01/1959	23/06/1964	Scrapped at Dunsfold
FB.11	WZ632	G-9-45	21/01/1959	23/06/1964	Scrapped at Dunsfold

Mark	Serial	B-Reg	Arrived Dunsfold	Departed Dunsfold	Notes
FB.11	WZ654	G-9-58	27/01/1959	1964	Earmarked for Cuba. Lets Fire School Netherlands
FB.11	WZ655	G-9-59	04/02/1959	15/06/1964	Earmarked for Cuba. Lets Fire School Netherlands
35 total					
T.20	VX280	G-9-63	03/11/1960	02/07/1963	To Germany D-CACI
T.20	VX281	G-9-64	02/12/1960	10/6/1963	To Germany D-CACO
T.20	VX291	G-9-55	30/12/1958		To Germany D-CADA
T.20	VX291	G-9-55	30/12/1958	28/04/1960	To Germany D-CADA
T.20	VX300	G-9-24	22/07/1958	29/08/1958	To Germany D-CAMI
T.20	VX302	G-9-62	03/11/1960	05/04/1963	To Germany D-CACE
T.20	VX309	G-9-27	24/07/1958	29/08/1958	Winch tests Dunsfold. To Germany D-CIBO
T.20	VZ350	G-9-54	22/12/1958	11/08/1959	To Germany D-COCO
T.20	VZ351	G-9-53	22/12/1958		To Germany D-CEDO
T.20	VZ351	G-9-53	22/12/1958	11/08/1959	To Germany D-CEDO
T.20	VZ352		15/11/1960	20/04/1964	Scrapped at Dunsfold
T.20	VZ353	G-9-56	16/02/1959	05/05/1960	To Germany D-CABU
T.20	VZ364		24/11/1960	03/02/1964	Lets Fire School Netherlands
T.20	VZ365	G-9-61	29/11/1960	28/03/1963	To Germany D-CACA
T.20	VZ372	G-9-50	08/01/1959	12/07/1960	To Germany D-CAME

T.20	WE820	G-9-49	06/08/1958	26/08/1958	Dunsfold for T.T. mods. Ret. to SG. Germany D-COTE
T.20	WE824	G-9-60	29/11/1960	07/03/1963	To Germany D-CABY
T.20	WG652	G-9-57	03/02/1959	23/05/1960	To Germany D-CAFO
T.20	WG655	G-9-65	15/11/1960	07/08/1963	To Germany D-CACU

19 total

54 grand total

Courtesy of Peter Amos, 2019

Index

Aircraft manufacturing and servicing companies:

INDEX

INDEX